Lecture Notes in Computer Science 3474

Commenced Publication in 1973
Founding and Former Series Editors:
Gerhard Goos, Juris Hartmanis, and Jan van Leeuwen

Editorial Board

David Hutchison
Lancaster University, UK

Takeo Kanade
Carnegie Mellon University, Pittsburgh, PA, USA

Josef Kittler
University of Surrey, Guildford, UK

Jon M. Kleinberg
Cornell University, Ithaca, NY, USA

Friedemann Mattern
ETH Zurich, Switzerland

John C. Mitchell
Stanford University, CA, USA

Moni Naor
Weizmann Institute of Science, Rehovot, Israel

Oscar Nierstrasz
University of Bern, Switzerland

C. Pandu Rangan
Indian Institute of Technology, Madras, India

Bernhard Steffen
University of Dortmund, Germany

Madhu Sudan
Massachusetts Institute of Technology, MA, USA

Demetri Terzopoulos
New York University, NY, USA

Doug Tygar
University of California, Berkeley, CA, USA

Moshe Y. Vardi
Rice University, Houston, TX, USA

Gerhard Weikum
Max-Planck Institute of Computer Science, Saarbruecken, Germany

Clemens Grelck   Frank Huch
Greg J. Michaelson   Phil Trinder (Eds.)

Implementation and Application of Functional Languages

16th International Workshop, IFL 2004
Lübeck, Germany, September 8-10, 2004
Revised Selected Papers

 Springer

Volume Editors

Clemens Grelck
University of Lübeck, Institute of Software Technology and Programming Languages
Ratzeburger Allee 160, 23538 Lübeck, Germany
E-mail: grelck@isp.uni-luebeck.de

Frank Huch
University of Kiel, Institute of Computer Science and Applied Mathematics
Olshausenstr. 40, 24098 Kiel, Germany
E-mail: fhu@informatik.uni-kiel.de

Greg J. Michaelson
Phil Trinder
Heriot-Watt University Edinburgh, School of Mathematical and Computer Sciences
Riccarton, EH14 4AS, UK
E-mail: {greg, trinder}@macs.hw.ac.uk

Library of Congress Control Number: 2005926884

CR Subject Classification (1998): D.3, D.1.1, F.3

ISSN   0302-9743
ISBN-10   3-540-26094-3 Springer Berlin Heidelberg New York
ISBN-13   978-3-540-26094-3 Springer Berlin Heidelberg New York

This work is subject to copyright. All rights are reserved, whether the whole or part of the material is
concerned, specifically the rights of translation, reprinting, re-use of illustrations, recitation, broadcasting,
reproduction on microfilms or in any other way, and storage in data banks. Duplication of this publication
or parts thereof is permitted only under the provisions of the German Copyright Law of September 9, 1965,
in its current version, and permission for use must always be obtained from Springer. Violations are liable
to prosecution under the German Copyright Law.

Springer is a part of Springer Science+Business Media

springeronline.com

© Springer-Verlag Berlin Heidelberg 2005
Printed in Germany

Typesetting: Camera-ready by author, data conversion by Scientific Publishing Services, Chennai, India
Printed on acid-free paper   SPIN: 11431664   06/3142   5 4 3 2 1 0

Preface

The 16th International Workshop on Implementation and Application of Functional Languages (IFL 2004) was held in Lübeck, Germany, September 8–10, 2004. It was jointly organized by the Institute of Computer Science and Applied Mathematics of the University of Kiel and the Institute of Software Technology and Programming Languages of the University of Lübeck.

IFL 2004 was the sixteenth event in the annual series of IFL workshops. The aim of the workshop series is to bring together researchers actively engaged in the implementation and application of functional and function-based programming languages. It provides an open forum for researchers who wish to present and discuss new ideas and concepts, work in progress, preliminary results, etc., related primarily, but not exclusively, to the implementation and application of functional languages. Topics of interest cover a wide range from theoretical aspects over language design and implementation towards applications and tool support.

Previous IFL workshops were held in the United Kingdom (Southampton, Norwich, London, St Andrews, and Edinburgh), in the Netherlands (Nijmegen and Lochem), in Germany (Aachen and Bonn), in Sweden (Båstad and Stockholm), and in Spain (Madrid). In 2005, the 17th International Workshop on Implementation and Application of Functional Languages will be held in Dublin, Ireland.

As an innovation for IFL 2004, the term "application" was added to the workshop name; it was previously known as the International Workshop on Implementation of Functional Languages. This change was made after an intensive discussion following IFL 2003 in Edinburgh. Our aim was to reflect the broader scope IFL has gained over recent years and to make IFL even more attractive for researchers in the future. Continuity with previous workshops is expressed by keeping the well-known and familiar acronym IFL.

IFL 2004 attracted 59 researchers from 11 different countries. Most participants came from Europe: 13 from the United Kingdom, 6 from the Netherlands, 4 from Spain, 3 each from Denmark, Ireland, and France, 1 from Hungary, and 20 from Germany. We also welcomed 2 participants each from the United States, Mexico, and Australia. During the three days of the workshop 40 presentations were given, organized into 10 individual sessions. The draft proceedings distributed during the workshop contained 37 contributions. They were published as Technical Report 0408 of the Institute of Computer Science and Applied Mathematics of the University of Kiel.

This volume follows the IFL tradition since 1996 in publishing a high-quality subset of contributions presented at the workshop in the Springer Lecture Notes in Computer Science series. All participants who gave a presentation at the workshop were invited to resubmit revised versions of their contributions after the workshop. We received 27 papers, each of which was reviewed by four members of the international Programme Committee according to normal conference standards. Following an intensive discussion the Programme Committee selected 13 papers to be included in this volume.

Since 2002 the Peter Landin Prize has been awarded annually to the author or the authors of the best workshop paper. The Programme Committee was pleased to give this prestigious award to Olivier Danvy for his contribution *A Rational Deconstruction of Landin's SECD Machine*. Previous Peter Landin Prize winners were Arjen van Weelden, Rinus Plasmeijer, and Pedro Vasconcelos.

IFL 2004 was generously sponsored by Deutsche Forschungsgemeinschaft (German Research Foundation), Innovationszentrum Lübeck, and the organizing institutes and universities. We are grateful to our sponsors for their financial and organizational support. We wish to thank all participants of IFL 2004 who made this workshop the successful event it was. Last but not least, we are indebted to the members of the Programme Committee who completed more than 100 reviews in a very short time frame.

March 2005   Clemens Grelck, Frank Huch,
                                               Greg Michaelson, Phil Trinder

Organization

Programme Committee

Matthias Blume	Toyota Technological Institute, Chicago, USA
Andrew Butterfield	Trinity College Dublin, Ireland
Manuel Chakravarty	University of New South Wales, Sydney, Australia
Clemens Grelck (Chair)	Universität zu Lübeck, Germany
Frank Huch (Chair)	Christian-Albrechts-Universität zu Kiel, Germany
Hans-Wolfgang Loidl	Ludwig-Maximilians-Universität München, Germany
Frédéric Loulergue	Université de Paris XII, Val de Marne, France
Simon Marlow	Microsoft Research, Cambridge, UK
Greg Michaelson	Heriot-Watt University, Edinburgh, UK
Yolanda Ortega-Mallén	Universidad Complutense de Madrid, Spain
Rinus Plasmeijer	Radboud Universiteit Nijmegen, Netherlands
Colin Runciman	University of York, UK
Peter Thiemann	Albert-Ludwigs-Universität Freiburg, Germany
Phil Trinder	Heriot-Watt University, Edinburgh, UK
Germán Vidal	Universitat Politècnica de Valencia, Spain

Additional Reviewers

Peter Achten
Jost Berthold
Bernd Braßel
Olaf Chitil
Xiao Yan Deng
Santiago Escobar
David de Frutos
John van Groningen
Christian Haack
Michael Hanus
Mercedes Hidalgo-Herrero
Steffen Jost
Gabriele Keller
Pieter Koopman
Wolfgang Küchlin
Rita Loogen
Matthias Neubauer
Jan Henry Nyström

Ricardo Peña
Robert Pointon
José Guadalupe Ramos
André Rauber du Bois
John Reppy
Fernando Rubio
Clara Segura
Sven-Bodo Scholz
Wolfgang Schreiner
Sean Seefried
Josep Silva
Donald Stewart
Annette Stümpel
Arjen van Weelden
Simon Winwood
Patryk Zadarnowski
Abdallah Al Zain

Sponsoring Institutions

Deutsche Forschungsgemeinschaft (DFG)

Innovationszentrum Lübeck (IZL)

Christian-Albrechts-Universität zu Kiel
Institut für Informatik und Praktische Mathematik

Universität zu Lübeck
Institut für Softwaretechnik und Programmiersprachen

Table of Contents

Exploiting Single-Assignment Properties to Optimize Message-Passing Programs by Code Transformations

Alfredo Cristóbal-Salas[1], Andrey Chernykh[2], Edelmira Rodríguez-Alcantar[3], and Jean-Luc Gaudiot[4] [(*)]

[1] School of Chemistry Science and Engineering, Autonomous University of Baja California,
Tijuana, Baja California, Mexico, 22390
cristobal@uabc.mx
[2] Computer Science Department, CICESE Research Center,
Ensenada, Baja California, Mexico, 22830
chernykh@cicese.mx
[3] Computer Science; University of Sonora,Hermosillo, Sonora,
Mexico, 83000
edelmira@mat.uson.mx
[4] Electrical Engineering and Computer Science, University of California, Irvine,
Irvine, California, USA, 92697
gaudiot@uci.edu

Abstract. The message-passing paradigm is now widely accepted and used mainly for inter-process communication in distributed memory parallel systems. However, one of its disadvantages is the high cost associated with the data exchange. Therefore, in this paper, we describe a message-passing optimization technique based on the exploitation of single-assignment and constant information properties to reduce the number of communications. Similar to the more general partial evaluation approach, technique evaluates local and remote memory operations when only part of the input is known or available; it further specializes the program with respect to the input data. It is applied to the programs, which use a distributed single-assignment memory system. Experimental results show a considerable speedup in programs running in computer systems with slow interconnection networks. We also show that single assignment memory systems can have better network latency tolerance and the overhead introduced by its management can be hidden.

1   Introduction

The exchange of information remains as a critical bottleneck in distributed memory systems. Exchanging information by message passing is a popular technique in distributed environment. Furthermore, with the proliferation of clusters and GRID technology, the message passing paradigm has significantly increased in popularity. However, its major drawback is the inherently high communication costs. Communication cost depends on memory manipulation overhead (message preparation, message interpretation) and network communication delays.

(*) Authors are listed in alphabetical order.

C. Grelck et al. (Eds.): IFL 2004, LNCS 3474, pp. 1–16, 2005.
© Springer-Verlag Berlin Heidelberg 2005

There are several strategies to minimize this cost such as computation and communication overlapping, network optimization, or reduction of number of messages (message coalescing, caching messages, etc). Consequently, reducing this cost is vital to achieve good performance.

In this paper we present how to reduce communication cost of parallel programs for distributed memory systems. Technique eliminates synchronization issues by non-strict data access and fully asynchronous operations. It also combines functional programming techniques such: I-Structures [2] and partial evaluation [11] together with classical program optimization like constant-propagation, loop unrolling and dead-code elimination. As a contribution of this paper, we provide detailed description about code transformations needed to partially evaluate memory accesses when part of the program's input information is available. We use single-assignment I-Structures to facilitate asynchronous access when structure production and consumption can be allowed to proceed with a looser synchronization. When a read operation occurs before a write operation, the deferred request is queued on a linked list of that particular I-Structure element. When the write operation finally occurs, the system responds to the deferred reads by distributing the written value to the requesters, which have been received in the meantime.

On the other hand, partial evaluation [11,18] is an automatic program transformation technique which allows the partial execution of a program when only some of its input data are available (static), and specializes it by pre-computing parts of the program that depend on specific parameter settings. It has been shown in [9, 14] that the majority of communications in scientific programs are static, that is, the communication information can be determined at compile time. Some experiments which show how MPI parallel programs can be optimized by using static information can be found in [20]. These characteristics can be exploited in message passing paradigm to eliminate memory request at compile time. Elimination of memory accesses may improve performance of parallel programs running in architectures with high latency interconnection networks such as wide area networks or grids. Even though our technique works directly with MPI as communication layer, it can be applied to other communication libraries.

The rest of the paper is organized as follows: in section 2 a general description of proposed optimization technique is presented. In section 3, we provide detailed information how optimization technique works using an example of code transformation. Experimental results can be found in section 4. Related work is presented in section 5. Finally, some conclusions are presented.

2   General Description of the Optimization Technique

In [8], this optimization technique is proposed. This technique is based on a particular case of partial evaluation approach where parallel programs evaluation is performed when only part of their input is given. It reduces the number of messages in single-assignment distributed memory systems by exploiting constant information. For instance, matrix multiplication can be evaluated when matrices size and number of processes are known, but with unknown matrices elements values. Obviously, program evaluation cannot be completed but it is possible to create a residual program (optimized one). When remaining input data become available, residual program can continue evaluations. This residual program can be run as many times as needed, and it is expected to be faster than executing the original program.

Fig. 1 shows a general view of this new technique. Parallel program code and a set of constant values are given as an input. The output is a residual (optimized) code where all constant memory accesses have been eliminated. Two main steps are considered: *pre-processing* and *message elimination*.

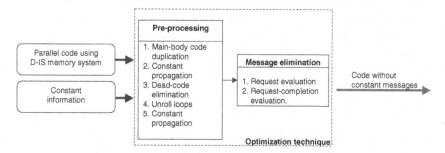

Fig. 1. General view of the optimization technique

In the *preprocessing* step, code is transformed to facilitate detection of static memory accesses. Main-body code is replicated in accordance with the number of processes given, constants are propagated, dead code is eliminated, and loops are unrolled.

In the *message elimination* step, static memory accesses are evaluated by inserting a special instruction in the corresponding remote process code to locally perform the remote request. After the evaluation of all static memory requests, a second review of code is performed to complete execution of all requests that refer to elements already defined. Before going into details, we review design of Distributed I-Structure memory system. More information about it can be found in [6, 7].

2.1 Distributed I-Structure Memory System (D-IS)

D-IS is a communication library for distributed memory systems that implements the functionality of I-Structures [2] on top of MPI (Fig. 2). Each MPI process manages a local I-Structure memory system arranged in a linked list. Remote operations are performed using split-phase transactions and they are implemented using MPI point-to-point routine calls. Exchange of information involves a *send-request*, *receive-value* on the requester side and *receive-request*, and *send-value* on the side of the owner of the I-Structure. D-IS permits consulting an I-Structure element even before a value is bound to that memory location. This feature breaks the restrictions unnecessarily imposed by sequential systems, which demand the complete production of data before consumption. The write policy is write-through to ensure data will be available as soon it is produced. D-IS is a further research of the I-Structure memory system presented in [15]. As D-IS runs on top of MPI, it has most of its features such as portability and efficient implementation in several architectures. The D-IS memory system has been tested in a NUMA S2MP ORIGIN 2000 and in a Pentium III cluster.

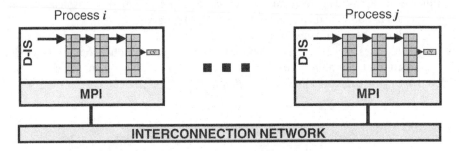

Fig. 2. Graphical representation of the D-IS

3   Functionality of Optimization Technique

Before presenting functionality of proposed technique, we first describe the syntax of the main function routines.

3.1   Syntax of Instructions to Manipulate D-IS Memory System

D-IS has four general routines to initialize memory system and to obtain general information from the communicator:

- `void DIS_Init(int argc, char **argv)`. Initializes the D-IS memory system. `argc` and `argv` are parameters taken from the command line.
- `void DIS_GetProcessRank(int *rank)`. Gets the rank of a process inside the current communicator.
- `void DIS_Finalize()`. Finalizes the D-IS memory system and stops the execution of all MPI routines.

The D-IS memory system also has the following instructions

- `int DIS_Request(int node, int id, int pos)`. It requests the element `pos` of the I-Structure `id` to process `node`. Remote requests are stored in a list whose index is attached to a MPI message as a continuation vector. This routine returns the position of the request in the list.
- `void DIS_RecvRequest(int node)`. This instruction is divided into three steps. First, an *MPI_Recv* instruction is executed to receive a request. Secondly, local D-IS is consulted to obtain information about the I-Structure element requested. If the I-Structure element is in the "empty" or "deferred" state, then the request is added to the end of the deferred-reads queue and no further action is taken. Finally, as soon the I-Structure element becomes available, the value is sent back to the requester by using another *MPI_Send* call.

- double DIS_RecvDatum(int index). An *MPI_Recv* instruction is executed to receive a message from node. Index specifies the position from the list of remote requests where the continuation vector is stored. This routine returns the value of the I-Structure element requested.

- Void DIS_Write(int id, int pos, double value). This instruction stores a value in the I-Structure id at position pos. If that element is in the "deferred" state the value stored is copied to all continuation vectors and state is changed to "full"; if element is in "empty" state the value is stored in that position and its state is changed to "full". If element is "full" state then the store operation cannot be completed and it causes a fatal error.

```
1    int main(int argc, char **argv ){
2    -CODE-
3    if (rank==0){
4       for (j=1; j<PROCS; j++)
5          for (i=0; i<n; i++)
6             index[i]=DIS_Request(j, ID, i);
7          for (j=1; j<PROCS; j++)
8             for (i=0; i<n; i++)
9                data[i]=DIS_RecvDatum(index[i]);
10      }
11      else{
12         for (i=0; i<n; i++)
13            DIS_Write(ID, i, value[i]);
14         for (i=0; i<n; i++)
15            DIS_RecvRequest(0);
16      }
17   -CODE-
18   }
```

Fig. 3. Original user code

3.2   Code Transformation Description Following an Example Code

An example of code transformation by exploiting constant information is presented next. Fig. 3 shows the original user code to be optimized. In this code, process 0 sends request for *n* elements to the rest of the processes in the communicator.

As constant input information, we provide the following parameters: PROCS=2, n=3, ID=3. For rank=1 we define I-Structure elements such as: ID=3, element=0, value=12.7 and ID=3, element=2, value=38.5

3.2.1   Main-Body Routine Code Duplication

In this step, the original main-body routine code is copied as many times as there are specified processes. The main-body routine code is substituted for a switch-case instruction that selects the appropriate code for each process. The code for a particular process is specified by the function main_process_X, where X is the rank number and it is an exact copy of the original main-body code. In Fig. 4, we see how this code transformation is done in the example code: a new main-body code is inserted (lines 1-12) and it contains a switch instruction where the variable rank has two possible options because it is intended to run with two processes. Also, two new functions have been inserted in the code, main_process_0 (lines 14-32) and main_process_1 (lines 34-52), these functions specify the code for each process.

```
1   Int main(int argc, char **argv ){        27   for (i=0; i<n; i++)
2   DIS_Init(&argc,&argv);                    28     DIS_RecvRequest(0);
3   DIS_GetProcessRank(&rank);                29   }
4   switch(rank) {                            30   -CODE-
5         case 0: main_process_0();           31   return 1 ;
6               break;                        32   }
7         case 1: main_process_1();           33
8               break;                        34   int main_process_1(){
9   };                                        35   -CODE-
10  DIS_Finalize();                           36   if (rank==0){
11  return 1;                                 37    for (j=1; j<PROCS; j++)
12  }                                         38     for (i=0; i<n; i++)
13                                            39      index[i]=DIS_Request(j, ID, i);
14  int main_process_0(){                     40    for (j=1; j<PROCS; j++)
15  -CODE-                                    41     for (i=0; i<n; i++)
16  if (rank==0){                             42      data[i]=DIS_RecvDatum(index[i]);
17   for (j=1; j<PROCS; j++)                  43   }
18    for (i=0; i<n; i++)                     44   else{
19     index[i]=DIS_Request(j, ID, i);        45    for (i=0; i<n; i++)
20   for (j=1; j<PROCS; j++)                  46     DIS_Write(ID, i, value[i]);
21    for (i=0; i<n; i++)                     47    for (i=0; i<n; i++)
22     data[i]=DIS_RecvDatum(index[i]);       48     DIS_RecvRequest(0);
23  }                                         49   }
24  else{                                     50   -CODE-
25   for (i=0; i<n; i++)                       51   Return 1 ;
26    DIS_Write(ID, i, value[i]);             52   }
```

Fig. 4. Main-body routine code duplication

```
1   Int main(int argc, char **argv ){        27   for (i=0; i<3; i++)
2   DIS_Init(&argc,&argv);                    28     DIS_RecvRequest(0);
3   DIS_GetProcessRank(&rank);                29   }
4   switch(rank) {                            30   -CODE-
5         case 0: main_process_0();           31   return 1;
6               break;                        32   }
7         case 1: main_process_1();           33
8               break;                        34   int main_process_1(){
9   };                                        35   -CODE-
10  DIS_Finalize();                           36   if (1==0){
11  return 1;                                 37    for (j=1; j<2; j++)
12  }                                         38     for (i=0; i<3; i++)
13                                            39      index[i]=DIS_Request(j, 3, i);
14  int main_process_0(){                     40    for (j=1; j<2; j++)
15  -CODE-                                    41     for (i=0; i<3; i++)
16  if (0==0){                                42      data[i]=DIS_RecvDatum(index[i]);
17   for (j=1; j<2; j++)                      43   }
18    for (i=0; i<3; i++)                     44   else{
19     index[i]=DIS_Request(j, 3, i);         45    for (i=0; i<3; i++)
20   for (j=1; j<2; j++)                      46     DIS_Write(3, i, value[i]);
21    for (i=0; i<3; i++)                     47    for (i=0; i<3; i++)
22     data[i]=DIS_RecvDatum(index[i]);       48     DIS_RecvRequest(0);
23  }                                         49   }
24  else{                                     50   -CODE-
25   for (i=0; i<3; i++)                       51   return 1;
26    DIS_Write(3, i, value[i]);              52   }
```

Fig. 5. Constant propagation to identify static loops

3.2.2   Constant Propagation

In this step, we propagate constant information throughout the code to detect any possible static loop. In the example (see Fig. 5 for details), we propagate for rank=0 the constants PROCS=2, n=3, ID=3 and for rank=1 we propagate: PROCS=2, n=3, ID=3.

3.2.3   Dead-Code Elimination

Instructions that will never be processed by a particular process are eliminated in this step (see Fig. 6 for resulting code); for instance, conditional expressions depending on the rank value. In the example, from Fig. 5, we see that lines 24-29 in function `main_process_0` will never be executed by process 0; the same happens in function `main_process_1` where lines 36-43 will never be processed by process 1.

3.2.4   Unrolling Loops

All loops involving memory accesses are unrolled to detect possible static instructions inside loops. In the example code (Fig. 6), there are six loops that can be unrolled (lines 14, 15, 17, 18, 26, and 28). Fig. 7 shows the code after the loops have been unrolled.

```
 1    int main(int argc, char **argv ){        17    for (j=1; j<2; j++)
 2    DIS_Init(&argc,&argv);                    18      for (i=0; i<3; i++)
 3    DIS_GetProcessRank(&rank);                19        data[i]=DIS_RecvDatum(index[i]);
 4    switch(rank) {                            20    -CODE-
 5       case 0: main_process_0(); break;       21    return 1;
 6       case 1: main_process_1(); break;       22    }
 7    };                                        23
 8    DIS_Finalize();                           24    int main_process_1(){
 9    return 1;                                 25    -CODE-
10    }                                         26    for (i=0; i<3; i++)
11                                              27      DIS_Write(3, i, value[i]);
12    int main_process_0(){                     28    for (i=0; i<3; i++)
13    -CODE-                                    29      DIS_RecvRequest(0);
14    for (j=1; j<2; j++)                       30    -CODE-
15      for (i=0; i<3; i++)                     31    return 1;
16        index[i]=DIS_Request(j, 3, i);        32    }
```

Fig. 6. Code after dead-code elimination

```
 1    int main(int argc, char **argv ){        19    data[0]=DIS_RecvDatum(index[0]);
 2    DIS_Init(&argc,&argv);                    20    data[1]=DIS_RecvDatum(index[1]);
 3    DIS_GetProcessRank(&rank);                21    data[2]=DIS_RecvDatum(index[2]);
 4    switch(rank) {                            22    -CODE-
 5        case 0: main_process_0();             23    return 1;
 6                break;                        24    }
 7        case 1: main_process_1();             25
 8                break;                        26    int main_process_1(){
 9    };                                        27    -CODE-
10    DIS_Finalize();                           28    DIS_Write(3, 0, value[0]);
11    return 1;                                 29    DIS_Write(3, 1, value[1]);
12    }                                         30    DIS_Write(3, 2, value[2]);
13                                              31    DIS_RecvRequest(0);
14    int main_process_0(){                     32    DIS_RecvRequest(0);
15    -CODE-                                    33    DIS_RecvRequest(0);
16    index[0]=DIS_Request(1, 3, 0);            34    -CODE-
17    index[1]=DIS_Request(1, 3, 1);            35    return 1;
18    index[2]=DIS_Request(1, 3, 2);            36    }
```

Fig. 7. Unroll loops inside each local_main functions

3.2.5   Final Constant Propagation

We propagate constants throughout the code to reach variables inside the loops that may not be processed during first propagation. In Fig. 8, we show the code after propagation; lines 28 and 30 have been modified specifying the values to be stored in the I-Structure 3 positions 0 and 2.

3.2.6   Constant Requests Evaluation for Remote I-Structure Elements

This step detects static memory accesses and eliminates them. Each constant request is erased from the code and a `DIS_RemoteRequest()` function is inserted instead in the `main_process_X()` function of the remote process code.

```
1    int main(int argc, char **argv ){        19    Data[0]=DIS_RecvDatum(index[0]);
2    DIS_Init(&argc,&argv);                    20    data[1]=DIS_RecvDatum(index[1]);
3    DIS_GetProcessRank(&rank);                21    data[2]=DIS_RecvDatum(index[2]);
4    switch(rank) {                            22    -CODE-
5            case 0: main_process_0();         23    return 1;
6                    break;                    24    }
7            case 1: main_process_1();         25
8                    break;                    26    int main_process_1(){
9    };                                        27    -CODE-
10   DIS_Finalize();                           28    DIS_Write(3, 0, 12.7);
11   return 1;                                 29    DIS_Write(3, 1, value[1]);
12   }                                         30    DIS_Write(3, 2, 38.5);
13                                             31    DIS_RecvRequest(0);
14   int main_process_0(){                     32    DIS_RecvRequest(0);
15   -CODE-                                     33    DIS_RecvRequest(0);
16   index[0]=DIS_Request(1, 3, 0);            34    -CODE-
17   index[1]=DIS_Request(1, 3, 1);            35    return 1;
18   index[2]=DIS_Request(1, 3, 2);            36    }
```

Fig. 8. Code after constant propagation

```
1    int main(int argc, char **argv ){        19    data[2]=DIS_RecvDatum(index[2]);
2    DIS_Init(&argc,&argv);                    20    -CODE-
3    DIS_GetProcessRank(&rank);                21    return 1;
4    switch(rank) {                            22    }
5        case 0: main_process_0();             23
6                break;                        24    int main_process_1(){
7        case 1: main_process_1();             25    -CODE-
8                break;                        26    base=0;
9    };                                        27    DIS_Write(3, 0, 12.7);
10   DIS_Finalize();                           28    DIS_Write(3, 1, value[1]);
11   return 1;                                 29    DIS_Write(3, 2, 38.5);
12   }                                         30    DIS_RemoteRequest(0,3,0,base+0);
13                                             31    DIS_RemoteRequest(0,3,1,base+1);
14                                             32    DIS_RemoteRequest(0,3,2,base+2);
15   int main_process_0(){                     33    base=3;
16   -CODE-                                     34    -CODE-
17   data[0]=DIS_RecvDatum(index[0]);          35    return 1;
18   data[1]=DIS_RecvDatum(index[1]);          36    }
```

Fig. 9. Static messages evaluation by inserting DIS_RemoteRequest()functions in the data-owner (process that stores data) text code

The introduction of the DIS_RemoteRequest() functions insert in local I-Structure elements a remote deferred read. From Fig. 8, lines 16-18 are constant requests and can be transformed into DIS_RemoteRequest() functions as can be seen in Fig. 9 in lines 30-32. Base is a variable that adjusts index when loops involving memory requests cannot be unrolled.

3.2.7   Constant Remote Request Completion

In this step, each main_process_X()function is analyzed to check if any of the DIS_RemoteRequest()functions refers to an I-Structure element already defined by a DIS_Write() function. If so, there is no need to wait until execution time to complete this evaluation, it can be evaluated during this optimization step. Then, the corresponding DIS_RecvDatum()function can be deleted and substituted by the constant value already defined. From Fig. 9, lines 30 and 32 refer to an I-Structure element already defined in lines 27 and 29 respectively.

Therefore, lines 30 and 32 (Fig. 9) can be evaluated by copying values 12.7 and 38.5 into the main_process_0() code as is shown in Fig. 10, lines 17 and 19.

In this section, we have shown above how to partially evaluate remote memory requests by exploiting the I-Structures' features and constant propagation prior to the execution of the parallel program. In this particular data independent example, three of the messages needed to perform remote memory requests can be fully evaluated while 2/3 of the messages that answer remote requests can be also fully evaluated. Hence, from six messages that were required to be evaluated at execution time, five of them were evaluated during the optimization technique.

```
1    int main(int argc, char **argv ){          18    data[1]=DIS_RecvDatum(index[1]);
2      DIS_Init(&argc,&argv);                   19    data[2]=38.5;
3      DIS_GetProcessRank(&rank);               20    -CODE-
4      switch(rank) {                           21    return 1;
5        case 0: main_process_0();              22  }
6             break;                            23
7        case 1: main_process_1();              24  int main_process_1(){
8             break;                            25    base=0;
9      };                                       26    -CODE-
10     DIS_Finalize();                          27    DIS_Write(3, 0, 12.7);
11     return 1;                                28    DIS_Write(3, 1, value[1]);
12   }                                          29    DIS_Write(3, 2, 38.5);
13                                              30    DIS_RemoteRequest(0,3,1,base+1);
14                                              31    base=3;
15   int main_process_0(){                      32    -CODE-
16     -CODE-                                   33    return 1;
17     data[0]=12.7;                            34  }
```

Fig. 10. Constant information in remote node is transferred to the requester

4   Experimental Results

This optimization technique has been tested with several algorithms such as matrix multiplication, conjugate gradient, and fast Fourier transform [7, 8] running in a SGI Origin 2000 with 10 MIPS R10000 processors and a PC Cluster with 8 Pentium III processors. In this section, we show experimental results for a 4 Dual-Pentium III PC Cluster in a 10/100 Fast Ethernet point-to-point interconnection and 512 MB of memory in each node. Programs presented in the section use no collective communication, cache mechanism, message coalescing, or data locality exploitation. These restrictions are set just to observe how much performance can be obtained just by the partial evaluation technique alone.

We present experimental results using the 2D Haar wavelet transform (2D-HWT) applied to a 1024x1024 image. The Haar wavelet transform is the first known wavelet, proposed in 1909 by Alfred Haar [17]. The Haar wavelet is also the simplest possible wavelet. As opposed to the functions sine and cosine used for Fourier transforms, a wavelet not only has locality in the frequency domain but also in the time or spatial domain. The algorithm produces as output a file containing the average of original image together with the detail information of the same image.

We chose 2D-HWT because it is a data independent algorithm. This feature makes it well suitable to show the advantages of our optimization technique. With this benchmark program, we intend to demonstrate how parallel programs can benefit when part of the input information is constant. In benchmark program, we assume that different percentages of the input image are known. This assumption is reasonable in digital image processing where images may contain a constant background or fixed objects. In experiments, we run the program that implements 2D-HWT and use D-IS memory system.

We show results for different percentages of the image, network latencies, and number of processing elements (PEs). We define the following notation:

DIS - Refers to the original program without any optimization.

DIS(p) - Refers to the optimized program running when *p* percentage of the image is known. When zero percentage of the image is known, technique can still be performed because the sending of requests can be evaluated if image size is provided.

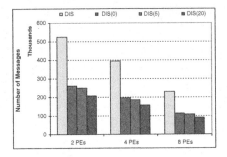
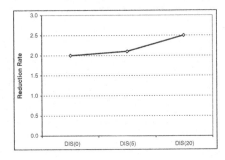

Fig. 11. Number of messages sent varying the number of processing elements and the percentage of the image that is known

Fig. 12. Reduction in the message rate when part of the image (0%, 5%, and 20%) is known

4.1   Number of Messages Analysis

Fig. 11 shows how the number of messages sent by optimized and non-optimized programs varies with respect to the number of PEs. Comparing *DIS* and *DIS(0)* from this figure, we can see that optimization technique can eliminate half of the messages just by knowing the image dimension and the number of processing elements available. Under these circumstances memory requests can be sent even without knowing the value of any pixels of the image.

These instructions represent half of the messages to send; the other half is required to send the value of elements when they become available.

We also see that the number of messages is reduced when the number of processing elements increases; this is an effect of parallelization and data distribution. Comparing *DIS(0)*, *DIS(5)* and *DIS(20)*; we also see the impact of the technique when part of the image is known. In this case, not only the requests can be performed which is the case between *DIS* and *DIS(0)*, but also some requests can be answered, thereby eliminating more messages, as seen in Fig. 11.

These results are confirmed in Fig. 12, which shows the reduction in the rate of message. This measurement is the ratio between the number of messages sent by the *DIS* program over the number of messages sent by the *DIS(k)* programs. As seen in the figure, this ratio is at least two and increases when part of the image is known. This happens for 2, 4, and 8 PEs.

4.2   Execution Time Reduction Analysis

Fig. 13 shows the execution time reduction rate obtained with *DIS* program varying the percentage of constant information, number of PEs and the interconnection network latency. Execution time reduction rate is the ratio between *DIS* execution time over *DIS(k)* execution time. From this figure, we see the impact of the technique with different interconnection network latencies.

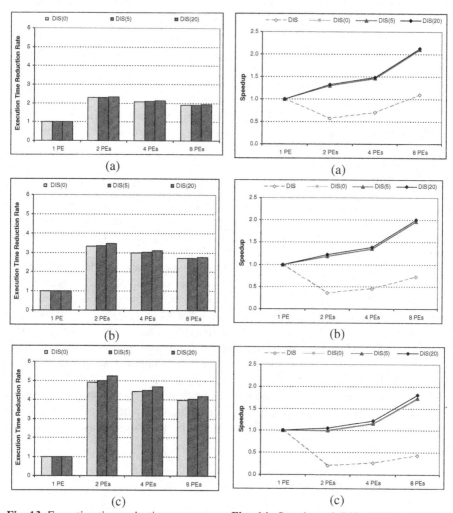

Fig. 13. Execution time reduction rate varying the number of PEs, the percentage of constant information and the interconnection network speed. We analyze (a) twice faster (b) original and (c) twice slower network speeds

Fig. 14. Speedup of *DIS, DIS(0), DIS(5), DIS(20)* programs with different numbers of PEs. We present data for (a) twice faster (b) original and (c) twice slower interconnection network

In Fig. 13a, the interconnection network is twice faster than network in Fig. 13b and four times faster than in Fig. 13c; while the network in Fig. 13b is twice faster than the network in Fig. 13c. Hence, from this figure we see that the reduction rate is higher when the interconnection network is slower. This means that technique makes single assignment memory system more robust and latency tolerant.

We also see that there is almost no optimization possible when there is just one PE because technique gets its real advantage from remote memory operations instead of local memory operations. Also, when we increase the percentage of constant input information from 0, 5, and 20, there is a small increment in the reduction ratio because a second message is eliminated; however, the processing of that message is not so time-consuming when compared with the time spent by sending and receiving requests. Moreover, optimization is reduced when the number of PEs is increased. This is due to the data distribution between PEs; in other words, when more PEs are added, then more messages are required to exchange information.

This effect does not mean that the optimized program runs slower; this only means that the original program execution time and the execution time of its optimized version are becoming similar.

4.3 Speedup

Fig. 14 shows the speedup obtained by benchmark programs when increasing the number of PEs and varying the interconnection network speed by a factor of two. We compare the time spent by parallel programs running in several PEs with respect to the same parallel implementation running in a single PE.

Fig. 14a, 14b, and 14c show that *DIS* programs have a speedup below one which means that programs with more than one PE run slower than their sequential counterpart. This is due to the exchange of messages, which are time consuming; however, with the introduction of more PEs, the program begins speeding up. When the interconnection network is fast enough, the speedup becomes higher than one (see Fig. 14a *DIS* with 8 PEs). However, when the technique is applied to *DIS* program even without any image values, which is the case of *DIS(0)*, we note a positive speedup. This tendency is also valid for *DIS(5)* and *DIS(20)* execution times.

In these cases, the overhead introduced by the management of I-Structures and the communication times can be masked by the technique, producing a faster optimized code. *DIS(0)*, *DIS(5)*, and *DIS(20)* display a similar speedup because the execution time is similar in these cases.

5   Related Work

In this section we review related work in the area of parallel program optimization. We analyze optimizations performed to the communication library (MPI) in software and hardware also we review optimizations performed at compiled time which exploits static information about network or communication patterns.

5.1   Optimization of Inter-process Communication

Optimizations of the MPI barrier operation are discussed in [19]. Moh *et al* propose a fast tree-based barrier synchronization scheme for 2-D meshes producing a reduction in the number of messages by combining the synchronization messages.

In [4], a design and implementation of the MPI collective communication instructions optimized for clusters of workstations is presented. The system consists of two main components: the MPI-CCL layer and a User-Level Reliable Transport Protocol (URTP). The MPI-CCL layer includes the collective communication functionality of MPI and the URTP works as an interface with the LAN Data-Link Layer. Their system is integrated with the operative system through a kernel extension mechanism. These operations reduce significantly the number of messages during the execution of a MPI program. However, the correct utilization of these instructions depends on the ability of programmer.

In [10], a prototype of the D-OSC, a SISAL compiler for distributed memory machines is presented. D-OSC is a further research of the Optimizing SISAL Compiler (OSC) [16]. D-OSC generates C code with MPI calls. In D-OSC, messages are eliminated using rectangular arrays, multiple-alignment, and block messages.

In [13], a library of collective communication operations, called MAGPIE, is presented. MAGPIE is optimized for wide area systems and its algorithms are designed to send the minimal amount of data over the slow wide area links, and to only incur singlewide area latency. MAGPIE implements the complete set of collective operations according to the MPI standard. Reduction operations with short data vectors are frequently used in parallel applications. The paper also discusses optimizations such as message vectorization, message coalescing, and redundancy elimination implemented in MAGPIE.

5.2   Optimizations at Compile-Time

Single assignment is a fundamental property of variables in functional languages. When a variable is only assigned to a value once, then an instance of that variable is thereafter semantically equivalent to the value. The single assignment property is used in compilers to implement a variety of optimizations [5]. One of the most attractive features of single-assignment in parallel systems is that cache coherence is already embedded in it [15].

The PARADIGM compiler [3], provides an automated mean to parallelize sequential programs for their efficient execution on distributed-memory multi-computers. PARADIGM performs a number of optimizations: automatic data partitioning and distribution, synthesis of high-level communication, and communication optimization. These are provided through a generic library interface (MPI is included). Regular computations are optimized by message coalescing, message vectorization, coarse grain pipelining, and message aggregation. It also supports functional, data parallelism, and multithreaded execution.

In [1], a compiler algorithm that automatically finds computation- and data-decompositions is presented. This algorithm optimizes both parallelism and data locality. Also, a mathematical framework to systematically derive decompositions is introduced. An optimization algorithm focuses on programs with nesting of parallel and sequential loops. The algorithm attempts to uncover a static decomposition that exploits the maximum degree of parallelism available in the program to minimize communication, such that there is no reorganization or pipeline communication. It can exploit parallelism in both fully parallelizable loops as well as loops that require explicit synchronization. If communication is needed, the algorithm will attempt to introduce the least expensive forms of communication into those parts of the program that are least frequently executed.

Another optimization technique performed at compile-time and applied to message-passing parallel programs is Compiled Communication (CC) [21]. In CC, the compiler determines the communication requirements in a program and manages network resources, such as multicast groups and buffer memory, statically using the knowledge of both the underlying network architecture and the application communication requirement. In this technique, the compiler analyzes the program and partitions it into phases. Each phase has a fixed communication pattern and the compiler inserts code to reconfigure the network at the end of each phase to manage network resources directly. CC can eliminate runtime communication overhead produced by group management. CC can also use prolonged connections for communications and amortize the startup overhead over a number of messages. However, CC cannot be applied to communications where information is not available at compile time. In other words, the programming style influences the effectiveness of the CC technique. Recently, CC has been proposed to improve the performance of MPI routines for clusters of workstations, and an MPI prototype called CC-MPI [12] has been designed. The CC-MPI supports compiled communication on Ethernet switched clusters. It allows the user to manage network resources such as multicast groups directly and to optimize communications based on the availability of the communication information. The CC-MPI optimizes one-to-all, one-to-many, all-to-all, and many-to-many collective communication routines using the CC technique.

6   Conclusions

In this paper, we have provided detailed information about how to perform code manipulations in order to optimize parallel programs by exploiting static information. This technique eliminates messages if the input data of MPI_Send() and MPI_Recv() routines are known. We show that code transformations can be considered as efficient optimization tool and they can be done by a partial evaluator using D-IS memory system. We have shown that partial evaluation can be extended to a wider class of program paradigms, and efficiently applied to distributed-applications, reducing the number of the most time-consuming operations in addition to the known optimizations of sequential programs. In some applications with a partially given input, the number of remote memory requests can be decreased dramatically by evaluating ready-to-execute MPI_Send() and MPI_Recv() routines. Traffic in the interconnection network and the network latency is also reduced and it makes the system more scalable especially with slow interconnection media.

Technique also improves design process avoiding hand-made optimization and exploiting features of parallel system automatically. Technique may also increase code and memory consumption while improving efficiency; however, the same occurs with traditional partial evaluation technique. The regulation of extra code inserted is made by limitation of unfolding or depth of recursion, or loop unrolling, etc. automatically or with human interaction during partial evaluation step. Moreover, code that handles transactions (send/receive routines) could grow with less speed than specialized code for each processor. In any case, elimination of the messages is much more time saving than time increasing by code growing.

Acknowledgements. The authors are pleased to acknowledge the anonymous referees whose valuable remarks and comments helped improve the paper. This work is supported in part by the UC-Mexus under 2003-2004 post doctorate program, by UABC under grant #371, by SEP-PROMEP under grant #PTC-UABC-16, by the NSF under Grants #CCR-0234444 and INT-0223647, and by CONACYT under grant #32989. Any opinions, findings, conclusions, or recommendations expressed in this material are those of the authors and do not necessarily reflect the views of the UC-Mexus, UABC, SEP, NSF, or of CONACYT.

References

1. Amarasinghe S-P and Lam M-S. Communication optimization and code generation for distributed memory machines. In Proceedings of the SIGPLAN '93 Conference on Programming Language Design and Implementation. 1993.
2. Arvind, Nikhil R-S, Pingali K-K. I-Structures: Data Structures for Parallel Computing. ACM Transaction on PLS, Vol. 11 No. 4 pp. 598-632. 1989.
3. Banerjee P., Chandy J-A, Gupta M., Holm J-G, Lain A, Palermo D-J, Ramaswamy S., Su E. The PARADIGM compiler for distributed-memory message multicomputers. In proceedings of the first international workshop on parallel processing. 1994.
4. Bruck J., Dolev D., Ho C-T, Roşu M-C, Strong R. Efficient Message-passing Interface (MPI) for Parallel Computing on Clusters of Workstations. Journal of Parallel and Distributed Computing, Vol. 40 No. 1 pp. 19-34. 1997.
5. Champeaux D., Lea D., and Faure P. Object-Oriented System Development. Addison Wesley, ISBN 0-201-56355-X. 1993.
6. Cristóbal-Salas A, and Tchernykh A. I-Structure Software Cache for distributed applications. Dyna, Year 71, No. 141. pp. 67 – 74. Medellín, March 2004. ISSN 0012-7353. 2004
7. Cristóbal-Salas A., Tchernykh A., Gaudiot J-L., Lin WY. Non-Strict Execution in Parallel and Distributed Computing, International Journal of Parallel Programming, Kluwer Academic Publishers, New York, U.S.A., Vol. 31, 2, p. 77-105. 2003.
8. Cristóbal-Salas A., Tchernykh A., Gaudiot J-L. Incomplete Information Processing for Optimization of Distributed Applications. Proceedings of the Fourth ACIS International Conference on Software Engineering, Artificial Intelligence, Networking, and Parallel/Distributed Computing (SNPD'03), ACIS, pp. 277-284, 2003.
9. Faraj A-A. Communication characteristics in the NAS parallel benchmarks. Master thesis, college of arts and sciences, Florida State University. October 2002.
10. Garza-Salazar D-A, Bohm W. D-OSC: A sisal compiler for distributed memory machines. In proceedings of the International Workshop on PCS. 1997.
11. Jones, N-D. An introduction to Partial Evaluation. ACM computing surveys, Vol. 28, No. 3. 1996.

12. Karwande A., Yuan X., and Lowenthal D-K. CC-MPI: A Compiled Communication Capable MPI Prototype for Ethernet Switched Clusters. ACM SIGPLAN Symposium on Principles and Practice of Parallel Programming (PPoPP), pp. 95-106. 2003.
13. Kielmann T., Hofman F-H, Bal H-E, Plaat A., and Bhoedjang A-F. MagPIe: MPI's Collective Communication Operations for Clustered Wide Area Systems, 7th ACM SIGPLAN Symposium on Principles and Practice of Parallel Programming (PPOPP'99). 1999.
14. Lahaut D. and Germain C. Static Communications in Parallel Scientic Programs. In PARLE'94, Parallel Architec-ture & Languages, LNCS 817, pp. 262-276. 1994.
15. Lin W-Y, and Gaudiot J-L. 1996. I-Structure Software Cache - A split-Phase Transaction runtime cache system, Proceedings of PACT '96 Boston, MA. 1996.
16. McGraw J., Skedzielewski S., Allan S., Grit D., Oldehoeft R., Glauert J., Dobes I., and Hohensee P. SISAL-Streams and Iterations in a Single Assignment Language, Language Reference Manual, version 1. 2. Technical Report TR M-146, University of California - Lawrence Livermore Laboratory. 1985.
17. Mikulic Emil. Haar wavelet transform. http://dmr.ath.cx/gfx/haar/index.html. 2004.
18. Mogensen and P Sestoft. Partial evaluation. In A. Kent and J.G. Williams, editors, Encyclopedia of Computer Science and Technology, Vol. 37, pp. 247-279. 1997.
19. Moh S., Yu C., Lee B., Youn H-Y, Han D., Lee D. 4-ary Tree-Based Barrier Synchronization for 2-D Meshes without Nonmember Involvement. IEEE Transactions on Computers, Vol. 50, No. 8. 2001.
20. Ogawa H., Matsuoka S. OMPI: Optimizing MPI programs using Partial Evaluation. Proceedings of the 1996 IEEE/ACM Supercomputing Conference, Pittsburgh. 1996.
21. Yuan X., Melhem R. and Gupta R., Algorithms for Supporting Compiled Communication. IEEE Transactions on Parallel and Distributed Systems, Vol. 14, No. 2, pp. 107-118. 2003.

The Feasibility of Interactively Probing
Quiescent Properties of GUI Applications

Peter Achten

Department of Software Technology, Radboud University Nijmegen, Toernooiveld 1,
6525ED Nijmegen, The Netherlands
P.Achten@science.ru.nl

Abstract. In this paper we explore how application-users can, in an interactive way, test properties about the state of GUI applications that can be classified as local state transition systems with quiescence. These properties can be added and removed at run-time. It is guaranteed that they are type-correct. We investigate the consequences of such an approach for one particular functional GUI library, Object I/O. The goal is to gain confidence in the quality of interactive applications, and to seek properties that can be proven correct, perhaps using formal proof tools.

1 Introduction

Programming an effective Graphical User Interface (GUI) is a challenging task because of the myriad of details that need to be controlled and managed: the set of possible events, knowledge of the API, general design rules for GUIs, life-cycle maintenance of GUI objects, and so on.

However, if we ignore this plethora of details, it turns out that the structure of a typical GUI program is basically a *nested while-case loop*. The *while* structure reflects the obligation of a GUI application to poll for *events* until termination; the *case* structure reflects the need to perform case distinction on the events and act according to the needs of the application; this structure is *nested* due to the use of constructs such as modal dialogues and synchronous message passing.

A second characteristic feature of GUI applications is that they use a *structured state*, usually relying on scope rules. This structured state evolves dynamically, as parts of the state are associated with GUI objects. The data itself is in general not very complicated. We call the state *stable* when the application is polling for the next available event, because it can not modify the state in any way until an event is actually been given to it. In testing theory, this state of the application is also known as *quiescence* [17], i.e.: the application can not proceed without further input.

Although the structure of GUI programs is clear, it is hard to reason about GUI applications thoroughly and rigidly. This is caused by the following reasons:

1. The actions that are triggered by the case distinctions operate on the same (parts of the) state structure, thereby interfering with each other. When there

C. Grelck et al. (Eds.): IFL 2004, LNCS 3474, pp. 17–34, 2005.
© Springer-Verlag Berlin Heidelberg 2005

are many such actions it is hard to keep track of each of their effects. Even a small application such as *Notepad* on Windows has at least 100 actions.

2. Reasoning about a particular program run boils down to reasoning about a particular *event trace*, an ordered sequence of events. Applications modify the set of admissible events dynamically by techniques such as enabling/disabling, hiding/showing, opening/closing of GUI objects, in order to provide the user with proper feedback on allowed actions on his part. This means that one cannot assume that an event trace is a sequence of random events.

3. The case distinction done by applications is *partial*: a program does not respond to all possible events because that would make even the simplest application unreasonably large. Instead, the underlying system takes standard actions if the application is not interested or chooses to ignore events. As a consequence, one can not rely solely on the code as the specification, but one must also take the behavior of the operating system into account.

When designing the state structure, the programmer usually has some properties in mind that the values of the state structure should satisfy whenever the application is in a stable state. A property is *invariant* for a specific event trace if it holds during all stable states along this trace. Ideally, we would like to *prove* that a property is invariant for every possible event trace because this promotes such a property to an invariant of the application. Unfortunately, for the reasons mentioned above, this is infeasible.

In this paper we take a pragmatic approach to the problem of establishing (hopefully invariant) properties of GUI applications. We want to encourage GUI programmers to develop as many properties as possible (including false ones!) to any GUI object of an application under construction or one that has been finished long ago by perhaps somebody else. This is known as *run-time assertion checking* [12, 10]. However, for reasons of flexibility, we want to be able to *interactively* add and remove properties. The application, whenever in a stable state, checks all currently added properties and notifies the user whenever a property is violated. In this way, the developer can *probe* the application for properties.

The concrete research questions this feasibility study should give an answer to are:

- Can we assign properties to any GUI object in the application, and even to the whole application? Can this be done at compile-time and at run-time?
- Are properties that are added always of the correct type?
- Can we store properties on disk?
- Is there no loss in efficiency when no properties are probed?

Based on the results of this feasibility study, we intend to implement this system for the Object I/O library [2, 4, 1, 5], a comprehensive GUI library that is available for the functional programming languages Clean [16] and Haskell [14].

This paper is structured as follows. We first present our technique for *local state transition systems* in general in Section 2. In Section 3 we show that Object I/O is a local state transition system. We then explain the expected issues when adding property probing to Object I/O in Section 4. We discuss related work in Section 5 and conclude in Section 6.

2 Probing Local State Transition Systems

The bare bones structure of the class of GUI applications that we investigate is that of a *local state transition system* [3], which is basically the same as that of a nested while-case as discussed in the introduction. In this section we reveal this structure (Section 2.1) in order to point out the technical problems that need to be resolved when adding/removing (Section 2.2) and testing (Section 2.3) properties in a type-safe and dynamic way.

2.1 Local State Transition Systems

The set of types is very similar to those presented in [3], except that here we do include interactive processes (in order to reason about complete programs). A program (`Program`) is a collection of processes (`Process`), each of which encapsulates a state `ps` via an existential quantifier ($\exists$ `ps:`). This state is shared by all of its elements. It effectively models the global data that is accessible by every element. To enforce this, the type (`Proc ps`) is used.

```
::¹ Program :== [Process]
:: Process = ∃ps: Process (Proc ps)
```

Every process (the record type `Proc ps` below) has a number of actions that respond to process related events. These are modelled by the list of functions in the field `pcbfs`. Note that the type of an action, ((`Proc ps`) $\rightarrow$ (`Proc ps`)) provides it with full access to all elements of a program. In particular, the other processes are also an element of a process (`pcontext`). Processes are identified by an `ID`, which is a simple integer. An event (`id,i`)::`Event` identifies the `i`-th action of the process `id`. This is of course a very simplified form of events.

```
:: Proc ps    = {² pstate   :: ps
               , pid        :: ID
               , pcbfs      :: [(Proc ps) → (Proc ps)]
               , pobjs      :: [Object (Proc ps)]
               , pcontext   :: [Process] }
:: ID         :== Int
:: Event      :== (ID,Int)
```

Processes have top-level objects (these correspond with menus, windows, and so on), stored in `pobjs`, each of which again encapsulate their piece of local state `ls` and operate on the same state of the program `pst`, which is always (`Proc ps`):

```
:: Object pst = ∃ls: Object ls [Comp ls pst]
```

Top-level objects have components with access to the shared state (`Proc ps`) and the local state of the top-level object (`ls`). A component (`Comp ls pst`)

---

[1] All Clean type definitions are introduced by thekeyword `::`. Synonym types are indicated with separatorsymbol `:==`. Algebraic and record types are indicated with-separator symbol `=`.

[2] $\{f_0 :: t_0, \ldots, f_n :: t_n\}$ denotes a record type with field names f_i and typet_i.

is either a concrete object (`Obj ls pst`), or it replaces the current local state (`NewLS ls pst`), or it extends the current local state (`AddLS ls pst`).

```
:: Comp ls pst = Obj   (Obj   ls pst)
               | NewLS (NewLS ls pst)
               | AddLS (AddLS ls pst)
:: NewLS ls pst = ∃new: {newLS :: new, newDef :: [Comp  new      pst]}
:: AddLS ls pst = ∃new: {addLS :: new, addDef :: [Comp  (new,ls) pst]}
```

Analogous to processes, concrete objects are identified via an ID, have actions, and can contain other objects. An event (`id,i`) identifies the `i`-th action of the concrete object identified by `id`.

```
:: Obj ls pst = { oid   :: ID
                , ocbfs :: [(ls,pst) → (ls,pst)]
                , oobjs :: [Comp ls pst] }
```

With this collection of types we can model scoped state structures. A value `p::Program` represents the complete quiescent state of a program. When an application successfully polls for an event `e = (id,i)`, then the next quiescent state of the program is computed by (`eval e`).

```
eval :: Event Program → Program³
```

We will not discuss its implementation: it is basically a recursive function that searches for a process or concrete object that is identified by `id` and applies the `i`-th action to the current program state. Details can be found in [3].

Example. In order to make this discussion more concrete, consider the following small example of a local state transition system that has a few 'bugs':

```
program :: Program
program
  = [Process                                // the process
       { pstate  = []                       // shared [Int] state of process
       , pid     = 1                         // identification value of process
       , pcbfs   = []                        // process has no actions
       , pobjs   = [Object                   // top-level object
                      0                      // local Int state of top-level object
                      [Obj { oid   = 2       // identification value of child object
                           , ocbfs = [ λ(n,pst=:{pstate=1})    // action 1
                                         → (n+1,{pst &⁴ pstate=[n+1:1]⁵})
                                     , λ(n,pst=:{pstate=1})    // action 2
                                         → (n-1,{pst & pstate=tl 1}) ]
                           , oobjs = [] }]]
       , pcontext = [] }]
```

---

³ Clean separates function arguments by whitespace, instead of →.
⁴ {r & f₀ = v₀,..., fₙ = vₙ} is a record equal to r, except that fields fᵢ have value vᵢ.
⁵ Clean lists are always delimited by [and].

The process maintains and shares a list of integers, `pstate :: [Int]`. The concrete object, identified by `oid = 2`, has two actions: the first adds one element to the list, and the second shortens the list. The object has a local integer state which value should reflect the length of the shared integer list. The second action contains two bugs caused by unrestricted uses of `tl` in `tl l` and `-` in `n-1`.

2.2   Adding and Removing Properties at Run-Time

A *property* of some data type `st` is a boolean function:

```
:: Prop st :== st → Bool
```

In Section 2.1 we have introduced the elements that we want to probe:

- Complete programs, of type `[Process]` are probed with `(Prop [Process])`.
- Processes, of type `(Proc ps)`, with `ps` the type of the shared state, are probed with `(Prop (Proc ps))`.
- Concrete objects, of type `(Obj ls (Proc ps))`, with `ls` the type of the local shared state of the concrete object. Note that, due to `NewLS` and `AddLS`, `ls` can be a nested tuple composition of several local states. They are probed with `(Prop (ls,Proc ps))`.

In order to test any of these elements at run-time with an appropriate property one needs to provide a property of the *correct type*. Unfortunately, only the type of complete programs is immediately accessible; the types of the scoped state of processes and concrete objects can not be retrieved, even though we, as program developer, are well aware of their concrete types. The deliberate existential quantification has rendered it impossible for us to check properties afterwards using a solution within the *static* type system.

We need to resort to *dynamic* type checking if we are to solve this issue. For several years now, Clean has had dynamic types [15, 18]. There are basically two ways to use dynamic types for our problem:

1. Do not use existential types to hide the types of the states but use dynamic types. In that case, checking for type equality is straightforward, using run-time type unification.
2. Use existential types to hide the types of the states, but do the type equality match inside the object's scope where the types are known.

Alternative 1 is alien to the philosophy of working in a strongly typed language. Instead, we show that alternative 2 can be used within the framework.

First we wrap properties in a dynamic, and give such a property a name:

```
:: UserProp    = { name :: PropName
                 , prop :: PropDynamic }
:: PropName    :== String    // A sensible name
:: PropDynamic :== Dynamic   // A (Prop st) function
```

We need to make a few modifications to the data types that we have introduced in Section 2.1. We store the properties of each object in an association list. Its key value is (Just id) with id::ID of processes and concrete objects, and Nothing for complete programs. The association list is stored globally in the Program type, which now becomes a record.

```
:: Program    = { procs :: [Process]      // As before
                , props :: [Property] }  // The property list
:: Property := (Maybe ID,[UserProp])     // For each element, all its properties
```

The second change that we need to make is related with the dynamic type system. We are going to match the type of a property encapsulated in a PropDynamic with the state in scope of concrete objects and processes. This is done by a *type dependent* function [15]. A type dependent function can match a dynamic type with a static type, provided the static type belongs to the TC type class. We need to impose this restriction to the type variables of Proc and Obj. Because Clean does not support type class restrictions on data type definitions, we do this with an explicit dictionary (DictTC) which amounts to the same thing:

```
:: DictTC  a  = { unpack :: Dynamic → (Bool,Prop a) }

:: Proc    ps = { ..., pdict :: DictTC (Proc ps) }
:: Obj ls pst = { ..., odict :: DictTC (ls,pst)  }
```

The unpack member is a function that returns the content of its dynamic argument if it correctly contains a property of the right type. It is easy to define a type dependent function that creates a dictionary of the desired type:

```
dictTC :: DictTC a |⁶ TC a
```

dictTC :: DictTC a $|^6$ TC a

dictTC = { unpack = λdx → case dx of

$$(x :: Prop\ a^{\wedge 7}) = (True,\ x)$$
$$\_ = (False, \bot) \}$$

We can now proceed by defining the function addProperty that associates a property with an element:

```
addProperty :: (Maybe ID) UserProp Program → (Bool,Program)
```

The task of (addProperty mid prop prog) is to extend the prog.props list with an entry for (mid,prop) either by extending an existing entry or creating a new one. The function fails (returns False) if the type of the property does not match. The key challenge of this function is the check for type equality. Let us assume that this function, propertyTypeMatches, exists. Then the definition of addProperty is straightforward:

```
addProperty :: (Maybe ID) UserProp Program → (Bool,Program)
addProperty mid p=:⁸{prop} program=:{props}
```

addProperty mid p=:^{8}{prop} program=:{props}

---

[6] In a function type, | introducesall overloading class restrictions.

[7] $a^{\wedge}$ refers to a in the parent function type, in this case DictTC a.

[8] x =: e binds x to e.

```
   | not (propertyTypeMatches mid prop program)
              = (False,program)
   | otherwise = (True,{program & props=new_props})
where
   new_props   = case span (λ(mid',_) = mid≠mid') props of
                   (otherProps,[])                  // no properties yet
                      = otherProps++[(mid,[p])]
                   (otherProps,[(_,ps):otherProps2])  // extend properties
                      = otherProps++[(mid,ps++[p]):otherProps2]
```

Note that `addProperty` maintains the order of registered properties, so properties are tested in the same order all the time.

The function application (`propertyTypeMatches mid p program`) must decide whether the indicated object operates on the type as given by p. If `mid`=`Nothing`, then it must be a program property, and hence the dynamic content should be matched with type (`Prop [Process]`):

```
propertyTypeMatches :: (Maybe ID) PropDynamic Program → Bool
propertyTypeMatches Nothing dp _ = case dp of
                            (_ :: Prop [Process]) = True
                            otherwise             = False
```

If (`mid` == (`Just id`)), then it must either correspond with a process or with a concrete object.

```
propertyTypeMatches (Just id) dp {procs} = any (processMatches id dp) procs
```

A process matches if its `pid` matches `id` *and* the dynamic property `dp` matches the dictionary `pdict`. A process also matches if any of its components matches:

```
processMatches :: ID PropDynamic Process → Bool
processMatches id dp (Process proc) = procMatches id dp proc
where
   procMatches :: ID PropDynamic (Proc ps) → Bool | TC ps
   procMatches id dp { pid,pobjs,pdict }
     = id=pid && fst (pdict.unpack dp) || any (objectMatches id dp) pobjs
```

The search for the proper concrete object is handled recursively. The interesting case is the match on a concrete object, which proceeds analogously to matching a process: either the concrete object matches or any of its children.

```
objectMatches :: ID PropDynamic (Object (Proc ps)) → Bool | TC ps
objectMatches id dp (Object _ cs) = any (compMatches id dp) cs
where
   compMatches :: ID PropDynamic (Comp ls (Proc ps)) → Bool | TC ls
   compMatches id dp (Obj {oid,odict,oobjs})
     = id=oid && fst (odict.unpack dp) || any (compMatches id dp) oobjs
   compMatches id dp (NewLS {newDef})  = any (compMatches id dp) newDef
   compMatches id dp (AddLS {addDef})  = any (compMatches id dp) addDef
```

Finally, it is convenient to have a version of `addProperty` that aborts in case the property type does not match the indicated object's state:

```
add :: (Maybe ID) UserProp Program → Program add mid prop program
    #⁹ (ok,program) = addProperty mid prop program
    | ok           = program
    | otherwise    = abort ("Could not add "+++¹⁰prop.name)
```

Because properties are stored globally in `Program`, it is trivial to define the function that removes properties by name:

```
delProperty :: PropName Program → Program
delProperty name program=:{props}
  = {program & props=[(mid,[p \\ p←ps | p.name≠name]) \\ (mid,ps)←props]}
```

Example. We continue our running example given at the end of Section 2.1 by extending it with properties. The only change of definition of `program` is the extension with two record fields `pdict=dictTC` and `odict=dictTC` at the appropriate places, as well as an empty properties list (`props=[]`).

We introduce one property for the program and process, and two for the concrete object. They are:

```
singleProp              // Program property
= { name="singleProcess"
  , prop=dynamic¹¹ (λprocs → length procs==1)::Prop [Process]          }
sortedProp              // Process property
= { name="sortedProp"
  , prop=dynamic (λ{pstate=l} → l==reverse $ sort l)::Prop (Proc [Int]) }
lengthProp              // Object property
= { name="lengthProp"
  , prop=dynamic (λ(n,{pstate=l}) → n==length l)::∀a:Prop (Int,Proc [a])}
definedProp             // Object property
= { name="definedProp"
  , prop=dynamic (λ(_,{pstate=l}) → 0≤length l)::∀a b:Prop (a,Proc [b]) }
```

`singleProp` states that there is one single process at every stable state; `sorted-Prop` says that the integer list of the process is in reverse order; `lengthProp` defines that the integer value of the concrete object correctly keeps track of the length of the list of its parent object; `definedProp` defines that the list spine does not contain ⊥. Note that the polymorphism in the types of the latter two functions makes them suitable for probing other objects.

2.3   Testing Properties at Quiescence

In the previous section we have explained how properties of programs, processes, and concrete objects can be added and removed at run-time. In this section we show how these properties can be tested when the application is in a stable state,

---

⁹ This is Clean's 'do-notation' for explicit environment passing.
¹⁰ +++ is the Clean string concatenation operator.
¹¹ **dynamic** $e :: t$ turns expression e of type t into a value of type Dynamic.

is quiescent. The function `reportProperties` evaluates all current properties of its program argument and collects the results in a report:

```
reportProperties :: Program → PropertiesReport
```

The report assigns, for each step in a run, a *verdict* for each tested property. A verdict is a simple boolean, which is true iff the property holds.

```
:: PropertiesReport = { run      :: Int
                      , reports :: [PropertyReport] }
:: PropertyReport  :== (Maybe ID,[(UserProp,Verdict)])
:: Verdict         :== Bool
```

To keep track of the run, the program type is extended with a run-count that is incremented by `eval`:

```
:: Program = { ..., run :: Int }
```

The purpose of (`reportProperties program`) is to test every property in the `props` field of `program`. Recall that properties are boolean functions on the particular state of the object with which they are associated. This means that `reportProperties` must construct the appropriate state of each object at which the property function can be applied. The function can then compute the verdict simply by application of the property to the constructed state.

The top-level of this function is easily defined:

```
reportProperties :: Program → PropertiesReport
reportProperties program=:{run,props}
  = foldl (programProperties program) {run=run,reports=[]} props
```

Note that this implies that if no properties are added to a program, the only computational overhead is generated by incrementing the run count by the modified `eval` function.

The function application (`programProperties program pr prop`) needs to test a program property in case `prop` = (`Nothing,props`). We know that `props` contains (`Prop [Process]`) property functions because `addProperty` is type-safe.

```
programProperties :: Program PropertiesReport Property → PropertiesReport
programProperties program=:{procs} pr=:{reports} (Nothing,props)
  = {pr & reports=reports++[(Nothing,[ (p,programProperty p.prop procs)
                                      \\ p ← props
                                      ]
                            )]}
where programProperty :: PropDynamic → Prop Program
      programProperty (f :: Prop [Process]) = f
```

In case `prop` = (`Just id,props`) then the correct state context needs to be built for a process or a concrete object. First consider testing a process property. If a process is found with a `pid::ID` that matches `id` then we know that the list of properties `props` contains functions of type (`Prop (Proc ps)`), with `ps` the type of the current value of its state. We can safely unpack every such property using the dictionary of the process (`pdict`) and apply it to the process. Note that we need to filter itself from the list of all processes in the `pcontext` field before doing so.

```
programProperties program=:{procs} pr (Just id,props)
  = foldl processProperties pr procs
where
  processProperties :: PropertiesReport Process → PropertiesReport
  processProperties pr (Process proc) = procProperties pr proc
  where
    procProperties :: PropertiesReport (Proc ps) → PropertiesReport
    procProperties pr=:{reports=rs} proc=:{pid,pobjs,pdict}
      | id==pid
        = {pr & reports=rs++[(Just id,[ (p,snd (pdict.unpack p.prop) pst)
                                      \\ p ← props
                                      ])]}
      | otherwise
        = foldl (objectProperties pst) pr pobjs
    where
      pst = {proc & pcontext=[p \\ p=:(Process {pid}) ← procs | pid≠id]}

    objectProperties ... // see definition below
```

Testing concrete object properties proceeds in an analogous way, except that now a local state structure needs to be built to which the properties can be applied. This is a recursive definition that follows the nested structure of the objects and their state scopes, which makes it a bit verbose.

```
objectProperties :: (Proc ps) PropertiesReport (Object (Proc ps))
                                → PropertiesReport
objectProperties pst pr (Object ls cs)
  = foldl (compProperties ls pst) pr cs
where
  compProperties :: ls (Proc ps) PropertiesReport (Comp ls (Proc ps))
                                → PropertiesReport
  compProperties ls pst pr=:{reports=rs} (Obj {oid,odict,oobjs})
    | id==oid
      = {pr & reports=rs++[(Just id,[(p,snd (odict.unpack p.prop) (ls,pst))
                                    \\ p ← props
                                    ])]}
    | otherwise
      = foldl (compProperties ls pst) pr oobjs
  compProperties _ pst pr (NewLS {newLS,newDef})
    = foldl (compProperties newLS pst) pr newDef
  compProperties ls pst pr (AddLS {addLS,addDef})
    = foldl (compProperties (addLS,ls) pst) pr addDef
```

Given the `reportProperties` function, it is straightforward to define extended `eval` functions that produce property report(s) and next program(s):

```
step :: Event Program → (PropertiesReport,Program)
step event program = (reportProperties program,eval event program)
```

```
steps :: [Event] Program → ([PropertiesReport],Program)
steps es program = seqList (map step es) program
```

Finally, for decent output, we define an instance of the `toString` function for a `PropertiesReport` that displays the number of tested properties, and names those that have failed in a particular run. We do not want to print the `Program` value, but we are interested in the definedness of its state values. We realize this by adding appropriate strictness annotations in its type definitions.

Example. We finish our running example by mimicking a probing session of the faulty program. The `program` definition is extended with **run**=0 field. We start by running the program without any properties, given a particular scenario:

Start [12]

```
♯ (rs0,program) = steps scenario0 program
= map toString rs0
```

The scenario first picks the first action of concrete object with `ID` value equal to 2, then takes the second action twice, and ends with the first action:

$scenario_0 = [(2,1),(2,2),(2,2),(2,1)]$

This scenario reveals the first 'bug' in the program:

```
Step 0: tested 0 properties. 0 failing properties.
Step 1: tested 0 properties. 0 failing properties.
Step 2: tested 0 properties. 0 failing properties.
tl of []
```

This means that everything runs properly until just before the second invocation of the second action (step 2), but after doing that action apparently the tail of an empty list is taken. We want to probe the definedness of the integer list that can be accessed by concrete object identified by `ID` 2. For this purpose we use `definedProp` (Section 2.2).

Start

```
♯ program       = add (Just 2) definedProp program
♯ (rs0,program) = steps scenario0 program
= map toString rs0
```

Applying the same scenario provides evidence that the list was defined initially and after the first two steps:

```
Step 0: tested 1 property. 0 failing properties.
Step 1: tested 1 property. 0 failing properties.
Step 2: tested 1 property. 0 failing properties.
tl of []
```

---

[12] **Start** is the main function of a Clean program.

This bug is easily fixed by replacing `tl` with `tl'`:

```
tl' :: [a] → [a]
tl' xs = if (isEmpty xs) xs (tl xs)
```

Running the program through the same scenario confirms that the definedness property now holds for this trace:

```
Step 0: tested 1 property. 0 failing properties.
Step 1: tested 1 property. 0 failing properties.
Step 2: tested 1 property. 0 failing properties.
Step 3: tested 1 property. 0 failing properties.
```

At this stage we no longer wish to probe the definedness of the list, but instead probe the other properties that have been given in Section 2.2. This is specified as follows:

```
Start
  # program       = add (Just 2) definedProp program
  # (rs0,program) = steps scenario0 program
  # program       = delProperty definedProp.name program
  # program       = add Nothing  singleProp  program
  # program       = add (Just 1) sortedProp  program
  # program       = add (Just 2) lengthProp  program
  # (rs1,program) = steps scenario1 program
  = map toString (rs0++rs1)
```

$$scenario_1 = [(2,1)]$$

Running the program through this longer scenario reveals the second 'bug':

```
Step 0: tested 1 property. 0 failing properties.
Step 1: tested 1 property. 0 failing properties.
Step 2: tested 1 property. 0 failing properties.
Step 3: tested 1 property. 0 failing properties.
Step 4: tested 3 properties. 1 failing property.
        lengthProp
```

Although property `lengthProp` is actually violated immediately after the second invocation of the second action, this is not displayed because the property was not probed at that stage. Instead, violation of the property is detected immediately after it is added (after step 3). This is caused by the local integer that decreases below 0 and therefore incorrectly reflects the length of the integer list. We fix this bug by replacing `n-1` with `n.-.1`, defined as:

```
(.-.)¹³infixl 6 :: !¹⁴Int !Int ->Int
(.-.) m n = max 0 (m-n)
```

Running the scenario again renders the properties invariant with respect to this event trace.

---

[13] (f) *fix* n :: t defines a new operator f of type t with fixity *fix* ∈ {*infix, infixl, infixr*}and precedence n.

[14] In a typedefinition, `!t` puts type t in a strict context.

3   Object I/O Is a Local State Transition Systems

In this section we explain the relation between the local state transition systems of the previous section with Object I/O. We do this in an informal manner, by means of an Object I/O program that is equivalent to the one shown in Section 2. A different account has appeared earlier in [3].

As in the local state transition example, the program consists of a single interactive process. Instead of manipulating an integer list, this program manipulates an Id list (second argument of Process):

```
Start :: *¹⁵World -> *World
Start world = startProcesses
                [Process MDI [] initGUI [ProcessClose closeProcess]] world
```

In Object I/O the state of an interactive process is given by the record type (:: PSt ps = {ls :: ps, io :: IOSt ps}), with ps the state as discussed in the previous section. io is a combination of the fields pobjs and pcontext. It is an abstract data type by which the programmer must access all GUI elements and the external world. In this example, we have a (PSt [Id]) process state.

The Id values are used to identify windows that are opened and closed dynamically by the two actions open and close. These actions are the callback functions of two menu items, labelled "Open" and "Close" respectively. Their parent object is the top-level menu object that corresponds with the Object of the local state transition system, and indeed, it encapsulates an integer state (first argument of openMenu). Note that the Object I/O program below has exactly the same 'bugs' as the running example in the previous section.

```
initGUI :: (PSt [Id]) → PSt [Id]
initGUI pst = snd $ openMenu 0 mDef pst
where
  mDef :: Menu (:+: MenuItem MenuItem) Int (PSt [Id])
  mDef  = Menu "&File"
                (   MenuItem "&Open"  [MenuFunction open ]
                :+: MenuItem "&Close" [MenuFunction close]
                )   []

  open :: (Int,PSt [Id]) → (Int,PSt [Id])
  open (n,pst=:{ls=l})
    # (wid,pst) = openId pst
    # wDef      = Window ("Window "+++toString (n+1)) NilLS [WindowId wid]
    # pst       = snd $ openWindow ⊥ wDef pst
    = (n+1,{pst & ls=[wid:l]})

  close :: (Int,PSt [Id]) → (Int,PSt [Id])
  close (n,pst=:{ls}) = (n-1,closeWindow (hd ls) {pst & ls=tl ls})
```

---

[15] Clean uses the 'world-as-value' paradigm for I/O. An annotated type *t indicates that t is used in a single threaded way. This is guaranteed by the type system.

Recall that in the local state transition system there are three kinds of elements that can be probed:

Programs probed with (Prop [Process]). Object I/O has a data type similar to [Process] (viz. Context) but this is an internal data type and should not be accessed by the programmer. There are no retrieval operations defined on this data type, so basically, the programmer can not define program properties as in the previous section. (Note that this suggests that the API of Object I/O might be lacking functionality, so it is worthwhile to see what useful access functions can be added.)

Processes probed with (Prop (Proc ps)). Object I/O processes are probed by (Prop (PSt ps)); in the example by (Prop (PSt [Id])).

Objects probed with (Prop (1s,Proc ps)). The GUI objects in the program are mDef, its two MenuItem elements, and the dynamically created windows (wDef). The menu and its items share an integer local state, so they are probed by (Prop (Int,PSt [Id])). The window has no significant local state ($\perp$ :: $\forall$a:a), so it is probed by ($\forall$a:Prop (a,PSt [Id])).

4   Issues of Probing Object I/O Programs

In the previous section we have shown in a very informal way how Object I/O relates to local state transition systems. In this section we discuss the major issues that are likely to occur when Object I/O applications are dynamically probed. Firstly, dynamically adding/removing properties to an Object I/O program requires *identification* of the GUI elements at run-time (Section 4.1). Secondly, assertions should be *free of side-effects* (Section 4.2). Finally, this work contributes to an old debate about which state paradigm to use: *explicit* or *implicit* state passing (Section 4.3).

4.1   Run-Time Identification of GUI elements

From the account in Section 2.2 we know that it is sufficient to retrieve the Id value of an element in order to associate a property with it using addProperty. The example in Section 3 shows that these identification values are known only at run-time, which is a quite common approach in GUI APIs. When probing GUI elements dynamically, the user needs to identify them. For this purpose we include a *GUI browser* for each application with which the user can select a GUI element, and thereby its identification value. This browser can be defined in Object I/O using the API inspection functions, and a tree list control to present the hierarchical structure of the GUI. Fig. 1 gives screenshots of this browser for the example program at several stable states.

Clean dynamics can be stored on disk, so the user can browse the file system in search of interesting properties, or create them using the Clean IDE and store them on disk. This gives the two arguments of the addProperty function, which should allow us to associate a stored property with a given GUI element.

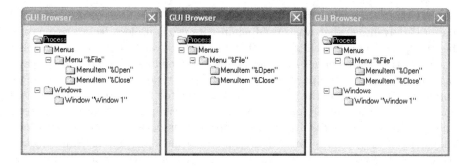

Fig. 1. The GUI browser after: [(2,1)], [(2,1),(2,2),(2,2)], and [(2,1),(2,2),(2,2),(2,1)]

4.2   Properties Should Have no Side-Effects

A fundamental problem with assertion checking systems is the *side-effect problem* [10]. It states that properties should, for obvious reasons, have no side-effects on the programs. In local state transition system terminology, this means that a property should not change the state that it inspects. In Section 2.2 this was effortlessly realized by defining a property over a state st as the simple function type $st \to Bool$. We would like to adopt this simple scheme to Object I/O, but unfortunately this is not possible. The main reason is that the types in Object I/O have been designed to allow the programmer to use *unique* state, i.e. state that can be destructively updated [6]. This requires the 'container types' to be at least as unique as their content. As a consequence, we are forced to use the following property type:

```
:: Prop st :== st → (Bool,st)
```

How can we guarantee that property functions have no side-effect? Such a function might have an effect on the custom states and on the GUI state. The latter can easily be eliminated by providing a 'mirror' library of Object I/O from which all functions are removed that have a side-effect. What is left is a *proof obligation* that property functions do not change the custom states. Systems with proof obligations require good support of proof tools such as Sparkle [9] in order to assist the programmer with these proofs.

4.3   The Influence of the State Paradigm

Object I/O uses an *explicit* state passing paradigm. One advantage of this paradigm is that each object carries in its type full information about which state it manipulates, so we can quickly check if a property that is to be associated with an object actually matches the type of the state.

However, it is also possible to use an *implicit* state passing paradigm using MVars [13]. This has been discussed in [1]. The used GUI monad is a regular IOSt state monad which uses MVars to hold the logical state. Advantages of this approach are the simpler types of Object I/O GUI elements, and the ability to have more complex state structures without loss of control over access. The major disadvantage that was raised against its use is its less declarative nature because programmers need to explicitly *take* and *put* values from these variables.

Interestingly, this paper identifies a new disadvantage of implicit state passing: in contrast with explicit state passing, the type of an object no longer contains information on the state that is manipulated by the object. This means that our approach of unifying the type of a dynamic property with the state of an object no longer works. Instead, one needs to associate properties over MVars that happen to be manipulated by objects. Identification and matching of MVars against property types can be done in a similar way as object identification in Sections 4.1 and 2.2, but is more complicated because all MVars must be retraceable for identification purposes, and a property of type $(st_1 \ldots st_n \rightarrow \text{GUI Bool})$ must be matched against $(\text{MVar } st_1) \ldots (\text{MVar } st_n)$.

5   Related Work

Assertion checking has been integrated in the object-oriented languages Eiffel [12] and JML– Java Modelling Language [10]. The Objective Caml language [11] has an **assert** statement. In a recent experiment, assertion checking has been added to Haskell [7]. We have in common with the Eiffel approach that we want to use *executable* properties. With the JML approach we share the reuse of the host language and libraries in order to encourage programmers to probe their applications. The **assert** statement in Objective Caml evaluates boolean expressions. These have no effect in case of true statements, but an exception is thrown in case of false statements. The latter aspect is different from our approach: false properties increase ones understanding of an application as much as true properties, and therefore do not terminate the application.

The main differences are: because of the side-effect problem, JML can't handle I/O methods, which is clearly a must in our case; we do not annotate source code for our properties, but rather probe the application at run-time using dynamically associated properties; this requires properties to be persistent; we do not yet intend these properties to be subject to formal verification as in JML; in contrast with the Haskell approach in which properties are not asserted over unevaluated expressions, we think that an assertion should evaluate an unevaluated expression if needed. The reason for this is that our assertions are meant to express properties of a program: a list must be sorted, a length invariant should hold, and so on. Such properties do not stop at unevaluated expressions, but refer to the complete value.

Probing application properties dynamically has the same flavor as using a *tracing/debugging tool* such as Freja, Hat, and Hood [8] or those used in more conventional programming languages such as C. With such tools one inspects the run-time values of an application whereas we focus on relations between run-time values expressed as properties.

Another area that is related to our work is that of *testing* [17] because in both areas it is the *application* itself that is subject to probing and we can give verdicts only for specific event traces, which in practice will not exhaust the possible event trace search space. At this moment the theory and practice of testing of GUI applications is starting to grow. Our project is a first step to investigate what can be done in this area.

6   Conclusions and Future Work

In this paper we have shown how systems that are based on local state transition systems can be probed at run-time for their stable state based properties. These properties can be added and removed at any stable state of the application. There are no limitations to the size of the application. We have shown what needs to be done additionally for one particular instance of local state transition systems, the Object I/O library. This provides us with a directly usable means to probe GUI applications of arbitrary size.

There are many directions of research to take based on this framework. Among others these are: adding good property management functionality to the framework; extend it with value-inspection and back-tracing in case a property is found to be invalid; explore the formal verification potential of our approach.

Acknowledgements

The author would like to thank Marko van Eekelen and the anonymous referees.

References

1. P. Achten and S. Peyton Jones. Porting the Clean Object I/O library to Haskell. In M. Mohnen and P. Koopman, editors, *Proceedings of the 12th International Workshop on the Implementation of Functional Languages, IFL'00, Selected Papers*, volume 2011 of *LNCS*, pages 194–213. Aachen, Germany, Springer, Sept. 2001.
2. P. Achten and R. Plasmeijer. Interactive Functional Objects in Clean. In C. Clack, K. Hammond, and T. Davie, editors, *Proc. of the 9th International Workshop on the Implementation of Functional Languages, IFL 1997, Selected Papers*, volume 1467 of *LNCS*, pages 304–321. St.Andrews, UK, Springer, Sept. 1998.
3. P. Achten and R. Plasmeijer. The implementation of interactive local state transition systems in Clean. In P. Koopman and C. Clack, editors, *Proceedings of the 11th International workshop on the Implementation of Functional Languages, IFL'99*, number LNCS 1868, pages 115–130. Springer-Verlag, Sept. 2000.
4. P. Achten and M. Wierich. A Tutorial to the Clean Object I/O Library - Version 1.2. Technical Report CSI-R0003, Computing Science Institute, Faculty of Mathematics and Informatics, University of Nijmegen, The Netherlands, Feb. 2000. 294 pages.
5. K. Angelov. ObjectIO for Haskell. Description and Sources at www.haskell.org/ObjectIO/, Applications at /free.top.bg/ka2_mail/, 2003.

6. E. Barendsen and S. Smetsers. Uniqueness typing for functional languages with graph rewriting semantics. In *Mathematical Structures in Computer Science*, volume 6, pages 579–612, 1996.

7. O. Chitil, D. McNeill, and C. Runciman. Lazy Assertions. In Greg Michaelson and Phil Trinder, editors, *Draft Proceedings of the 15th International Workshop on the Implementation of Functional Languages, IFL'03*, pages 31–46. Edinburgh, UK, Sept. 2003.

8. O. Chitil, C. Runciman, and M. Wallace. Freja, Hat and Hood – A Comparative Evaluation of Three Systems for Tracing and Debugging Lazy Functional Programs. In M. Mohnen and P. Koopman, editors, *Proceedings of the 12th International Workshop on the Implementation of Functional Languages, IFL'00, Selected Papers*, volume 2011 of *LNCS*, pages 176–193. Aachen, Germany, Springer, Sept. 2001.

9. M. de Mol, M. van Eekelen, and R. Plasmeijer. Theorem proving for functional programmers - Sparkle: A functional theorem prover. In T. Arts and M. Mohnen, editors, *The 13th International Workshop on Implementation of Functional Languages, IFL 2001, Selected Papers*, volume 2312 of *LNCS*, pages 55–72, Stockholm, Sweden, 2002. Springer.

10. G. T. Leavens, Y. Cheon, C. Clifton, C. Ruby, and D. R. Cok. How the Design of JML Accomodates Both Runtime Assertion Checking and Formal Verification. In *Formal Methods for Components and Objects*, volume 2852 of *LNCS*, pages 262–284. Springer Verlag, 2003. Also available as Technical Report TR 03-04a, Department of Computer Science, 226 Atanasoff Hall, Iowa State University, Ames, Iowa, USA.

11. X. Leroy. *The Objective Caml system – release 3.08; Documentation and user's manual*. Institut National de Recherche en Informatique et en Automatique, July 2004.

12. B. Meyer. *Eiffel: The Language*. Prentice Hall, 1992.

13. S. Peyton Jones, A. Gordon, and S. Finne. Concurrent Haskell. In *23rd ACM Symposium on Principles of Programming Languages (POPL'96)*, pages 295–308, St.Petersburg Beach, Florida, 1996. ACM.

14. S. Peyton Jones and Hughes J. et al. *Report on the programming language Haskell 98*. University of Yale, 1999. http://www.haskell.org/definition/.

15. M. Pil. Dynamic types and type dependent functions. In D. Hammond and Clack, editors, *Implementation of Functional Languages (IFL '98)*, LNCS, pages 169–185. Springer Verlag, 1999.

16. R. Plasmeijer and M. van Eekelen. *Concurrent CLEAN Language Report (version 2.0)*, December 2001. http://www.cs.kun.nl/~clean/contents/contents.html.

17. J. Tretmans. Test Generation with Inputs, Outputs, and Quiescence. In T. Margaria and B. Steffen, editors, *Second Int. Workshop on Tools and Algorithms for the Construction and Analysis of Systems (TACAS'96)*, volume 1055 of *Lecture Notes in Computer Science*, pages 127–146. Springer-Verlag, 1996.

18. M. Vervoort and R. Plasmeijer. Lazy dynamic input/output in the lazy functional language Clean. In R. Peña and T. Arts, editors, *The 14th International Workshop on the Implementation of Functional Languages, IFL'02, Selected Papers*, volume 2670 of *LNCS*, pages 101–117. Springer, Sept. 2003.

A Functional Programming Technique for Forms in Graphical User Interfaces

Sander Evers[1], Peter Achten[1], and Jan Kuper[2]

[1] Radboud University Nijmegen, Department of Software Technology,
Toernooiveld 1, 6525 ED Nijmegen, The Netherlands.
[2] University of Twente, Department of Computer Science,
P.O.Box 217, 7500 AE Enschede, The Netherlands.
{s.evers,p.achten}@cs.ru.nl, jankuper@cs.utwente.nl

Abstract. This paper presents FunctionalForms, a combinator library for constructing fully functioning *forms* in a concise and flexible way. A form is a part of a graphical user interface (GUI) restricted to displaying a value and allowing the user to modify it. The library is built on top of the medium-level GUI library wxHaskell. To obtain complete separation between the structure of a form's layout and that of the edited values, we introduce a novel use of *compositional functional references*.

1 Introduction

In many applications, the graphical user interface (GUI) contains parts which can be considered *forms*: they show a set of values, and allow the user to update them. For example, the omnipresent dialogs labeled *Options*, *Settings* and *Properties* are forms. Also, an address book can be considered a form. (Note that in our sense of the word, a form is not only used for input but also for output.)

Despite their simple functionality, programming these forms is often a time-consuming task. A lot of code is spent on converting values and passing them around; furthermore, creating even the smallest form requires quite some knowledge about the architecture of the GUI library. For larger forms, the code tends to get monolithic, badly readable and inflexible.

In this paper we present the combinator library (or *embedded domain-specific language*) FunctionalForms, built on top of the GUI library wxHaskell[1] (while our earlier work[2] shows that the ideas are general enough to build it on top of another library, Object I/O[3]). It is dedicated for building forms in a concise and compositional way, and abstracts over low-level implementation details. A form built with FunctionalForms can be used as an action on initial data; it returns the modified data in the IO monad.

We take special care to preserve the expressivity of wxHaskell's layout combinators, and to separate the look of a form (what are its constituent forms and what is their relative layout) from the structure of the edited value. It is especially this part of FunctionalForms that is the most important contribution

C. Grelck et al. (Eds.): IFL 2004, LNCS 3474, pp. 35–51, 2005.
© Springer-Verlag Berlin Heidelberg 2005

of our framework: we present a technique which uses *compositional functional references* in a novel way to completely separate the two structures.

To indicate the need for a combinator library for forms, we start with a small form programming example in wxHaskell (Sect. 2). Next, FunctionalForms is developed in two stages. In Sect. 3, we define the form abstraction and construct a naïve combinator library for it; in Sect. 4, we transform this library using compositional functional references in order to obtain the desired layout freedom. An elaborate example of programming with FunctionalForms is presented in Sect. 5. Related 'work is discussed in Sect. 6 and we conclude in Sect. 7.

2   Form Programming with **wxHaskell**

A recent GUI library for Haskell is wxHaskell[1], an interface to the extensive cross-platform C++ library wxWidgets[4]. Since wxHaskell (intentionally) does not introduce a complete new programming model, programming follows an object oriented style. We show what this means by giving an example of form programming in wxHaskell.[1] It illustrates the problems of programming forms at a too low level (see Sect. 2.2) and serves as running example throughout the paper.

2.1   Example: A Door Information Form

The form we define shows and alters information about a certain door: the name of the person who works behind it and whether s/he is available. This information is exchanged with the rest of the system using a pair of type (*String, Bool*). The GUI (see Fig. 1) consists of a small dialog window with four *controls*: a text entry control to show and alter the name, a drop-down choice control showing either 'come on in' or 'do not disturb' and two buttons to close the dialog: *OK* to confirm the changes we made and *Cancel* to reject them.

Figure 2 shows the code producing this dialog. We give a short overview:

- The program starts by creating an empty dialog[2] and the four controls to populate it. For every object, a pointer (*pdialog, pentry, ...*) is returned. Controls have dynamic attributes which can be manipulated by the user and/or the program during their lifetime. In particular, the *text* and *selection* attributes (on the *entry* and *choice* control, resp.) are set[3] to the form's initial values (contained in *initDoor*). We have to convert the *Bool* value into an *Int* first.
- Next, the dialog's layout is specified. The function *widget* creates layout information from a control pointer; the combinators *margin, column, row*

---

[1] The version of wxHaskell used throughout this paper is 0.8.

[2] Although the terms *dialog, window* and *frame* have slightly different technical meanings, we will use them interchangeably.

[3] The 'assignment operator' := looks like a language construct, but is actually just an infix data constructor defined in the wxHaskell library.

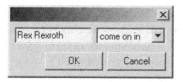

Fig. 1. Door information form

```
doorForm parentWindow initDoor =
  do let (initName, initAvail) = initDoor

        — create dialog and controls
     pdialog  ← dialog parentWindow []
     pentry   ← entry pdialog [text := initName]
     pchoice  ← choice pdialog
                  [ items     := ["come on in", "do not disturb"]
                  , selection := bool2int initAvail
                  ]
     pok      ← button pdialog [text := "OK"]
     pcancel  ← button pdialog [text := "Cancel"]
        — set layout
     let mylayout =
       margin 6 $ column 10
         [ row 5 [widget pentry, widget pchoice]
         , alignRight $ row 5 [widget pok, widget pcancel]
         ]
     set pdialog [layout := mylayout]

        — define event handlers
     let getFinalDoor =
       do finalName  ← get pentry text
          finalAvail ← liftM int2bool $ get pchoice selection
          return (finalName, finalAvail)
     let setclose close =
       do set pok [on command :=
                    do finalDoor ← getFinalDoor; close $ Just finalDoor]
          set pcancel [on command := close Nothing]
        — run dialog
     maybeDoor ← showModal pdialog setclose
     return $ case maybeDoor of
                Just finalDoor → finalDoor
                Nothing        → initDoor
  where bool2int b = if b then 0 else 1
        int2bool i = (i == 0)
```

Fig. 2. wxHaskell code for door information form

and *alignRight* join and transform this information. All layout information is of type *Layout* (we will encounter this type again in Sect. 3.1). Note that the integers 6, 10 and 5 only specify margin widths between controls; actual coordinates are determined by wxHaskell's layout system, which also takes care of resizing controls.

- Both buttons are assigned an *event handler*: a call-back function (IO action) invoked when the user presses the button. It can access the dynamic properties of another control by calling a *get* or *set* function with the corresponding control pointer and property. In the *OK* button's event handler, we obtain the current *String* and *Int* values from the *pentry* and *pchoice* controls, convert the latter back into a *Bool* and join them into a tuple again.
- The last few lines run the dialog modally[4] and determine the function's result: the new values from the controls if the dialog was closed using the *OK* button, and the initial value *initDoor* otherwise.

This *doorForm* function can be used as an IO action in a wxHaskell program.

2.2   Programming Problems Identified

The first thing one may notice about the above example is that, considering the minimal functionality that our dialog provides, 39 lines of code is rather sizable. In the light of defining a form, the only original decisions we express are:

1. We are editing a (*String*, *Bool*) pair; its components are associated with a text entry control and a choice control, respectively.
2. Regarding the latter, the value *True* is associated with the first item, labeled 'come on in', and *False* with the second item, labeled 'do not disturb'.
3. The choice control is placed to the right of the text entry control.

These decisions are encompassed within a lot of procedural code. Moreover, we see that the first two are encoded twice:

1. (i) During control creation, the *text* attribute of control *pentry* is set to the pair's first element; the *selection* attribute of *pchoice* is set to the second.
   (ii) In the button event handler, the values of the same two attributes are retrieved, and a pair is constructed in the same way.
2. (i) During control creation, the *Bool* is converted to *Int*.
   (ii) In the button event handler, the *Int* is converted to *Bool*.

This reduces the modularity and flexibility of our program: if we want to change, say, the choice control into a check box control, we need to make consistent adaptations at two different places.

A third problem, pointed out by Leijen[1], is the possibility to create incorrect layout specifications: forgetting or duplicating a control causes run-time errors.

All three symptoms are evidence that the programming level is too low for forms. In the next section, we design a combinator library to abstract over this level.

---

[4] i.e. the dialog blocks interaction with the rest of the application until it is closed.

3   A Naïve Combinator Library for Forms

In this section, we develop the first stage of FunctionalForms, which focuses on abstracting over low-level form programming details. Structured as a typical combinator library, it revolves around a central data type (*FForm*) that represents both the smallest (atomic) and largest parts of the constructed program; combinators combine and transform these parts.

A value of this type is a *form*: a part of the GUI that is only able to display and alter a certain value. A form lives within a surrounding dialog with *OK* and *Cancel* buttons. When this dialog appears, the form has an *initial value* which is provided by its environment; subsequently, the user can read and alter this value; at the end, the user closes the dialog with one of the buttons, and the form passes the *final value* to the environment. The type of this value is called the *subject type* of the form. It appears as type parameter t in the *FForm* type:

$$\textbf{type } FForm\ t\ w\ =\ Window\ w\ \rightarrow\ t\ \rightarrow\ IO\ (Layout,\ IO\ t)$$

The top-level IO action, provided with a pointer to a parent window and an initial value, creates the controls which make up the form. It returns a *Layout* value for this form and another IO action. This action is used when the dialog is closed with the *OK* button; it retrieves the form's current value at that moment.

3.1   Components of the Library

Atomic forms correspond to single wxHaskell controls which contain an editable value, such as *entry*. This value is held in some attribute of the control, in this case *text*. The definition of the corresponding form *entry′* simply joins the creation, layout, and attribute-reading functions for this control:

$$entry′\ ::\ FForm\ String\ w$$
$$entry′\ =\ \lambda w\ init\ \rightarrow$$
$$\quad \textbf{do } pentry\ \leftarrow\ entry\ w\ [text := init]$$
$$\quad\quad return\ (widget\ pentry,\ get\ pentry\ text)$$

In Fig. 3, some other atomic forms, their subject types, and the corresponding wxHaskell attributes are shown. They are defined analogously. We follow the convention that all exported library functions are underlined.

Forms can be combined into larger forms: taken together, an *entry′* and a *checkBox′* edit a composite value (containing a *String* and a *Bool*). Naïvely, a combinator for joining forms therefore joins their subject types as well as their *Layout* values. However, this will turn out to be a source of trouble for the library (see Sect. 3.2). We demonstrate this with the combinator ⊞, which conveniently suits our *doorForm* example:

$$(⊞)\ ::\ FForm\ t_1\ w\ \rightarrow\ FForm\ t_2\ w\ \rightarrow\ FForm\ (t_1, t_2)\ w$$
$$form_1\ ⊞\ form_2\ =\ \lambda w\ (init_1, init_2)\ \rightarrow$$
$$\textbf{do } (lay_1, getfin_1)\ \leftarrow\ form_1\ w\ init_1$$
$$\quad (lay_2, getfin_2)\ \leftarrow\ form_2\ w\ init_2$$
$$\quad return\ (\ row\ 5\ [lay_1, lay_2],\ liftM2\ (,)\ getfin_1\ getfin_2\ )$$

Name	Appearance	Subject type	wxHaskell attribute
entry'	foo	_String_	_text_
choice'	first / second	_Int_	_selection_
radioBox'	first / second	_Int_	_selection_
checkBox'	☑	_Bool_	_checked_
spinCtrl'	5	_Int_	_selection_

Fig. 3. Some atomic forms and their subject types

As the type signature shows, the composite form's subject type is a pair of its components' subject types. Its initial value $(init_1, init_2)$ is split up and fed to the two component forms; likewise, the two final values are joined back into a pair (we lift the pair constructor into the IO monad). Regarding layout, both components are put next to each other with a five-pixel gap in between.

Using only ⊞ and atomic forms, we can already concisely define a fully functioning form for any combination of simple types expressed in nested pairs. For example, a form for $(String, (Bool, Bool))$ can be defined like:

$$composite = \underline{entry'} \boxplus (\underline{checkBox'} \boxplus \underline{checkBox'})$$

To actually use this form in a wxHaskell program, we would provide it with an initial value _init_ of type $(String, (Bool, Bool))$ and run it:

do ...
$\quad final \leftarrow \underline{runInDialog}\ parentWindow\ composite\ init$
$\quad$ ...

The function _runInDialog_, when given a parent window, a form and an initial value of the form's subject type, yields an IO action producing a modal dialog which contains the form, an _OK_ button and a _Cancel_ button. This is accomplished by:

1. Setting up the dialog with the buttons.
2. Executing the form's IO action, which creates the controls in the dialog.
3. Augmenting the layout returned by (2) with the layout of the buttons, and attaching it to the dialog.
4. Using the IO action returned by (2) in the _OK_ button event handler to retrieve the form's final value.

The result of _runInDialog_'s IO action equals the form's final value if the _OK_ button is used, and the initial value otherwise. We omit the implementation; it is very similar to the corresponding fragments in Fig. 2.

As the last addition to the combinator library, we define the function _convert_[5] and its specialization _convertL_. They transform a form's subject type into an 'isomorphic' type, given the corresponding bijection.

$$\underline{convert} :: (t_1 \rightarrow t_2, t_2 \rightarrow t_1) \rightarrow \textit{FForm } t_2\ w \rightarrow \textit{FForm } t_1\ w$$

Often, a concept from the data domain, like _week day_ or _eye color_, can be captured with a simple enumerated type. To convert between such a type and the zero-based _Int_ index used in some atomic forms, we don't need to write out a full bijection; it suffices to enumerate the values in a list. The function _convertL_ then maps the first value to 0, the second to 1, etc.:

$$\underline{convertL} :: Eq\ t \Rightarrow [t] \rightarrow \textit{FForm Int } w \rightarrow \textit{FForm } t\ w$$
$$\underline{convertL}\ items = \underline{convert}\ (f, f_{inv})$$
$$\mathbf{where}\ f\ a\ = fromJust\ \$\ elemIndex\ a\ items$$
$$f_{inv}\ i\ = items!!i$$

We are now ready to define the form example from Sect. 2.1 in only three lines:

$$doorForm = \underline{entry}\ ⊞\ availForm$$
$$availForm = \underline{convertL}\ [True, False]\ \$$$
$$\underline{choice}\ [items := [\text{"come on in"}, \text{"do not disturb"}]]$$

3.2   Evaluation of the Combinator Library

An important thing to notice is that the combinator library we defined solves all the problems mentioned in Sect. 2.2. Along with providing a very concise way of specifying the relevant decisions, it also rules out the possibility of forgetting or duplicating controls in the layout specification: an atomic form associates a control with exactly one layout specification, and the combinators maintain this invariant.[6] However, the library has a disadvantage: ⊞ is a bad template for form combinators, because it introduces a dependency between the subject type structure and the layout structure of a form. This manifests itself in two ways:

Incompatible types: To increase the layout possibilities for composite forms, the obvious solution would be to introduce combinators which mimic wx-Haskell's layout combinators. When we follow the ⊞ template, these combinators also have to construct a subject type, but this often causes trouble:
  - For one-argument combinators (which transform a single _Layout_) such as _margin_, it is indeed no problem to 'lift' them into the _FForm_ domain: we just let them alter the form's layout and leave the subject type alone.
  - Lifting a zero-argument combinator such as _label_, which _produces_ a _Layout_ by itself, is a little more problematic: the lifted combinator should produce a form with a certain subject type and final value. In principle, these can be the unit type and value (). However, every label used in a composite form will then clutter its subject type with another ().

---

[5] The implementation of _convert_ can be found in Fig. 4.

[6] In fact, a similar technique is briefly mentioned in [1] (section _Safety_).

- Combinators of the form $[Layout] \to Layout$, such as *row*, cause even more problems: providing the lifted combinator with a list of forms would force them to have the same subject type. In principle, we could solve this problem by extending the *FForm* type to also accommodate *lists* of *Layout*s, and introducing combinators *nilF* and *consF* to produce such forms, but then our *doorForm* example would turn into

$$doorForm \ = \ row' \ 5 \ \$ \ \underline{entry'} \ `consF` \ (availForm \ `consF` \ nilF)$$

with subject type $(String, (Bool, ()))$. In practice, this is rather awkward.

Dependency between layout and values: Say we want to swap the two controls in the *doorForm* layout. If we just swap the two operands of ⊞, we also unintentionally change *doorForm*'s subject type from $(String, Bool)$ to $(Bool, String)$. One way to hack around this would be to $\underline{convert}$ the new form's subject type back:

$$doorForm \ = \ \underline{convert} \ (mirror, mirror) \ (availForm \ ⊞ \ \underline{entry'})$$
$$\textbf{where} \ mirror \ (a, b) \ = \ (b, a)$$

... but this is no real solution: with larger forms—say we want to permute eight controls instead of two—the programmer is heavily burdened by these kind of 'plumbing' bijections. Not only is this much work, but it also has an impact on the flexibility of the program: if later we decide to alter the layout structure, we also need to alter the bijection functions again.

The cause of both problems is that we cram too much functionality into the combinators, thereby creating dependencies between two structures which are, in essence, largely unrelated. In the next section, we show how to factor the ⊞ combinator into a layout combinator and a subject type combinator.

4   Separating Subject Type and Layout Combinators Using Compositional Functional References

This section presents the second stage of FunctionalForms. It allows the user to explicitly manage the subject type of a form, separate from its layout, using two types of combinators: subject type combinators, like $\underline{declare2}$ for a pair, and layout combinators, like $\underline{row'}$ and $\underline{margin'}$ (derived from their wxHaskell counterparts). This enables the definition of forms such as

$$\underline{declare2} \ \$ \ \lambda(name, avail) \to$$
$$\underline{row'} \ 5 \ [availForm \ avail, \ \underline{entry'} \ name]$$

to specify a door information form with the name at the first position in the subject type, and at the last position in the layout structure. The connection between the two structures is formed by special values (*name* and *avail* in the example) which we call *compositional functional references*.

4.1 Introducing Compositional Functional References

Reference values are members of an algebraic data type containing two functions:

$$\textbf{data } Ref \; cx \; t \; = \; Ref\{ \; val \; :: \; cx \rightarrow t$$
$$, \; app \; :: \; (t \rightarrow t) \rightarrow cx \rightarrow cx$$
$$\}$$

Type variable cx denotes the type of the *context*, a structure of values, which contains some sub-structure of type t. The first function retrieves a t value from a cx structure, while the second updates a cx structure by applying a $t \rightarrow t$ update function to the t value at the right spot. An example reference value is *reffst*, a reference to the first element of a pair:

$$reffst \; :: \; Ref \; (t_1, t_2) \; t_1$$
$$reffst \; = \; Ref \; fst \; appfst$$
$$\textbf{where } appfst \; f \; (x, y) \; = \; (f \; x, \; y)$$

Using *reffst* and *refsnd*, which is defined analogously, we can retrieve or update the values in $initcx = (39, "foo")$:

$$(val \; reffst) \; initcx \qquad\qquad \Rightarrow \; 39$$
$$(app \; reffst) \; (+3) \; initcx \qquad \Rightarrow \; (42, "foo")$$
$$(app \; refsnd) \; (const \; "bar") \; initcx \Rightarrow \; (39, "bar")$$

Note that when we partially apply the *app* functions by removing *initcx* in the last two examples, we obtain functions of type $cx \rightarrow cx$: a context update. We include such a function in the new *FForm* type, which we now present.

4.2 Forms with References

In the transformed library, shown in the right-hand side of Fig. 4, every form has access to the same context, whose type equals the subject type of the topmost form composition. The new *FForm* type clearly shows this: a form no longer depends on an initial *value* for itself, but rather on an initial *context*; and instead of producing a final *value*, it produces a final *context update*. In the *OK* button event handler, this update will be applied to the initial context, yielding a final context.

As the new definition of *entry* shows, an atomic form is now provided by the programmer with a reference value. This determines which part of the context it edits: the *val* function retrieves an initial value from this part and the *app* function writes the final value to this part. The *Ref* type contains the form's subject type, in this case *String*. How the programmer obtains such a reference value is explained in Sect. 4.3.

The combinator ⊞ is replaced by □. The resulting composite form distributes the initial context among its components unaltered, instead of splitting it. Conversely, instead of pairing two final component values, it constructs a joint context update by sequencing both component updates (this time, the function composition operator is lifted into the IO monad).

FunctionalForms stage 1	FunctionalForms stage 2
type $FForm\ t\ w\ =$ $\quad Window\ w\ \rightarrow\ t\ \rightarrow$ $\quad IO\ (Layout,\ IO\ t)$	**type** $FForm\ cx\ w\ =$ $\quad Window\ w\ \rightarrow\ cx\ \rightarrow$ $\quad IO\ (Layout,\ IO\ (cx\ \rightarrow\ cx))$
$\underline{entry'}\ ::\ FForm\ String\ w$ $\underline{entry'}\ =\ \lambda w\ init\ \rightarrow$ $\quad$**do** $pentry\ \leftarrow\ entry\ w\ [text := init]$ $\qquad return\ (\ widget\ pentry$ $\qquad\qquad,\ get\ pentry\ text$ $\qquad\qquad)$	$\underline{entry'}\ ::\ Ref\ cx\ String\ \rightarrow\ FForm\ cx\ w$ $\underline{entry'}\ (Ref\ val\ app)\ =\ \lambda w\ init_{cx}\ \rightarrow$ $\quad$**do** $pentry\ \leftarrow\ entry\ w\ [text := val\ init_{cx}]$ $\qquad return\ (\ widget\ pentry$ $\qquad\qquad,\ $**do** $t\ \leftarrow\ get\ pentry\ text;$ $\qquad\qquad\qquad return\ \$\ app\ \$\ const\ t$ $\qquad\qquad)$
$(⊞)\ ::\ FForm\ t_1\ w\ \rightarrow\ FForm\ t_2\ w$ $\qquad\rightarrow\ FForm\ (t_1, t_2)\ w$ $form_1\ ⊞\ form_2\ =\ \lambda w\ (init_1, init_2)\ \rightarrow$ $\quad$**do** $(lay_1, getfin_1)\ \leftarrow\ form_1\ w\ init_1$ $\qquad(lay_2, getfin_2)\ \leftarrow\ form_2\ w\ init_2$ $\qquad return\ (\ row\ 5\ [lay_1, lay_2]$ $\qquad\qquad,\ liftM2\ (,)\ getfin_1\ getfin_2\ )$	$(□)\ ::\ FForm\ cx\ w\ \rightarrow\ FForm\ cx\ w$ $\qquad\rightarrow\ FForm\ cx\ w$ $form_1\ □\ form_2\ =\ \lambda w\ init_{cx}\ \rightarrow$ $\quad$**do** $(lay_1, getupd_1)\ \leftarrow\ form_1\ w\ init_{cx}$ $\qquad(lay_2, getupd_2)\ \leftarrow\ form_2\ w\ init_{cx}$ $\qquad return\ (\ row\ 5\ [lay_1, lay_2]$ $\qquad\qquad,\ liftM2\ (.)\ getupd_1\ getupd_2\ )$ — actually a template for deriving: $\underline{row'}\ ::$ $\quad Int\ \rightarrow\ [FForm\ cx\ w]\ \rightarrow\ FForm\ cx\ w$ $\underline{margin'}\ ::$ $\quad Int\ \rightarrow\ FForm\ cx\ w\ \rightarrow\ FForm\ cx\ w$ $\underline{label'}\ ::\ String\ \rightarrow\ FForm\ cx\ w$ $\vdots$
	$\underline{declare2}\ ::\ ((Ref\ cx\ t_1,\ Ref\ cx\ t_2)\ \rightarrow\ z)$ $\qquad\rightarrow\ Ref\ cx\ (t_1, t_2)\ \rightarrow\ z$ $\underline{declareL}\ ::\ ([Ref\ cx\ t]\ \rightarrow\ z)$ $\qquad\rightarrow\ Ref\ cx\ [t]\ \rightarrow\ z$ $\vdots\quad$ — implementation: see running text
$\underline{runInDialog}\ ::\ Window\ w\ \rightarrow$ $\quad FForm\ t\ (CPanel\ ())\ \rightarrow$ $\quad t\ \rightarrow\ IO\ t$	$\underline{runInDialog}\ ::\ Window\ w\ \rightarrow$ $\quad (Ref\ cx\ cx\ \rightarrow\ FForm\ cx\ (CPanel\ ()))\ \rightarrow$ $\quad cx\ \rightarrow\ IO\ cx$
$\underline{convert}\ ::\ (t_1\ \rightarrow\ t_2,\ t_2\ \rightarrow\ t_1)\ \rightarrow$ $\quad FForm\ t_2\ w\ \rightarrow\ FForm\ t_1\ w$ $\underline{convert}\ (f, f_{inv})\ form\ =\ \lambda w\ init\ \rightarrow$ $\quad$**do** $(lay, getfin)\ \leftarrow\ form\ w\ \$\ f\ init$ $\qquad return\ (lay,\ liftM\ f_{inv}\ getfin)$	$\underline{convert}\ ::\ (t_1\ \rightarrow\ t_2,\ t_2\ \rightarrow\ t_1)\ \rightarrow$ $\quad (Ref\ cx\ t_2\ \rightarrow\ z)\ \rightarrow\ (Ref\ cx\ t_1\ \rightarrow\ z)$ $\underline{convert}\ (f, f_{inv})\ refToForm\ ref\ =$ $\quad refToForm\ (refiso\ \bullet\ ref)$ $\quad$**where** $refiso\ =\ Ref\ f\ (\lambda g\ \rightarrow\ f_{inv}\ .\ g\ .\ f)$

Fig. 4. Transforming the combinator library

Since the arguments of ⊡ are of the same type, the first problem in Sect. 3.2 is solved: ⊡ can easily be generalized to take a list of forms instead of two (and a margin width value), thereby implementing the lifted version _row′_ of wxHaskell's layout combinator _row_. As the context update for base case [], we return _id_, the unit value for function composition. This is also the solution for lifting zero-argument layout combinators like _label_.

The second problem is also solved: the two operands of ⊡ (and for _row′_: all the forms in the list) can be freely swapped without any effect on the initial value for the components or the final value for the composite form.[7] We can conclude that this combinator has no influence on the functionality of a form anymore; indeed it is merely a lifted layout combinator.

In fact, using ⊡ as a template, we have lifted _all_ of wxHaskell's layout combinators into the _FForm_ domain.[8] However, for simplicity's sake, we will still restrict our use of layout combinators to ⊡ in the rest of this section.

4.3   Constructing the Subject Type with References

Since the new layout combinators do not construct the subject type, it has to be done in another way: using reference values. For now, we are mainly concerned with subject types consisting of nested pairs. We can derive the reference values to their elements using the reference values to the elements of a simple pair, _reffst_ and _refsnd_. This is done by 'normally' composing their _val_ functions (_fst_ and _snd_), while composing their _app_ functions (_appfst_ and _appsnd_) in the reverse order. For example, a reference to the c value in $(a, (b, (c, d)))$ is constructed with:

$$Ref\ (fst\ .\ snd\ .\ snd)\ (appsnd\ .\ appsnd\ .\ appfst)$$

This pattern of constructing new reference values can be captured with the operator • for composition of references:

$$(•)\ ::\ Ref\ b\ c\ \rightarrow\ Ref\ a\ b\ \rightarrow\ Ref\ a\ c$$
$$w\ •\ v\ =\ Ref\ (val\ w\ .\ val\ v)\ (app\ v\ .\ app\ w)$$

The reference value above can now be written _reffst_ • _refsnd_ • _refsnd_. With the • operator, we can also construct new _forms_ in a compositional way. We illustrate this by means of the _doorForm_ example, which is _not_ compositional when defined in a naïve way:

$$doorFormNC\ ::\ FForm\ (String, Bool)\ w$$
$$doorFormNC\ =\ \underline{entry'}\ reffst\ ⊡\ availForm\ refsnd$$

---

[7] Provided that some conditions hold, e.g. that none of the atomic forms is supplied with the same reference value. A formal proof of this can be found in [2].

[8] Alternatively, the _FForm_ domain can be structured as a monad. The monadic lifting functions can then be used for this purpose.

This form can only be used as a top-level form; it cannot be usefully joined with another form, because *doorFormNC* ⊡ *otherForm* would force the context type of *otherForm* to be (*String*, *Bool*) as well. Compare this with the compositional way of defining *doorForm*:

> *doorForm* :: *Ref cx* (*String*, *Bool*) → *FForm cx w*
> *doorForm ref* = *entry* (*reffst* • *ref*) ⊡ *availForm* (*refsnd* • *ref*)

This form *can* be used as a component of a larger form. Just like the atomic forms, it should be supplied with a reference value pointing to its subject type (*String*, *Bool*) in a larger context *cx*. It uses this to derive reference values to a *String* and a *Bool* for its sub-forms.

To enforce this pattern of form construction, the library does not export reference creation functions, but only the subject type combinator *declare2*:

> *declare2* :: ((*Ref cx t*$_1$, *Ref cx t*$_2$) → *z*) → *Ref cx* (*t*$_1$, *t*$_2$) → *z*
> *declare2 refsToForm ref* = *refsToForm* (*reffst* • *ref*, *refsnd* • *ref*)

Using this combinator, the same *doorForm* definition can be written as:

> *doorForm* = *declare2* $ λ(*name*, *avail*) →
>   *entry name* ⊡ *availForm avail*

To enable the use of a compositional form like *doorForm* (i.e. parameterized by a reference value) at the top level, the new *runInDialog* is defined to take just this kind of form as its argument. It applies it to *refid* = *Ref id id*, the unit element for • (turning *doorForm* back into *doorFormNC*). This is what equates the context type of every form to the subject type of this topmost form.

The new *convert* function also transforms compositional forms. It does this by transforming the reference value that gets passed to a form. Interestingly, this transformation can be performed by composing it with the appropriate *isomorphism reference*; see Fig. 4 for details. Although the type of *convertL* changes due to the type change of *convert*, its textual definition remains the same. The same holds for the user-defined *availForm* in the *doorForm* example.

4.4   Reference Values for Other Subject Types

Up to this point, we have restricted the composite subject types to pairs. Of course, we can easily extend the approach to tuples of higher arity by defining *declare3* et cetera.[9] Using the same scheme as before, it is also possible to define references to the head and tail of a list:

> *refhead* :: *Ref* [*t*] *t*
> *refhead* = *Ref head apphead* **where** *apphead f* (*x* : *xs*) = *f x* : *xs*

---

[9] Using Template Haskell[5], these definitions can be generated automatically. Furthermore, Haskell's type classes can be used to unite the *declare* functions.

$$reftail \;\; :: \;\; Ref\ [t]\ [t]$$
$$reftail \;\; = \;\; Ref\ tail \quad apptail \;\; \textbf{where}\ apptail \;\; f\ (x:xs) = x\ :\ f\ xs$$

Subsequently, we can define the list of references to all possible list elements, and a subject type combinator for a list (note how _declareL_ resembles _declare2_):

$$refslist \;\; :: \;\; [Ref\ [t]\ t]$$
$$refslist \;\; = \;\; refhead\ :\ map\ (\bullet\ reftail)\ refslist$$

$$\underline{declareL} \;\; :: \;\; ([Ref\ cx\ t] \to z) \; \to \; Ref\ cx\ [t]\ \to\ z$$
$$\underline{declareL}\ refsToForm\ ref \;\; = \;\; refsToForm\ \$\ map\ (\bullet\ ref)\ refslist$$

The following example illustrates the use of the functions defined in this section.

5   Elaborate Example

To give an impression of the concise declarative style of form programming with FunctionalForms, we present a more elaborate example. While we have thus far kept the atomic form _entry_ as simple as possible for clarity, we use a more flexible version here, with a small adaptation: every atomic form is extended with a property list, which it passes on to its corresponding control.

The form we define is shown in Fig. 6; it edits a list of three alarms. Every alarm consists of three components: a value indicating whether the alarm is enabled, a time setting and a message. This information is encoded in a value of type $(Bool, Int, String)$, where the integer represents the number of minutes elapsed since midnight.

The corresponding code can be found in Fig. 5. In _alarmListForm_, an infinite list of references is generated by _declareL_ and bound to _refs_. Then, _makeBox_ assigns each reference to an _alarmForm_ and puts a box around it. Finally, the first three boxes are taken from the list and put in a column.

An _alarmForm_ splits its reference into three parts, which it distributes over a _checkBox'_, a _timeForm_ and an _entry'_. The last two are arranged in a grid, together with two labels (which are aligned middle-left in their cell). The check box is placed left of the grid.

A _timeForm_ converts the total number of minutes into a value for hours and a value for minutes using _div_ and _mod_, and assigns the corresponding two references to a pair of spin controls. For these controls, minimum and maximum values are set, as well as a custom size.

6   Related Work

The notion of _compositional references_ was introduced by Kagawa[6] as a means to compose mutable (i.e. destructively updatable) data structures, such as arrays, in a functional language. Although it was proposed as a primitive data type,

```
alarmListForm  ::  Ref cx [(Bool, Int, String)]  →  FForm cx w
alarmListForm  =  declareL $ λrefs →
  column' 10 $ take 3 $ zipWith makeBox [1..] refs
    where
      makeBox nr ref  =  boxed' ("Alarm" ++ show nr) (alarmForm ref)

alarmForm  ::  Ref cx (Bool, Int, String)  →  FForm cx w
alarmForm  =  declare3 $ λ(enab, time, msg) →
  margin' 3 $ row' 8 [ checkBox' [] enab
                     , grid' 5 5
                         [ [floatLeft' $ label' "time :",     timeForm time]
                         , [floatLeft' $ label' "message :", entry' [] msg]
                         ]
                     ]

timeForm  ::  Ref cx Int  →  FForm cx w
timeForm  =  convert (splittime, jointime) $ declare2 $ λ(hrs, mins) →
  row' 2
    [ spinCtrl' 0 23 [outerSize := sz 40 20] hrs
    , spinCtrl' 0 59 [outerSize := sz 40 20] mins
    ]
  where splittime total  =  (total 'div' 60, total 'mod' 60)
        jointime (hours, minutes)  =  60 * hours + minutes
```

Fig. 5. Definition code for alarm list form

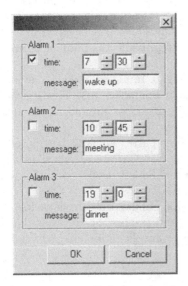

Fig. 6. Appearance of alarm list form

```
module Alarms(main) where

import Graphics.UI.WX
import FForms

main  =  start $
  do f  ←  frame []
     final  ←  runInDialog f
                         alarmListForm init
     print final
     close f
init =
  [ (True,  450,  "wake up")
  , (False, 645,  "meeting")
  , (False, 1140, "dinner")
  ]
```

Fig. 7. Startup code for alarm list form

Kagawa also gives a functional account of the reference type. Our references resemble this (except that we use an *apply* function instead of a *write* function to facilitate composition) so we use the name *compositional functional references*.

Closely related are *lenses*[7], which are also pairs of accessor and modificator functions. Several operators, including composition, are used to combine lenses into a large lens which *is* the program; this program specifies a bidirectional transformation between model and view.

Although we have chosen for an underlying GUI library with an object oriented style (which is more widely accepted), declarative form programming is probably achieved most easily on top of a declarative GUI library like FranTK[8] or Fudgets[9]. The latter even defines a form combinator >·< which closely resembles ⊞ (see the corresponding PhD thesis[10], chapter 29). To obtain a layout flexibility similar to ours, a unique name can be assigned to each sub-fudget; these names are used in a *name layout combinator* which is applied to the composite fudget. They play the same role as our references, but:

- Fudget names refer to parts of the layout. We believe that from a top-down design perspective, it is more natural to name the parts of a data structure, because this is designed first and less susceptible to change.
- Fudget names are identifier values. Generating these (unique) values is an extra responsibility for the programmer that our approach does not have.

In functional GUI libraries which are more or less 'object oriented', GUI parts are related using pointers to the controls themselves, instead of to the data structures they edit (our approach) or their layout (the Fudgets approach). Like we have shown in Sect. 2, the wxHaskell control creation functions return these pointers as values in the IO monad. In Clean Object I/O[3], they are generated by a shared environment at user request; in a GUI library for the Curry language[11] (which has a more declarative flavour), these pointers are implemented using free logic variables.

There are several functional libraries for Web form programming. We mention WASH/CGI[12] here; this article provides an overview of the others. With WASH/CGI, the programmer can refer to the (typed) value in a Web form using *input handles*; like wxHaskell's control pointers, these are returned as monadic values by creation functions.

XForms[13], the recent W3C standard for declarative Web forms, also takes the approach of naming parts (XML elements) of the data structure. This is done in the first part of an XForms definition, the *XForms Model*. It also provides every element with an initial value and possibly type or value constraints. In a separate second part, the *XForms User Interface*, GUI controls are bound to these elements by referring to their names.

Generic *Graphical Editor Components* (GECs)[14] use their 'subject type' to convey layout information. A generic function[15] automatically derives the GUI for any given subject type; to create a different GUI for a certain type, one can specialize this function. In order to release this rigid coupling between subject type and layout, *abstract GECs*[16] differentiate between a *domain type* and a *view type*. The GUI is derived from the view type; mapping functions relate domain values to view values, quite like in our *convert* function. Like Fudgets, GECs differ from forms in their ability to react to user events during their whole lifetime and to dynamically create new GECs for editing new values.

7   Conclusions and Future Work

We have introduced FunctionalForms, a combinator library which facilitates the programming of forms in a functional language. (Alternatively, it can be seen as an *embedded domain-specific language* for forms.) First we showed how to build a combinator library capturing the form abstraction on top of an underlying GUI library with an object oriented programming style. This solved the problems of low-level programming like verbosity, but had a drawback: it coupled subject type structure and layout combinator structure together. Then we used compositional functional references in a novel way to release this dependency; this also allowed us to exploit the full power of the layout combinators from the underlying library wxHaskell.

Forms have limited functionality: value editing only affects the rest of the system after the lifetime of a form, and forms can only edit a static, finite, product-like structure of values. While we have already investigated the use of sum-like structures[2] and synchronizing forms briefly, these are yet to be integrated into one framework. However, our results are already of practical use.[10]

A major advantage of our technique is that it does not depend on a special GUI library or language construct. Our earlier work[2], in which we applied the technique to the Clean Object I/O library[3], supports this statement. In fact, the key characteristic of our use of compositional functional references is very general: it allows two different structures to be built from the same set of elements. Therefore, we believe that it can be applied in other areas of functional programming as well.

Acknowledgements

The authors would like to thank Marko van Eekelen, Rinus Plasmeijer and the anonymous referees for their comments on this paper, and Maarten Fokkinga for co-supervising the Master's thesis from which it partially resulted.

References

1. Leijen, D.: wxHaskell – a portable and concise GUI library for Haskell. In: ACM SIGPLAN Haskell Workshop (HW'04), ACM Press (2004)
2. Evers, S.:   Form follows function: Editor GUIs in a functional style.   Master's thesis, University of Twente (2004) Permanently available at http://doc.utwente.nl/fid/2101.
3. Achten, P., Plasmeijer, R.: Interactive Functional Objects in Clean. In Clack, C., Hammond, K., Davie, T., eds.: Proc. of 9th International Workshop on Implementation of Functional Languages, IFL'97. Number 1467 in LNCS, Springer-Verlag, Berlin (1998) 304–321

---

[10] The library can be downloaded at http://www.sandr.dds.nl/FunctionalForms.

4. The wxWidgets home page can be found at http://www.wxwidgets.org.
5. Sheard, T., Peyton Jones, S.: Template metaprogramming for Haskell. In Chakravarty, M.M.T., ed.: ACM SIGPLAN Haskell Workshop 02, ACM Press (2002) 1–16
6. Kagawa, K.: Compositional references for stateful functional programming. In: Proceedings of the second ACM SIGPLAN International Conference on Functional Programming (ICFP'97). Volume 32(8) of SIGPLAN Notices., ACM Press (1997) 217–226
7. Foster, J.N., Greenwald, M.B., Moore, J.T., Pierce, B.C., Schmitt, A.: Combinators for bi-directional tree transformations: A linguistic approach to the view update problem. Technical Report MS-CIS-04-15, University of Pennsylvania (2004) An earlier version appeared in the *Workshop on Programming Language Technologies for XML (PLAN-X)*, 2004, under the title "A Language for Bi-Directional Tree Transformations".
8. Sage, M.: FranTk - a declarative GUI language for Haskell. In: ICFP '00: Proceedings of the fifth ACM SIGPLAN International Conference on Functional programming, ACM Press (2000) 106–117
9. Carlsson, M., Hallgren, T.: FUDGETS - a graphical user interface in a lazy functional language. In: Proceedings of the ACM Conference on Functional Programming and Computer Architecture, Copenhagen, DK, FPCA '93, New York, NY, ACM (1993)
10. Carlsson, M., Hallgren, T.: Fudgets – Purely Functional Processes with applications to Graphical User Interfaces. PhD thesis, Chalmers University of Technology (1998) http://www.cs.chalmers.se/~hallgren/Thesis/.
11. Hanus, M.: A functional logic programming approach to graphical user interfaces. In: Proc. of the Second International Workshop on Practical Aspects of Declarative Languages (PADL'00). Volume 1753 of LNCS., Springer-Verlag (2000) 47–62
12. Thiemann, P.: WASH/CGI: Server-side web scripting with sessions and typed, compositional forms. In: Proceedings of the 4th International Symposium on Practical Aspects of Declarative Languages. Volume 2257 of LNCS., Springer-Verlag (2002) 192–208
13. The XForms home page can be found at http://www.w3.org/MarkUp/Forms/.
14. Achten, Peter, van Eekelen, Marko and Plasmeijer, Rinus: Generic Graphical User Interfaces. In Greg Michaelson, Phil Trinder, eds.: Selected Papers of the 15th Int. Workshop on the Implementation of Functional Languages, IFL03. Volume 3145 of LNCS., Edinburgh, UK, Springer (2003)
15. Alimarine, A., Plasmeijer, R.: A Generic Programming Extension for Clean. In Arts, T., Mohnen, M., eds.: The 13th International workshop on the Implementation of Functional Languages, IFL'01, Selected Papers. Volume 2312 of LNCS., Älvsjö, Sweden, Springer (2002) 168–186
16. Achten, Peter, van Eekelen, Marko and Plasmeijer, Rinus: Compositional Model-Views with Generic Graphical User Interfaces. In: Practical Aspects of Declarative Programming, PADL04. Volume 3057 of LNCS., Springer (2004) 39–55

A Rational Deconstruction
of Landin's SECD Machine

Olivier Danvy

BRICS*, Department of Computer Science, University of Aarhus,
IT-parken, Aabogade 34, DK-8200 Aarhus N, Denmark
danvy@brics.dk

Abstract. Landin's SECD machine was the first abstract machine for
the λ-calculus viewed as a programming language. Both theoretically as a
model of computation and practically as an idealized implementation, it
has set the tone for the subsequent development of abstract machines for
functional programming languages. However, and even though variants
of the SECD machine have been presented, derived, and invented, the
precise rationale for its architecture and modus operandi has remained
elusive. In this article, we deconstruct the SECD machine into a λ-
interpreter, i.e., an evaluation function, and we reconstruct λ-interpreters
into a variety of SECD-like machines. The deconstruction and reconstruc-
tions are transformational: they are based on equational reasoning and
on a combination of simple program transformations—mainly closure
conversion, transformation into continuation-passing style, and defunctionalization.

The evaluation function underlying the SECD machine provides a
precise rationale for its architecture: it is an environment-based eval-
apply evaluator with a callee-save strategy for the environment, a data
stack of intermediate results, and a control delimiter. Each of the components of the SECD machine (stack, environment, control, and dump)
is therefore rationalized and so are its transitions.

The deconstruction and reconstruction method also applies to other
abstract machines and other evaluation functions.

1 Introduction

Forty years ago, Peter Landin wrote a profoundly influencial article, "The Mechanical Evaluation of Expressions" [27], where, in retrospect, he outlined a
substantial part of the functional-programming research programme for the following decades. This visionary article stands out for advocating the use of the
λ-calculus as a meta-language and for introducing the first abstract machine
for the λ-calculus (i.e., in Landin's terms, applicative expressions), the SECD
machine. However, and in addition, it also introduces the notions of 'syntactic

---

* Basic Research in Computer Science (www.brics.dk), funded by the Danish National
Research Foundation.

C. Grelck et al. (Eds.): IFL 2004, LNCS 3474, pp. 52–71, 2005.
© Springer-Verlag Berlin Heidelberg 2005

sugar' over a core programming language; of 'closure' to represent functional values; of circularity to implement recursion; of thunks to delay computations; of delayed evaluation; of partial evaluation; of disentangling nested applications into where-expressions at preprocessing time; of what has since been called de Bruijn indices; of sharing; of what has since been called graph reduction; of call by need; of what has since been called strictness analysis; and of domain-specific languages—all concepts that are ubiquitous in programming languages today. The topic of this article is the SECD machine.

Since "The Mechanical Evaluation of Expressions," many other abstract machines for the λ-calculus have been invented, discovered, or derived [16]. In fact, the literature simply abounds with derivations of abstract machines—though with one remarkable exception: there is no derivation of Landin's original SECD machine, even though it was the first such abstract machine. Since its inception, the SECD machine has been the starting point of many university courses and textbooks and the topic of many variations and optimizations, be it for its source language (call by name, call by need, other syntactic constructs, including control operators), for its environment (de Bruijn indices, de Bruijn levels, explicit substitutions, higher-order abstract syntax), or for its control (proper tail recursion, one stack instead of two). Yet in forty years of existence, it has not been derived or reconstructed. The common agreement is that there is something special, something original and still unexplained about the SECD machine.

The goal of this article is to pinpoint and explain the originality of the SECD machine. To this end, we show how to mechanically deconstruct the SECD machine into an evaluator for applicative expressions and then how to rationally reconstruct a variety of SECD-like machines. This deconstruction–reconstruction is actually interesting in itself because it provides a bridge between small-step operational semantics (in the form of an abstract machine) and denotational semantics (in the form of a compositional evaluation function). It is also general because it applies to other evaluators and other abstract machines [1]. The derivation is based on a combination of simple, correct, and well-known program-transformation tools: CPS transformation [13, 41], delimited continuations [12], defunctionalization [14, 37], and closure conversion [27]. In fact, these transformations are so classical that one could almost say that the present work could have been carried out years ago, would it be only for Piet Hein's gentle reminder that Things Take Time [24].

1.1   Deconstruction of the SECD Machine

Let us outline our deconstruction of the SECD machine, before substantiating it in Section 2. The SECD machine is defined as one transition function over a quadruple—a stack of intermediate values (of type S), an environment (of type E), a control stack (of type C), and a dump (of type D):

```
run : S * E * C * D -> value
```

This transition function is complicated because it has several induction variables. Our single creative step is to first disentangle it into four transition functions, each of which has one induction variable, i.e., operates on one element of the quadruple:

```
run_c : S * E * C * D -> value
run_d : S * D -> value
run_t : term * S * E * C * D -> value
run_a : S * E * C * D -> value
```

Depending on the control stack, run_c dispatches towards run_d if the control stack is empty, run_t if the top of the control stack contains a term, and run_a if the top of the control stack contains an apply directive.

– We observe that these four functions are in defunctionalized form (the control stack and the dump are defunctionalized data types and two of the four functions are the corresponding apply functions), and we refunctionalize them, eliminating the two apply functions:

```
run_t : term * S * E * C * D -> value
run_a : S * E * C * D -> value
where C = S * E * D -> value
      D = S -> value
```

– We observe that the result is in continuation-passing style, and we transform it back to direct style, eliminating the dump continuation:

```
run_t : term * S * E * C -> S
run_a : S * E * C -> S
where C = S * E -> S
```

– We observe that the result is almost in continuation-passing style, modulo the reinitialization of a continuation when evaluating the body of a λ-abstraction, and we transform it back to direct style with a control delimiter, eliminating the control continuation:

```
run_t : S * E -> S * E
run_a : S * E -> S * E
```

– We observe that the result threads a data stack of intermediate results, and we rewrite it to do without, eliminating the stack:

```
run_t : term * E -> value * E
run_a : value * value * E -> value * E
```

– We observe that the result is in closure-converted form, and we unconvert it, eliminating the closures.
– We observe that the result is a compositional evaluator in direct style.

Given a disentangled transition function for the SECD machine, all the observations above are in some sense unavoidable (though the author is well aware that to a man with a hammer, the world looks like a nail). The order of these transformations, however, is not fixed. Both closure unconversion and data-stack elimination could occur earlier in the deconstruction.

1.2   Denotational Content of the SECD Machine

The end result of the deconstruction outlined in Section 1.1 shows that the denotational content of the SECD machine is a (curried) evaluation function of type

$$\texttt{term -> E -> value * E}$$

where `term` is the type of a term, `value` is the type of a value, and `E` is the type of an environment mapping variables to values. This evaluator maps a term `t` into an ML function. This denotation maps an environment `e` in which to evaluate `t` into a pair `(v, e')`, where `v` is the value corresponding to `t` and `e'` is the same environment as `e`.

This evaluator is traditional in that it is composed of one 'eval' function (`run_t` above) to evaluate terms, and one 'apply' function (`run_a` above) to apply functions. (An alternative to this traditional eval–apply model is the push-enter model of Krivine's machine [26] and of the spineless tagless G-machine [33].) This evaluator, however, is also unconventional in that:

1. its environment is managed in a callee-save fashion (witness the environment paired with the resulting value), and
2. it uses a control delimiter to evaluate the body of λ-abstractions.

It seems to us that these two properties account both for the specificity and for the intriguing originality of Landin's SECD machine:

Specificity: The two properties show that the evaluation mechanism of the SECD machine is environment-based, that the environment is threaded and saved in a callee-save fashion, and that the body of each λ-abstraction is evaluated afresh. The rest—closures, stack, control, and dump—are inessential programming artefacts.

Originality: Environments are usually managed in a caller-save fashion in interpreters, and relatively rare are programs that use delimited continuations. (In fact, control delimiters were invented a quarter of a century after the SECD machine [12, 18].)

1.3   Overview

We first detail the deconstruction of the SECD machine into a compositional evaluator in direct style (Section 2). We then illustrate how to reconstruct a variety of SECD-like machines (Section 3), including one with an instruction set, and we conclude.

1.4   Prerequisites and Domain of Discourse

We use pure ML as a meta-language. We assume a basic familiarity with Standard ML and with reasoning about ML programs. In particular, given two ML expressions e and e' we write e $\cong$ e' to express that e and e' are observationally equivalent.

The source language. The source language is the λ-calculus, extended with literals (as observables). A program is a closed term.

```
structure Source
= struct
    type ide = string
    datatype term = LIT of int
                  | VAR of ide
                  | LAM of ide * term
                  | APP of term * term
    type program = term
  end
```

The (polymorphic) environment. We make use of a structure `Env` satisfying the following signature:

```
signature ENV
= sig
    type 'a env
    val empty : 'a env
    val extend : Source.ide * 'a * 'a env -> 'a env
    val lookup : Source.ide * 'a env -> 'a
  end
```

The empty environment is denoted by `Env.empty`. The function extending an environment with a new binding is denoted by `Env.extend`. The function fetching the value of an identifier from an environment is denoted by `Env.lookup`.

Expressible and denotable values. There are three kinds of values: integers, the successor function, and function closures:

```
datatype value = INT of int
               | SUCC
               | CLOSURE of value Env.env * Source.ide * Source.term
```

Following Landin [27], function closures pair a λ-abstraction (i.e., its formal parameter and its body) and the environment of its declaration.

The initial environment. We define the successor function in the initial environment:

```
val e_init = Env.extend ("succ", SUCC, Env.empty)
```

2   Deconstruction of the SECD Machine

We now substantiate the deconstruction outlined in Section 1.1.

Section 2.1 presents the SECD machine as originally specified and classically presented in the literature, i.e., as one tail-recursive transition function run. Section 2.2 presents an alternative specification where run is disentangled into four mutually (tail) recursive transition functions run_c, run_d, run_t, and run_a, each of which has one induction variable. This disentangled definition is in defunctionalized form, and Section 2.3 presents its higher-order counterpart. This counterpart is in continuation-passing style, and Section 2.4 presents its direct-style equivalent. This equivalent is almost in continuation-passing style, which is characteristic of delimited control. Section 2.5 presents the corresponding direct-style evaluator, which uses a control delimiter. This evaluator uses a data stack of intermediate results. Section 2.6 presents the corresponding stackless evaluator. This evaluator is in closure-converted form. Section 2.7 present the corresponding higher-order evaluator. This evaluator is compositional and assessed in Section 2.8.

2.1   The Original Specification of the SECD Machine

The SECD machine is a transition function over a state with four components:

- A *stack* register holding a list of intermediate results. This component has type value list.
- An *environment* register holding the current environment. This component has type value Env.env.
- A *control* register holding a list of control directives. This component has type directive, where directive is defined as follows:

      datatype directive = TERM of Source.term
                         | APPLY

- A *dump* register holding a list of triples. Each triple contains snapshots of the stack, environment, and control registers. This component has type (value list * value Env.env * directive list) list.

The SECD machine is defined with a set of transitions between its four components. Here is its transitive closure:

```
(*   run : S * E * C * D -> value   *)
(*   where S = value list           *)
(*         E = value Env.env         *)
(*         C = directive list        *)
(*         D = (S * E * C) list       *)
fun run (v :: nil, e', nil, nil)                          (* 1 *)
      = v
  | run (v :: nil, e', nil, (s, e, c) :: d)               (* 2 *)
      = run (v :: s, e, c, d)
  | run (s, e, (TERM (LIT n)) :: c, d)                     (* 3 *)
      = run ((INT n) :: s, e, c, d)
  | run (s, e, (TERM (VAR x)) :: c, d)                     (* 4 *)
      = run ((Env.lookup (x, e)) :: s, e, c, d)
  | run (s, e, (TERM (LAM (x, t))) :: c, d)                (* 5 *)
      = run ((CLOSURE (e, x, t)) :: s, e, c, d)
```

```
  | run (s, e, (TERM (APP (t0, t1)))) :: c, d)                    (* 6 *)
    = run (s, e, (TERM t1) :: (TERM t0) :: APPLY :: c, d)
  | run (SUCC :: (INT n) :: s, e, APPLY :: c, d)                  (* 7 *)
    = run ((INT (n+1)) :: s, e, c, d)
  | run ((CLOSURE (e', x, t)) :: v' :: s, e, APPLY :: c, d)       (* 8 *)
    = run (nil, Env.extend (x, v', e'), (TERM t) :: nil, (s, e, c) :: d)

(*  evaluate0 : Source.program -> value  *)
fun evaluate0 t                                                   (* 9 *)
    = run (nil, e_init, (TERM t) :: nil, nil)
```

The SECD machine does not terminate for divergent source terms. If it becomes stuck, an ML pattern-matching error is raised (alternatively, the co-domain of run could be made value option and an else clause could be added). Otherwise, the result of the evaluation is v for some ML value v : value.

In the full version of this article [11], we analyze each of the transitions above; this analysis is however inessential for what follows.

2.2   A More Structured Specification

In the definition of Section 2.1, all the possible transitions are meshed together in one recursive function, run. Let us factor run into several mutually recursive functions, each of them with one induction variable.

In this disentangled definition,

- run_c interprets the list of control directives, i.e., it specifies which transition to take if the list is empty, starts with a term, or starts with an apply directive. If the list is empty, it calls run_d. If the list starts with a term, it calls run_t, caching the term in an extra component (the first parameter of run_t). If the list starts with an apply directive, it calls run_a.
- run_d interprets the dump, i.e., it specifies which transition to take if the dump is empty or non-empty, given a valid stack.
- run_t interprets the top term in the list of control directives.
- run_a interprets the top value in the current stack.

```
(*   run_c : S * E * C * D -> value                    *)
(*   run_d : S * D -> value                            *)
(*   run_t : Source.term * S * E * C * D -> value      *)
(*   run_a : S * E * C * D -> value                    *)
(*      where S = value list                           *)
(*            E = value Env.env                         *)
(*            C = directive list                        *)
(*            D = (S * E * C) list                      *)
fun run_c (s, e, nil, d)
    = run_d (s, d)
  | run_c (s, e, (TERM t) :: c, d)
    = run_t (t, s, e, c, d)
  | run_c (s, e, APPLY :: c, d)
    = run_a (s, e, c, d)
```

```
and run_d (v :: nil, nil)
     = v
  | run_d (v :: nil, (s, e, c) :: d)
     = run_c (v :: s, e, c, d)
and run_t (LIT n, s, e, c, d)
     = run_c ((INT n) :: s, e, c, d)
  | run_t (VAR x, s, e, c, d)
     = run_c ((Env.lookup (x, e)) :: s, e, c, d)
  | run_t (LAM (x, t), s, e, c, d)
     = run_c ((CLOSURE (e, x, t)) :: s, e, c, d)

  | run_t (APP (t0, t1), s, e, c, d)
     = run_t (t1, s, e, (TERM t0) :: APPLY :: c, d)
and run_a (SUCC :: (INT n) :: s, e, c, d)
     = run_c ((INT (n+1)) :: s, e, c, d)
  | run_a ((CLOSURE (e', x, t)) :: v' :: s, e, c, d)
     = run_t (t, nil, Env.extend (x, v', e'), nil, (s, e, c) :: d)

(*  evaluate1 : Source.program -> value  *)
fun evaluate1 t
     = run_t (t, nil, e_init, nil, nil)
```

Proposition 1 (full correctness). *Given a source program,* evaluate0 *and* evaluate1 *either both diverge or yield expressible values that are structurally equal.*

2.3   A Higher-Order Counterpart

In the disentangled definition of Section 2.2, there are two possible ways to construct a dump (nil and cons) and three possible ways to construct a list of control directives (nil, cons'ing a term, and cons'ing an apply directive). (We could phrase these constructions as two data types rather than as two lists.)

These data types, together with run_d and run_c, are in the image of defunctionalization (run_d and run_c are the apply functions of these two data types). The corresponding higher-order evaluator reads as follows.

```
(*  run_t : Source.term * S * E * C * D -> value  *)
(*  run_a : S * E * C * D -> value                *)
(*    where S = value list                        *)
(*          E = value Env.env                     *)
(*          C = (S * E * D) -> value              *)
(*          D = S -> value                        *)
fun run_t (LIT n, s, e, c, d)
     = c ((INT n) :: s, e, d)
  | run_t (VAR x, s, e, c, d)
     = c ((Env.lookup (x, e)) :: s, e, d)
  | run_t (LAM (x, t), s, e, c, d)
     = c ((CLOSURE (e, x, t)) :: s, e, d)
```

```
  | run_t (APP (t0, t1), s, e, c, d)
    = run_t (t1, s, e,
              fn (s, e, d) => run_t (t0, s, e,
                                      fn (s, e, d) => run_a (s, e, c, d),
                                      d),
              d)
  and run_a (SUCC :: (INT n) :: s, e, c, d)
    = c ((INT (n+1)) :: s, e, d)
  | run_a ((CLOSURE (e', x, t)) :: v' :: s, e, c, d)
    = run_t (t, nil, Env.extend (x, v', e')),
              fn (s, _, d) => d s,
              fn (v :: nil) => c (v :: s, e, d))

(*  evaluate2 : Source.program -> value  *)
fun evaluate2 t
    = run_t (t, nil, e_init,
              fn (s, _, d) => d s,
              fn (v :: nil) => v)
```

The resulting evaluator is in continuation-passing style, with two nested continuations. It inherits the characteristics of the SECD machine, i.e., it threads a stack of intermediate results, an environment, a control continuation, and a dump continuation. As an evaluator, it is a bit unusual in that:

1. it has two continuations (c and D),
2. it threads a stack of intermediate results (S), and
3. the environment is saved by the recursive callees, not by the callers. (Usually, the environment is not threaded but saved across recursive calls.)

Otherwise the interpreter follows the traditional eval–apply schema identified by McCarthy in his definition of Lisp in Lisp [30], by Reynolds in his definitional interpreters [37], and by Steele and Sussman in their lambda-papers [40, 41, 42, 43]: run_t is eval and run_a is apply.

Proposition 2 (full correctness). *Given a source program,* evaluate1 *and* evaluate2 *either both diverge or yield expressible values that are structurally equal.*

2.4   A Dump-Less Direct-Style Counterpart

The evaluator of Section 2.3 is in continuation-passing style and therefore it is in the image of the CPS transformation [9]. Its direct-style counterpart reads as follows, renaming run_t as eval and run_a as apply.

```
(*   eval : Source.term * S * E * C -> stack  *)
(*  apply : S * E * C -> S                     *)
(*    where S = value list                     *)
(*          E = value Env.env                   *)
(*          C = S * E -> S                       *)
```

```
fun eval (LIT n, s, e, c)
     = c ((INT n) :: s, e)
  | eval (VAR x, s, e, c)
     = c ((Env.lookup (x, e)) :: s, e)
  | eval (LAM (x, t), s, e, c)
     = c ((CLOSURE (e, x, t)) :: s, e)
  | eval (APP (t0, t1), s, e, c)
     = eval (t1, s, e, fn (s, e) =>
       eval (t0, s, e, fn (s, e) =>
       apply (s, e, c)))
and apply (SUCC :: (INT n) :: s, e, c)
     = c ((INT (n+1)) :: s, e)
  | apply ((CLOSURE (e', x, t)) :: v' :: s, e, c)
     = let val (v :: nil) = eval (t, nil, Env.extend (x, v', e')),
                            fn (s, _) => s)
       in c (v :: s, e)
       end

(*  evaluate3 : Source.program -> value  *)
fun evaluate3 t
     = let val (v :: nil) = eval (t, nil, e_init, fn (s, _) => s)
       in v
       end
```

Proposition 3 (full correctness). *Given a source program,* evaluate2 *and* evaluate3 *either both diverge or yield expressible values that are structurally equal.*

2.5   A Control-Less Direct-Style Counterpart

All but two of the calls to eval are tail calls in the evaluator of Section 2.4. Thus, except for these two calls, the evaluator is in CPS. These two calls are characteristic of delimited continuations [12, 18]. To account for them, we use the control delimiter reset. Operationally, this control delimiter is moot here because no continuations are captured [12, 25]. It can therefore simply be defined as taking a thunk and forcing it, as we do below; in general of course, the definition is not as simple [20]. (Omitting reset leads to a dump-less variant of the SECD machine [11, Section 3.6].) With such a definition of reset, the direct-style counterpart of the evaluator reads as follows:

```
(*  (* mock-up *) reset : (unit -> 'a) -> 'a  *)
fun reset thunk
     = thunk ()

(*   eval : Source.term * S * E -> S * E   *)
(*   apply : S * E -> S * E                *)
(*     where S = value list                *)
(*           E = value Env.env             *)
```

```
fun eval (LIT n, s, e)
    = ((INT n) :: s, e)
  | eval (VAR x, s, e)
    = ((Env.lookup (x, e)) :: s, e)
  | eval (LAM (x, t), s, e)
    = ((CLOSURE (e, x, t)) :: s, e)
  | eval (APP (t0, t1), s, e)
    = let val (s, e) = eval (t1, s, e)
          val (s, e) = eval (t0, s, e)
      in apply (s, e)
      end
and apply (SUCC :: (INT n) :: s, e)
    = ((INT (n+1)) :: s, e)
  | apply ((CLOSURE (e', x, t)) :: v' :: s, e)
    = let val (v :: nil, _)
              = reset (fn () => eval (t, nil, Env.extend (x, v', e')))
      in (v :: s, e)
      end

(*  evaluate4 : Source.program -> value  *)
fun evaluate4 t
    = let val (v :: nil, _)
              = reset (fn () => eval (t, nil, e_init))
      in v
      end
```

Proposition 4 (full correctness). *Given a source program,* evaluate3 *and* evaluate4 *either both diverge or yield expressible values that are structurally equal.*

2.6   A Stack-Less Counterpart

In the evaluator of Section 2.5, eval and apply thread a data stack of intermediate results. The stackless counterpart of this evaluator reads as follows.

```
(*   eval : Source.term * E -> value * E   *)
(*   apply : value * value * E -> value * E  *)
(*    where E = value Env.env             *)
fun eval (LIT n, e)
    = (INT n, e)
  | eval (VAR x, e)
    = (Env.lookup (x, e), e)
  | eval (LAM (x, t), e)
    = (CLOSURE (e, x, t), e)
  | eval (APP (t0, t1), e)
    = let val (v1, e) = eval (t1, e)
          val (v0, e) = eval (t0, e)
      in apply (v0, v1, e)
      end
```

```
and apply (SUCC, INT n, e)
      = (INT (n+1), e)
  | apply (CLOSURE (e', x, t), v', e)
      = let val (v, _)
                = reset (fn () => eval (t, Env.extend (x, v', e')))
        in (v, e)
        end

(*  evaluate5 : Source.program -> value  *)
fun evaluate5 t
      = let val (v', _)
                = reset (fn () => eval (t, e_init))
        in v'
        end
```

Proposition 5 (full correctness). *Given a source program,* evaluate4 *and* evaluate5 *either both diverge or yield expressible values that are structurally equal.*

2.7   A Compositional Counterpart

The evaluators of Sections 2.3, 2.4, 2.5, and 2.6 represent functional values with closures. In Section 1.4, this representation was epitomized by the definition of values:

```
datatype value = INT of int
               | SUCC
               | CLOSURE of value Env.env * Source.ide * Source.term
```

A function closure pairs a source λ-abstraction and the environment of its declaration.

Because of this representation, none of the evaluators above are compositional in the sense of denotational semantics [38, 44, 45].[1] On the other hand, because they use closures, these evaluators are in closure-converted form. We closure-unconvert the latest one as follows.

```
datatype value = INT of int
               | SUCC
               | FUN of value -> value

(*   eval : Source.term * E -> value * E    *)
(*  apply : value * value * E -> value * E  *)
(*    where E = value Env.env               *)
fun eval (LIT n, e)
      = (INT n, e)
```

---

[1] To be compositional, they should solely define the meaning of each compound term as a composition of the meaning of its parts.

```
    | eval (VAR x, e)
      = (Env.lookup (x, e), e)
    | eval (LAM (x, t), e)
      = (FUN (fn v
                 => reset (fn ()
                              => let val (v', _)
                                      = eval (t, Env.extend (x, v, e))
                                 in v'
                                 end)),
          e)
    | eval (APP (t0, t1), e)
      = let val (v1, e) = eval (t1, e)
            val (v0, e) = eval (t0, e)
        in apply (v0, v1, e)
        end
  and apply (SUCC, INT n, e)
      = (INT (n+1), e)
    | apply (FUN f, v, e)
      = (f v, e)

  (*  evaluate6 : Source.program -> value  *)
  fun evaluate6 t
      = reset (fn () => let val (v', _) = eval (t, e_init)
                        in v'
                        end)
```

Proposition 6 (full correctness). *Given a source program,* evaluate5 *and* evaluate6 *either both diverge or yield expressible values that are related by closure conversion.*

The evaluator above is not unique, though. We can also choose a callee-save representation of functions, as developed in Section 2.7 of the full version of this article [11].

2.8   Assessment

Through a series of meaning-preserving steps, we have transformed the SECD machine (i.e., the transitive closure of a state-transition function) into an evaluator (i.e., a compositional evaluation function). For each of these language processors—the original one, the intermediate ones, and the final one—evaluating an ill-typed source term is undefined (i.e., in ML, evaluation gets stuck and a pattern-matching error is raised); evaluating a divergent source term diverges; and evaluating a well-typed and convergent source term converges to a value.

It seems to us that this deconstruction of the SECD machine into an evaluation function sheds a new light on it. Its stack, environment, control, and dump registers are explained as artefacts of a particular evaluation algorithm: environment-based with a callee-save strategy, left-to-right call by value, and with one data stack for intermediate results and two continuations, the inner one for the current λ-abstraction.

3   Reconstructions of SECD-Like Machines

Each of the deconstruction steps of Section 2 is reversible. In the full version of this article [11], we review briefly how to rationally reconstruct a variety of SECD-like machines: the original SECD machine, a left-to-right SECD machine, a properly tail-recursive SECD machine, a call-by-name SECD machine, a call-by-need SECD machine, an SEC machine, an EC machine, an SC machine, a C machine, an SCD machine, and an SECD machine with an instruction set.

4   Related Work

In his famous 700 follow-up article [28,31], Morris presents a "shorter equivalent" of the SECD machine as an interpreter written in an applicative language. We note, though, that while Morris's interpreter is definitely shorter, it is not strictly equivalent to the SECD machine. (For example, its environment is saved by the callers, not by the callees.) Indeed, defunctionalizing the CPS counterpart of Morris's interpreter yields a different abstract machine that has one control stack and no dump. (In fact, this abstract machine coincides with Felleisen et al.'s CEK abstract machine [17, 19].)

In a similar way, in "Call-by-name, call-by-value, and the λ-calculus" [34], Plotkin formalized the SECD machine with respect to a canonical, caller-save, evaluation function that is similar to Morris's. In the light of the reconstruction presented here, the correctness proof of the SECD machine reduces to proving the equivalence between a caller-save and a callee-save evaluation function, which is simpler.

In his formalization of (a tail-recursive version of) the SECD machine [35], Ramsdell also observes that this machine uses callee-save convention.

5   Conclusion

We have characterized the denotational content of the SECD machine as an evaluator with a callee-save strategy for the environment and a control delimiter.[2] In doing so, we have outlined a methodology for extracting the denotational content of abstract machines in the form of a compositional evaluation function. This methodology is reversible and enables one to extract the (small-step) operational content of evaluation functions in the form of an abstract machine in a fairly mechanical way: one closure-converts its expressible and denotable values to make them first-order; one CPS-transforms the closure-converted evaluation function to make it tail-recursive, i.e., iterative, and to materialize its control flow into a continuation; and one defunctionalizes this continuation to make the

---

[2] Landin was aware that abstract machines are interpreters, witness his introduction of the SECD machine as a way of "interpreting" applicative expressions. (The quotes are his. The other quotes in the abstract of his article occur when he wrote that his article contributes to the "theory" of computing.)

evaluation function first order, thereby obtaining a transition function, i.e., a finite-state, iterative abstract machine. Optionally, one introduces a data stack to hold intermediate results. The methodology also scales to other evaluation functions and other abstract machines; in particular, it applies directly to λ-calculi extended with computational effects à la Moggi, e.g., control and state, and to other language paradigms than functional programming [1, 3, 4, 7].

In passing, we have also presented a new application of defunctionalization and a new example of control delimiters in programming practice.

Acknowledgments

The rational deconstruction presented here arose because of a discussion with Mayer Goldberg in July 2002, at the occasion of our joint work on compilation and decompilation [2]. The author is also grateful to Mads Sig Ager, Dariusz Biernacki, and Jan Midtgaard for our subsequent joint study of the functional correspondence between evaluation functions and abstract machines [1, 3, 4, 7].

A first version of this article was written in the early fall of 2002. It gave rise to presentations at the University of Tokyo in September 2002, at INRIA-Rocquencourt in December 2002, at the University of Rennes in December 2002, and at the 2.8 Working Group on functional programming in January 2003. At the time, there was no data-stack elimination.

The present article contains data-stack elimination and is a shorter version of a BRICS technical report [11]. This technical report was written during the summer of 2003. It has benefited from the comments of Mads Sig Ager, Małgorzata Biernacka, Dariusz Biernacki, Julia Lawall, Jan Midtgaard, and Henning Korsholm Rohde. The present shortened version has benefited from the sagacity of four anonymous IFL reviewers. Thanks are also due to Harry Mairson, John Reynolds, and Mitchell Wand for their input about the title as well as for their encouraging words. Last but not least, thanks are due to Peter Landin himself for his feedback and for the historical explanations he kindly provided me at Queen Mary in May 2004.

This work is supported by the ESPRIT Working Group APPSEM II (`http://www.appsem.org`) and by the Danish Natural Science Research Council, Grant no. 21-03-0545.

References

1. M. S. Ager, D. Biernacki, O. Danvy, and J. Midtgaard. A functional correspondence between evaluators and abstract machines. In D. Miller, editor, *Proceedings of the Fifth ACM-SIGPLAN International Conference on Principles and Practice of Declarative Programming (PPDP'03)*, pages 8–19. ACM Press, Aug. 2003.
2. M. S. Ager, O. Danvy, and M. Goldberg. A symmetric approach to compilation and decompilation. In T. Æ. Mogensen, D. A. Schmidt, and I. H. Sudborough, editors, *The Essence of Computation: Complexity, Analysis, Transformation. Essays Dedicated to Neil D. Jones*, number 2566 in Lecture Notes in Computer Science, pages 296–331. Springer-Verlag, 2002.

3. M. S. Ager, O. Danvy, and J. Midtgaard. A functional correspondence between call-by-need evaluators and lazy abstract machines. *Information Processing Letters*, 90(5):223–232, 2004. Extended version available as the technical report BRICS-RS-04-3.

4. M. S. Ager, O. Danvy, and J. Midtgaard. A functional correspondence between monadic evaluators and abstract machines for languages with computational effects. *Theoretical Computer Science*, 2005. Accepted for publication. Extended version available as the technical report BRICS RS-04-28.

5. A. Banerjee, N. Heintze, and J. G. Riecke. Design and correctness of program transformations based on control-flow analysis. In N. Kobayashi and B. C. Pierce, editors, *Theoretical Aspects of Computer Software, 4th International Symposium, TACS 2001*, number 2215 in Lecture Notes in Computer Science, pages 420–447, Sendai, Japan, Oct. 2001. Springer-Verlag.

6. J. M. Bell, F. Bellegarde, and J. Hook. Type-driven defunctionalization. In M. Tofte, editor, *Proceedings of the 1997 ACM SIGPLAN International Conference on Functional Programming*, pages 25–37, Amsterdam, The Netherlands, June 1997. ACM Press.

7. D. Biernacki and O. Danvy. From interpreter to logic engine by defunctionalization. In M. Bruynooghe, editor, *Logic Based Program Synthesis and Transformation, 13th International Symposium, LOPSTR 2003*, number 3018 in Lecture Notes in Computer Science, pages 143–159, Uppsala, Sweden, Aug. 2003. Springer-Verlag.

8. H.-J. Boehm, editor. *Proceedings of the Twenty-First Annual ACM Symposium on Principles of Programming Languages*, Portland, Oregon, Jan. 1994. ACM Press.

9. O. Danvy. Back to direct style. *Science of Computer Programming*, 22(3):183–195, 1994.

10. O. Danvy. Type-directed partial evaluation. In G. L. Steele Jr., editor, *Proceedings of the Twenty-Third Annual ACM Symposium on Principles of Programming Languages*, pages 242–257, St. Petersburg Beach, Florida, Jan. 1996. ACM Press.

11. O. Danvy. A rational deconstruction of Landin's SECD machine. Technical Report BRICS RS-03-33, DAIMI, Department of Computer Science, University of Aarhus, Aarhus, Denmark, Oct. 2003.

12. O. Danvy and A. Filinski. Abstracting control. In M. Wand, editor, *Proceedings of the 1990 ACM Conference on Lisp and Functional Programming*, pages 151–160, Nice, France, June 1990. ACM Press.

13. O. Danvy and A. Filinski. Representing control, a study of the CPS transformation. *Mathematical Structures in Computer Science*, 2(4):361–391, 1992.

14. O. Danvy and L. R. Nielsen. Defunctionalization at work. In H. Søndergaard, editor, *Proceedings of the Third International ACM SIGPLAN Conference on Principles and Practice of Declarative Programming (PPDP'01)*, pages 162–174, Firenze, Italy, Sept. 2001. ACM Press. Extended version available as the technical report BRICS RS-01-23.

15. O. Danvy and L. R. Nielsen. On one-pass CPS transformations. Technical Report BRICS RS-02-3, DAIMI, Department of Computer Science, University of Aarhus, Aarhus, Denmark, Jan. 2002. Accepted for publication in the Journal of Functional Programming.

16. S. Diehl, P. Hartel, and P. Sestoft. Abstract machines for programming language implementation. *Future Generation Computer Systems*, 16:739–751, 2000.

17. M. Felleisen. *The Calculi of λ-v-CS Conversion: A Syntactic Theory of Control and State in Imperative Higher-Order Programming Languages*. PhD thesis, Department of Computer Science, Indiana University, Bloomington, Indiana, Aug. 1987.

18. M. Felleisen. The theory and practice of first-class prompts. In J. Ferrante and P. Mager, editors, *Proceedings of the Fifteenth Annual ACM Symposium on Principles of Programming Languages*, pages 180–190, San Diego, California, Jan. 1988. ACM Press.

19. M. Felleisen and M. Flatt. Programming languages and lambda calculi. Unpublished lecture notes. http://www.ccs.neu.edu/home/matthias/3810-w02/readings.html, 1989-2003.

20. A. Filinski. Representing monads. In Boehm [8], pages 446–457.

21. D. P. Friedman, M. Wand, and C. T. Haynes. *Essentials of Programming Languages, second edition*. The MIT Press, 2001.

22. M. Gasbichler and M. Sperber. Final shift for call/cc: direct implementation of shift and reset. In S. Peyton Jones, editor, *Proceedings of the 2002 ACM SIGPLAN International Conference on Functional Programming*, SIGPLAN Notices, Vol. 37, No. 9, pages 271–282, Pittsburgh, Pennsylvania, Sept. 2002. ACM Press.

23. J. Hatcliff and O. Danvy. A generic account of continuation-passing styles. In Boehm [8], pages 458–471.

24. P. Hein. *Grooks*. The MIT Press, 1966.

25. Y. Kameyama and M. Hasegawa. A sound and complete axiomatization of delimited continuations. In O. Shivers, editor, *Proceedings of the 2003 ACM SIGPLAN International Conference on Functional Programming*, pages 177–188, Uppsala, Sweden, Aug. 2003. ACM Press.

26. J.-L. Krivine. Un interprète du λ-calcul. Brouillon. Available online at http://www.pps.jussieu.fr/~krivine, 1985.

27. P. J. Landin. The mechanical evaluation of expressions. *The Computer Journal*, 6(4):308–320, 1964.

28. P. J. Landin. The next 700 programming languages. *Commun. ACM*, 9(3):157–166, 1966.

29. J. L. Lawall and O. Danvy. Continuation-based partial evaluation. In C. L. Talcott, editor, *Proceedings of the 1994 ACM Conference on Lisp and Functional Programming*, LISP Pointers, Vol. VII, No. 3, pages 227–238, Orlando, Florida, June 1994. ACM Press.

30. J. McCarthy, P. W. Abrahams, D. J. Edwards, T. P. Hart, and M. I. Levin. *LISP 1.5 Programmer's Manual*. The MIT Press, Cambridge, Massachusetts, 1962.

31. L. Morris. The next 700 formal language descriptions. *Lisp and Symbolic Computation*, 6(3/4):249–258, 1993.

32. L. R. Nielsen. A denotational investigation of defunctionalization. Technical Report BRICS RS-00-47, DAIMI, Department of Computer Science, University of Aarhus, Aarhus, Denmark, Dec. 2000.

33. S. L. Peyton Jones. Implementing lazy functional languages on stock hardware: The spineless tagless G-machine. *Journal of Functional Programming*, 2(2):127–202, 1992.

34. G. D. Plotkin. Call-by-name, call-by-value and the λ-calculus. *Theoretical Computer Science*, 1:125–159, 1975.

35. J. D. Ramsdell. The tail-recursive SECD machine. *Journal of Automated Reasoning*, 23(1):43–62, July 1999.

36. J. C. Reynolds. The discoveries of continuations. *Lisp and Symbolic Computation*, 6(3/4):233–247, 1993.

37. J. C. Reynolds. Definitional interpreters for higher-order programming languages. *Higher-Order and Symbolic Computation*, 11(4):363–397, 1998. Reprinted from the proceedings of the 25th ACM National Conference (1972), with a foreword.

38. D. A. Schmidt. *Denotational Semantics: A Methodology for Language Development.* Allyn and Bacon, Inc., 1986.

39. O. Shivers. *Control-Flow Analysis of Higher-Order Languages or Taming Lambda.* PhD thesis, School of Computer Science, Carnegie Mellon University, Pittsburgh, Pennsylvania, May 1991. Technical Report CMU-CS-91-145.

40. G. L. Steele Jr. Lambda, the ultimate declarative. AI Memo 379, Artificial Intelligence Laboratory, Massachusetts Institute of Technology, Cambridge, Massachusetts, Nov. 1976.

41. G. L. Steele Jr. Rabbit: A compiler for Scheme. Master's thesis, Artificial Intelligence Laboratory, Massachusetts Institute of Technology, Cambridge, Massachusetts, May 1978. Technical report AI-TR-474.

42. G. L. Steele Jr. and G. J. Sussman. Lambda, the ultimate imperative. AI Memo 353, Artificial Intelligence Laboratory, Massachusetts Institute of Technology, Cambridge, Massachusetts, Mar. 1976.

43. G. L. Steele Jr. and G. J. Sussman. The art of the interpreter or, the modularity complex (parts zero, one, and two). AI Memo 453, Artificial Intelligence Laboratory, Massachusetts Institute of Technology, Cambridge, Massachusetts, May 1978.

44. J. E. Stoy. *Denotational Semantics: The Scott-Strachey Approach to Programming Language Theory.* The MIT Press, 1977.

45. G. Winskel. *The Formal Semantics of Programming Languages.* Foundation of Computing Series. The MIT Press, 1993.

A   Toolbox

In this appendix, we review the elements of the toolbox mentioned in Section 1.

A.1   CPS Transformation

A λ-term is transformed into continuation-passing style (CPS) by naming each of its intermediate results, by sequentializing the computation of these results, and by introducing continuations. Equivalently, such a term can be first transformed into monadic normal form and then translated into the term model of the continuation monad [23]. The CPS transformation is abundantly described in the literature [15, 21, 36, 41].

For example, a term such as $\lambda f.\lambda g.\lambda x.f\ x\ (g\ x)$ is named and sequentialized into

$$\lambda f.\lambda g.\lambda x.\mathsf{let}\ v_1 = f\ x\ \mathsf{in}\ \mathsf{let}\ v_2 = g\ x\ \mathsf{in}\ v_1\ v_2$$

and its call-by-value CPS counterpart reads as

$$\lambda k.k\ (\lambda f.\lambda k.k\ (\lambda g.\lambda k.k\ (\lambda x.f\ x\ \lambda v_1.g\ x\ \lambda v_2.v_1\ v_2\ k))).$$

In both the sequentialized version and the CPS version, v_1 names the result of $f\ x$ and v_2 names the result of $g\ x$.

A.2   Delimited Continuations

A λ-term uses delimited continuations when some of its intermediate continuations are reinitialized to the identity function or when not all calls to a continuation are evaluation-order independent [12]. For example, in contrast to the CPS abstraction

$$\lambda f.\lambda k.f\ 42\ k$$

which is strictly in continuation-passing style (all calls are tail calls and all subterms are trivial), the non-CPS abstraction

$$\lambda f.\lambda k.k\ (f\ 42\ (\lambda a.a))$$

uses delimited continuations; the function denoted by f is passed an initial continuation, and the result of its application is sent to k. This term is therefore evaluation-order sensitive [34, 37]. The direct-style counterpart of the first abstraction,

$$\lambda f.f\ 42$$

is an ordinary λ-term, whereas the direct-style counterpart of the second,

$$\lambda f.reset(f\ 42)$$

uses the control delimiter *reset* [10, 12, 13, 20, 22, 25, 29]. Should the function denoted by f capture its continuation, it would capture all of it in the first case (and applying this captured continuation would be like a jump); in the second case, however, it would capture only a delimited part of the continuation (and applying this captured continuation would be like a call). In this article, we make no other use of reset than to reinitialize the continuation.

A.3   Defunctionalization

In a higher-order program, first-class functions occur as instances of function abstractions. Often, these function abstractions can be enumerated, either exhaustively or more discriminately using a control-flow analysis [39]. Defunctionalization is a transformation where function types are replaced by an enumeration of the function abstractions in this program.

Defunctionalization consumes the results of a control-flow analysis. A defunctionalizer replaces:

- function spaces by an enumeration, in the form of a data type, of the possible lambda-abstractions that can float there;
- function introduction by an injection into the corresponding data type; and
- function elimination by an apply function dispatching over elements of the corresponding data type.

For example, let us defunctionalize the following ML program:

```
fun aux f = (f 1) + (f 10)
```

```
fun main (x, y) = (aux (fn z => z)) * (aux (fn z => x + y + z))
```

The `aux` function is passed a first-class function, applies it to 1 and 10, and sums the results. The `main` function calls `aux` twice and multiplies the results. All in all, two function abstractions occur in this program, in `main`, as arguments of `aux`.

Defunctionalizing this program amounts to defining a data type with two constructors, one for each function abstraction, and its associated apply function. The first function abstraction contains no free variables and therefore the first data-type constructor is constant. The second function abstraction contains two free variables (`x` and `y`, of type integer), and therefore the second data-type constructor requires two integers.

In `main_def`, the first functional argument is thus introduced with the first constructor, and the second functional argument with the second constructor and the values of `x` and `y`. In `aux_def`, the functional argument is passed to a (second-class) function `apply` that eliminates it with a case expression dispatching over the two constructors.

```
datatype lam = LAM1
             | LAM2 of int * int

fun apply (LAM1, z)
     = z
  | apply (LAM2 (x, y), z)
     = x + y + z

fun aux_def f = (apply (f, 1)) + (apply (f, 10))

fun main_def (x, y) = (aux_def LAM1) * (aux_def (LAM2 (x, y)))
```

Defunctionalization was discovered by Reynolds thirty-two years ago [37]. Compared to closure conversion, it has been little used in practice since then, and has only been formalized over the last few years [5, 6, 32]. More detail can be found in Danvy and Nielsen's study [14]. The key observation here is that defunctionalizing a CPS program yields a transition function [1].

A.4   Closure Conversion

In retrospect, closure conversion is a particular case of defunctionalization, where the function space has only one constructor and the apply function is inlined.

Explaining ML Type Errors by Data Flows

Holger Gast

Wilhelm-Schickard-Institut für Informatik
Universität Tübingen
Sand 13, 72076 Tübingen, Germany
`gast@informatik.uni-tuebingen.de`

Abstract. We present a novel approach to explaining ML type errors:
Since the type system inhibits data flows that would abort the program
at run-time, our type checker identifies as explanations those data flows
that violate the typing rules. It also detects the notorious *backflows*,
which are artifacts of unification, and warns the user about the possibly
unexpected typing. The generated explanations comprise a detailed textual description and an arrow overlay to the source code, in which each
arrow represents one data flow. The description refers only to elementary
facts about program evaluation, not to the type checking process itself.
The method integrates well with unification-based type checking: Type-
correct programs incur a modest overhead compared to normal type
checking. If a type error occurs, a simple depth-first graph traversal yields
the explanation. A proof-of-concept implementation is available.

1   Introduction

Good explanations relate the unknown to the well-understood: The new insights
can be grasped more easily and they rest on a solid foundation. Unfortunately,
ML type errors seem to evade such desirable explanations, and for well-known
reasons: Types are not explicit, at least not pervasive, in the program source,
unification propagates them between possibly remote program locations and,
finally, the details of error messages are implementation-dependent. To the experienced programmer, this situation is a nuisance to be overcome by judicious
type annotations. To novice programmers, it is often an insurmountable obstacle,
for they must understand at least four items simultaneously to decode an error
message: the type system, the sources of types in the program, their propagation
by unification — and the type error itself, of course.

Data flows are the common ground on which the type system and the programmer meet: The type system is meant to inhibit data flows that would cause
the program to abort, while the programmer must at least have expectations
about the way that data is propagated through the program. Therefore, it is a
sensible goal that type errors make explicit the offending data flows that prove
the programmer's expectations wrong. Such an explanation does relate the error
to the programmer's preconceptions and good experience has been made with
similar tools [8].

C. Grelck et al. (Eds.): IFL 2004, LNCS 3474, pp. 72–89, 2005.
© Springer-Verlag Berlin Heidelberg 2005

The task addressed in this paper is to connect formally the intended data flows to unification-based ML type inference. The proposed method rests on two ideas:

- Type inference with subtyping [18, 1, 7] can be understood by elementary data flow reasoning. By augmenting the standard subtyping closure with *reversal* of constraints, we obtain a standard unification closure [2], where subtype relations replace equality. This essential addition distinguishes the proposed approach from MrSpidey [8]. Explanations for type errors are generated by annotating each subtyping constraint with a *reason* for its presence in the closure, the reason being essentially a trail of the closure computation.
- We avoid the inefficient direct closure computation [14] by extending standard ML type unification with a graph structure of *paths* between types. The paths are maintained at marginal cost and reasons can be reconstructed whenever a type error occurs.

The explanations thus obtained include a descriptive and detailed textual justification of single steps similar to type explanation engines [6, 3, 12, 5, 26]. They also yield program slices [23, 10, 19, 21] and arrow annotations as used in graphical debuggers [8] by omitting parts of the generated information.

The presentation of the paper assumes basic knowledge of type inference for both ML [17, 24] and subtyping [18, 1, 7].

1.1   Contributions

- We propose to use data flow reasoning to explain ML type errors.
- Our method can be integrated efficiently with a unification-based type checker.
- The generated explanations are detailed and refer only to elementary facts about evaluation. They have a meaning in terms of data flows that is independent of type checking.
- The mentioned source locations are akin to program slices, but carry more structure that can be employed in selecting among explanations.

1.2   Overview

The introduction continues with a motivation and intuitive justification in Section 1.3 and an example explanation in Section 1.4. Section 2 formally introduces the structure of explanations for subtyping as derived from the introduction. Section 3 shows how the same explanations can be computed efficiently during unification. Section 4 discusses the two main issues of future work: The treatment of let-bindings and a transfer from Martelli-Montanari unification [15] to graph algorithms. Section 5 discusses related work. Section 6 concludes.

1.3   Motivating the Approach

Our method of explanation rests on the intuition that type inference with subtyping captures data flows in programs and that these flows can be explained in elementary terms. We are now going to discuss these assumptions by stating several observations about subtyping that motivate the technical development in Section 2. The level of presentation is deliberately informal to give a self-contained, non-technical account of the method. For that purpose, we can restrict the expression language to a call-by-value λ-calculus.

$$e ::= x \mid \lambda x.e \mid f\,e$$

Standard type inference with subtypes [18, 1, 7] traverses an expression by the following syntax-directed rules to generate a set of initial $\leq$-constraints.

$$\frac{\Gamma_x, x : \alpha \vdash e : \beta \quad \alpha \to \beta \leq \gamma}{\Gamma \vdash \lambda x.e : \gamma}\ (\text{Abs}) \qquad \frac{\Gamma \vdash x : \alpha \quad \alpha \leq \beta}{\Gamma \vdash x : \beta}\ (\text{Var})$$

$$\frac{\Gamma \vdash f : \gamma \quad \Gamma \vdash e : \delta \quad \gamma \leq \alpha \to \beta \quad \delta \leq \alpha \quad \beta \leq \epsilon}{\Gamma \vdash f\,e : \epsilon}\ (\text{App})$$

In a second phase, these constraints are checked for satisfiability to establish type correctness. We now discuss the entire process with the aim of explaining all arising constraints in elementary terms.

Type Variables as Code References. The typing rules assign a fresh type variable to each bound variable and each expression. The mapping from program points to type variables is made one-to-one in the (Var) rule by using different variables for the binding location and the particular use. In references to the program, we therefore augment the source code with a *designator* that refers to the code's role. In (Var), for instance, we distinguish the "binding of variable x" (α) from the "use of variable x" (β). Type variables thus closely correspond to program locations and citations from the source code are detailed.

Interpreting Constraints. We argue subsequently that the following interpretation remains valid throughout type inference. (The word "may" accounts for the uncertainty induced by control flow in extended languages.)

$s \leq \alpha \equiv$ "a value of type s may reach location α"

$\alpha \leq t \equiv$ "a value emerging from location α may be expected to be of type t"

$\alpha \leq \beta \equiv$ "a value emerging from location α may reach location β"

$s \leq t \equiv$ "a value of type s may eventually be expected to be of type t"

Type errors occur from *inconsistent* constraints $s \leq t$, where the constructors of s and t are not in a subtype relationship. This definition is clear from the last case of the interpretation.

Initial Constraints describe Data Flows. It is straightforward to check that the initial constraints in the typing rules have a data flow explanation. The rule (App), for example, states that "the operator f" (γ) is used as a function, "the result of e" (δ) flows to "the argument of f" (α) and "the function result of f" (β) is the "result of ($f\,e$)" (ϵ). This explanation refers only to elementary parts of the language, it should be comprehensible to any modestly experienced programmer. The proposed interpretation is also fulfilled, the only expected and produced types concern the functions in (App) and (Abs).

Closure describes Data Flows. The initial constraints thus correspond to data flows in single evaluation steps. To account for their repeated application, standard type inference closes the initial constraints C under *transitivity* and *decomposition*. If the closure C^* still contains no inconsistent constraints, the expression is type-correct.

Transitivity requires that for each pair $s \leq \alpha, \alpha \leq t \in C^*$, also $s \leq t \in C^*$, which validates the proposed interpretation: If a value of type s may reach α, and a value from α may be expected to be of type t, then eventually a value of type s may be expected to be of type t. Simply concatenating the explanations for the input constraints explains the new constraint.

Decomposition relates the arguments of constructed types. With pairs, for instance, if $s \times t \leq s' \times t' \in C^*$, then $s \leq s', t \leq t' \in C^*$, satisfying the interpretation: Since a value of type $s \times t$ is expected to have type $s' \times t'$, extracting the first component yields an s-value where an s'-value is expected, and symmetrically for the second argument. We call this phenomenon an *implicit flow* [12–Section 6], because it occurs by values transported within a larger data structure. The implicit flow $s \leq s'$ is explained by explaining the original constraint $s \times t \leq s' \times t'$, with a prefix "type s is embedded to $s \times t$" and a suffix "type $s' \times t'$ contains s'".

Decomposition of function types requires for $s \rightarrow t \leq s' \rightarrow t' \in C^*$ that $t \leq t' \in C^*$ and $s' \leq s \in C^*$. The exchange of left- and right-hand side in $s' \leq s$ is known as *contravariance*, the second argument to $\rightarrow$ is treated *covariantly*. The interpretation remains valid: A function $f : s \rightarrow t$ expects a type s and returns t. Suppose f is called where a function from s' to t' is expected. The call will pass an argument of type s', although f expects s, and it receives a t result, although it expects t'. Such a detailed explanation is necessary, however, only if higher-order functions are used. In a normal application $f\,e$, the closure of the initial constraints relates the actual argument e to the formal argument of f, the explanation can skip the contravariant function constructor.

Remark 1. Decomposition also handles correctly the data flow through polymorphic functions, where it distinguishes input and output by variance. Calling the identity function $\mathrm{id} : \alpha \rightarrow \alpha$, for instance, with argument s and expected result ϵ yields constraints $s \leq \alpha$, $\alpha \leq \epsilon$, thus finally a data flow $s \leq \epsilon$.

Symmetry of Unification. We have thus explained subtyping by elementary data flows, but ML type inference uses type equality in all constraints [24]. We propose to stick to subtype constraints nevertheless, but to extend the closure operation: For each constraint $s \leq t$, we add $t \geq s$. Note that this *reversal* swaps the syntactic positions of the types, as symmetry of equality demands, but preserves the subtype relation. To explain the reversed constraint, we reverse the original explanation. The proposed interpretation remains valid if we read $t \geq s$ as $s \leq t$.

Upper and Lower Bounds. With the introduction of $\geq$, transitivity must combine constraints $s \leq \alpha$ and $\alpha \geq t$. If we read the second one as $t \leq \alpha$, the interpretation suggests that values of types s and t reach location α. The result constraint to be added by transitivity is thus

$$s \vee t \equiv \text{"values of types } s \text{ and } t \text{ may reach a common location"}$$

A valid explanation for this constraint is that any values reaching a common program point must have *consistent* types. (Note that the above two constraints could be generated for the branches of an if-expression as introduced below.) We also need a complementary constraint for the result of transitivity with $s \geq \alpha$ and $\alpha \leq t$.

$$s \wedge t \equiv \text{"a value from some location may be used as both } s \text{ and } t\text{"}$$

Having added these new relations, new transitivity rules are required. Consider for instance $s \vee \alpha, \alpha \geq t \in C^*$. By the interpretation, values of type s and from α may reach a common program point, and furthermore t-values may reach α. Hence, we add $s \vee t \in C^*$. Instead of continuing this case analysis with numerous transitivity rules, we abstract transitivity over relations $\Diamond_1, \Diamond_2 \in \{\leq, \geq, \wedge, \vee\}$ and use a single rule: For $s\Diamond_1\alpha, \alpha\Diamond_2 t$, we add $s(\Diamond_1 \star \Diamond_2)t$. The cases are factored into the multiplication table for $\star$, which turns out to be an associative operation.

In the very same manner, we need a case analysis for decomposition and reversal, which we again factor into operations $\overleftarrow{}$ (*reverse*) and $\overline{}$ (*dual*). The general reversal rule transforms $s\Diamond t$ into a new constraint $t\overleftarrow{\Diamond}s$, where the interpretation suggests $\overleftarrow{\leq} = \geq$, $\overleftarrow{\geq} = \leq$, $\overleftarrow{\vee} = \vee$, $\overleftarrow{\wedge} = \wedge$. Decomposition on the contravariant function argument then adds for $s \to t\Diamond s' \to t'$ a new constraint $s\overline{\Diamond}s'$, with $\overline{\leq} = \geq$, $\overline{\geq} = \leq$, $\overline{\vee} = \wedge$ and $\overline{\wedge} = \vee$.

Backflows. Unfortunately, the above development fails to deliver intuitive explanations for a class of ML type errors that are known in the literature as *backflows* [25] or *poisoning* [19]. They are characterized by type information that is propagated *against* the direction of data flows. Suppose we add an if-expression and type check

<code>if x then x else 3</code>

The type error `bool` $\neq$ `int` cannot be explained by the constraints introduced so far. Call α the type of x with uses β, β' and call γ the result of the entire expression. The closure with reversal contains a chain

$$\texttt{bool} \geq \beta \geq \alpha \leq \beta' \leq \gamma \geq \texttt{int}$$

in which due to the alternating $\leq$ and $\geq$ constraints no single program location with an inconsistency can be identified. We cannot avoid backflows without changing the type system, but we will warn the programmer that the typing may be unexpected. We introduce a new relation $\sim$ with

$$s \sim t \equiv \text{"} s \text{ must be consistent with } t \text{, but this is an artifact"}$$

Minimizing and Selecting Explanations. In general, there are several possible derivations for a constraint $s \Diamond t \in C^*$, hence different explanations can be produced for a type clash between s and t. The arising need to select among these is not peculiar to our approach. Slicing-based methods [19, 21, 10] use heuristics to minimize the reported slice in some sense to present a concise explanation to the programmer.

We argue, however, that the selection of a "best" explanation to be reported can rely on structural properties of our explanations. The most important one is that explanations are linear sequences, rather than sets, of program locations and data flows. In theses sequences, "detours" that explain a constraint $\alpha \Diamond \alpha$, which represents a "null" data flow, can obviously be elided without loosing information.

Consider the following example.[1] The argument type of f is constrained by `int`, `string` and by the type of x, although the latter constraint does not contribute to the type error. With the arrows below indicating single data flows, the error is explained as "Inconsistent values flow together." Note that x is not mentioned, because we discard the detour from the argument type of f to the type of x and back again.

$$\text{fun } f\, x \rightarrow$$
$$f\text{—}1; \quad f \ x; \quad f\text{—}"X"$$

Furthermore, we propose to sort constraints by their subtyping relation before displaying the explanations. First, constraints $s \le t$ or $s \ge t$ indicate possible data flows that would abort the program. Next, constraints $s \wedge t$ and $s \vee t$ are still understandable as elementary consistency requirements. Last, the backflows $s \sim t$ establish a type error, but their explanation is not based only on data flow reasoning. Within each group of constraints, the shorter explanations should be preferred. Furthermore, the user should be able to browse the arrow overlays and select an understandable explanation by visual impression.

1.4   An Example Explanation

We now discuss how a generated explanation would be used. The steps described in the text are supported by an (X)Emacs mode that lets the user select and highlight different portions of the explanation and source code interactively. The arrows are drawn by a patch to XEmacs-21.4.15. The overlays displayed below are generated by an alternative LATEX back-end in the prototype implementation.

Towards a comparison with related work in Section 5, we choose an example due to Haack and Wells [10–Section 1.2]. They highlight the program slice contributing to the type error as shown, but it remains the programmer's responsibility to understand the exact relations between the indicated locations.

```
val f = fn x => fn  y  => let val w =  y  +    in w  ::  y
```

---

[1] I am grateful to one of the reviewers for pointing out the difficulty of the example.

Consider now our explanation generated according to Section 1.3.[2] At the coars-
est level of display, it consists of a message "Inconsistent use of values" and an
arrow overlay to the source code. Each arrow links two consecutive program locations in the explanation, hence it represents roughly one elementary data flow
occurring at run-time. We simply choose the first characters of the mentioned
expressions for the start- and endpoints and refuse to start a new arrow if it has
zero length; in this case, one arrow may cover several elementary data flows.

```
let f = fun
    x -> fun y ->
       (fun w -> w :: y)
       (y +   1)
```

Note that the same source locations are mentioned as in the slicing output,
albeit with more precise relationships indicated. The two uses can be traced
directly from the origin y to the two operators + and :: .

If this version is not comprehensible, we can refer to the textual description
in Figure 1. The indentation level corresponds to decomposition steps and the
interactive mode hides text by indentation. First, only Line 1 and the arrow
overlay appear. Selecting Line 1 expands the next level with Lines 2–8 and 15–
23. We can then navigate to the line that corresponds to the incomprehensible
arrow. For now, the arrow numbers refer us to the correct explanations for the
represented data flows. The second display level thus shows the offending types
int and list(...) together with the offending data flows.

Selecting Line 8 expands Lines 9–14. This part of the explanation contains
the exact reasoning, in terms of decomposition, why the argument 1 of + must
an int. (A similar reason is not necessary for the constructor :: due to its internal, uncurried representation.) We have claimed earlier that such an explanation
should be hidden for normal function applications, and this is accomplished simply by indenting that part of the explanation: The undesirable output coincides
with the decomposition step.

2   Explanations in Subtyping

We are now going to formalize the ideas presented in Section 1.3 by type inference
with subtyping [18, 1, 7]. The main technical contribution of this section is to
extend the standard definitions to keep track of the *reason* why a constraint has
become necessary. The reason then permits a straightforward generation of the
explanations sought in Section 1.3.

2.1   Language, Types and Type Inference

We work in an applicative language with pattern matching and the ML type
system [17]. In the following grammar, c is a value constructor and T is a type

---

[2] We replace the "let val w =" with an application, see Section 4.

```
 1 Inconsistent use of values:
 2   Forward data flow
 3     "y"
 4     (type of variable from environment) 1
 5     result of "y"
 6     (argument 1 must match formal argument) 2
 7     argument 1 to "+"
 8     [which is contained in] 2
 9       (argument 1 to "+" -> (argument 2 to "+" -> function result of "+"))
10       (operator type must match the actual arguments) 2
11       result of "+"
12       (type of variable from environment)
13       (int -> (int -> int))
14       [which has the following part]
15     int
16   Forward data flow
17     "y"
18     (type of variable from environment) 3
19     result of "y"
20     (must match formal argument type) 4
21     constructor argument 1 "w :: y"
22     (must match formal argument type)
23     list(constructor "w :: y")
```

Fig. 1. An Example Explanation

constructor (including type constants, the function space $\rightarrow$, and pairing $\times$, which we write infix). For the present, only predefined polymorphic constants can have type schemes S, the polymorphic let is discussed in Section 4.

$$e ::= x \mid e\ e' \mid \lambda x.e \mid c(e_1 \ldots e_n) \mid \textbf{case } e \textbf{ of } p_1 \Rightarrow e_1 \ldots p_n \Rightarrow e_n$$
$$p ::= x \mid c(p_1 \ldots p_n)$$
$$t ::= \alpha \mid T(t_1 \ldots t_n)$$
$$S ::= \forall \alpha_1 \ldots \alpha_n.t$$

Type inference in constraint form is standard [24, 18, 7, 1]. The rules in Figure 2 use a typing judgment $\Gamma \vdash e : t \mid C$ to generate from type assumptions Γ and expression e a type t and a set C of *initial constraints*. (All type variables in the rules are fresh for each application. The notation $\tilde{\ }$ denotes sets or sequences.) Each of these constraints is annotated with an *initial reason*, an atomic token encoding the explanation of one initial data flow. A corresponding judgment $\Gamma \vdash_p e : t \mid C$ treats patterns by reversing the subtype relations to account for the data flow during pattern matching.

$$\Gamma, x : \forall \tilde{\alpha}.s \vdash x : \beta \,|\, s[\tilde{\gamma}/\tilde{\alpha}] \leq^{\text{Var}} \beta \qquad\qquad \text{(Var/use)}$$

$$\frac{\Gamma \vdash f : \alpha \,|\, C \qquad \Gamma \vdash e : \delta \,|\, C'}{\Gamma \vdash f\,e : \gamma \,|\, C \cup C' \cup \{\alpha \leq^{\text{Apply/op}} \beta \to \gamma, \delta \leq^{\text{Apply/arg}} \beta\}} \qquad\qquad \text{(Apply)}$$

$$\frac{\Gamma, x : \forall \varepsilon.\alpha \vdash e : \beta \,|\, C}{\Gamma \vdash \lambda x.e : \gamma \,|\, C \cup \{\alpha \to \beta \leq^{\text{Abs}} \gamma\}} \qquad\qquad \text{(Abs)}$$

$$\frac{i = 1..n : \ \Gamma \vdash e_i : \alpha_i \,|\, C_i \qquad c : \forall \tilde{\beta}.s_1 \times \cdots \times s_n \to t \in \Gamma}{\Gamma \vdash c(e_1 \ldots e_n) : \delta} \qquad\qquad \text{(Ctor)}$$
$$|\, (\bigcup_{i=1}^{n} C_i) \cup \{\alpha_i \leq^{\text{Ctor/arg}} s_i[\tilde{\gamma}/\tilde{\beta}]\}_{i=1}^{n} \cup \{t[\tilde{\gamma}/\tilde{\beta}] \leq^{\text{Ctor/res}} \delta\}$$

$$\begin{array}{c} \Gamma \vdash e : \alpha \,|\, C \\ i = 1..n : \ \Gamma_i = \Gamma \dot{\cup} \{x : \beta_{ix}\}_{x \in V(p_i)} \qquad \Gamma_i \vdash_p p_i : \alpha_i' \,|\, C_i \qquad \Gamma_i \vdash e_i : \gamma_i' \,|\, C_i' \\ \hline \Gamma \vdash \mathbf{case}\ e\ \mathbf{of}\ p_1 \Rightarrow e_1 \ldots p_n \Rightarrow e_n : \gamma \end{array} \qquad \text{(Case)}$$
$$|\, (\bigcup_{i=1}^{n} C_i \cup C_i') \cup \{\alpha \leq^{\text{Case/in}} \alpha_i\}_{i=1}^{n} \cup \{\gamma_i' \leq^{\text{Case/res}} \gamma\}_{i=1}^{n}$$

$$\Gamma, \{x : \alpha\} \vdash_p x : \beta \,|\, \{\beta \leq^{\text{Pvar/def}} \alpha\} \qquad\qquad \text{(PVar)}$$

$$\frac{i = 1..n : \ \Gamma \vdash_p p_i : \alpha_i \,|\, C_i \qquad c : \forall \tilde{\beta}.s_1 \times \cdots \times s_n \to t}{\Gamma \vdash_p c(p_1 \ldots p_n) : \gamma} \qquad\qquad \text{(PCtor)}$$
$$|\, (\bigcup_{i=1}^{n} C_i) \cup \{s_i[\tilde{\delta}/\tilde{\beta}] \leq^{\text{PCtor/arg}} \alpha_i\}_{i=1}^{n} \cup \{\gamma \leq^{\text{PCtor/res}} t[\tilde{\delta}/\tilde{\beta}]\}$$

Fig. 2. Type inference rules

2.2 Closure for Unification with Reasons

We now render directly the considerations from Section 1.3 in formal terms by defining a *closure for unification* $\cdot^U$. The goal of the technical development is to establish that for any constraint set $C = \{s_i \leq t_i\}_{i=1}^{n}$ the closure C^U is consistent iff unification of $\{s_i = t_i\}_{i=1}^{n}$ does not fail with a clash. (The occurs-check is treated in Section 3.5.)

Subtype Relations. We begin with the five relations occurring in constraints:

$$\Diamond ::= \leq \,|\, \geq \,|\, \vee \,|\, \wedge \,|\, \sim$$

With these relations, a case analysis on transitivity, reversal and decomposition rules became necessary which we avoided by abstracting over the exact relations and by introducing operations $\star$, $\overset{\leftarrow}{\cdot}$ and $\overline{\cdot}$. The latter two operations were already completely specified. For $\star$ we have derived $\vee\star \geq = \vee$ from the interpretation of subtyping constraints. By similar arguments, we complete the first of the following tables.

$\star$	$\leq$	$\geq$	$\vee$	$\wedge$	$\sim$
$\leq$	$\leq$	$\vee$	$\vee$	$\sim$	$\sim$
$\geq$	$\wedge$	$\geq$	$\sim$	$\wedge$	$\sim$
$\vee$	$\sim$	$\vee$	$\sim$	$\sim$	$\sim$
$\wedge$	$\wedge$	$\sim$	$\sim$	$\sim$	$\sim$
$\sim$	$\sim$	$\sim$	$\sim$	$\sim$	$\sim$

c	$\leq$	$\geq$	$\vee$	$\wedge$	$\sim$
$\overline{c}$	$\geq$	$\leq$	$\wedge$	$\vee$	$\sim$

c	$\leq$	$\geq$	$\vee$	$\wedge$	$\sim$
$\overset{\leftarrow}{c}$	$\geq$	$\leq$	$\vee$	$\wedge$	$\sim$

Proposition 1. $\star$, $\overleftarrow{\cdot}$, and $\overline{\cdot}$ satisfy the equalities:

$$(a \star b) \star c = a \star (b \star c) \qquad \overleftarrow{a \star b} = \overleftarrow{b} \star \overleftarrow{a} \qquad \overleftarrow{\overleftarrow{a}} = a \qquad \overline{\overline{a}} = a$$

Reasons. Section 1.3 generates explanations during the closure computation. We now introduce *reasons*, that trail the closure process instead. Herein, i is an argument position and v is a *variance* ($v = +$ for covariance, $v = -$ for contravariance) in decomposition, I is an initial reason and t, t' are types.

$$r ::= I \mid \uparrow^{i,v} (t, r', t') \mid r(t)r' \mid \overleftarrow{r}$$

The *depth* of reason r (depth(r)) is the maximal nesting depth of $\uparrow^{i,v}$ constructs in r.

The desired explanations are recovered by a recursive traversal: We decode initial reasons, report $\uparrow^{i,v}$ as a decomposition step at argument i with variance v, show $r(t)r'$ as transitivity through the point t and render $\overleftarrow{r}$ by generating an explanation in reverse order.

Closure Computation. Section 1.3 has generalized closure computation to the five possible constraints, the following rules merely add maintenance of reasons. Note that the constructor in the reason identifies the applied rule, while its arguments capture just those parts of the input constraints that are not present in the result, yet are required to generate the explanation.

$$s\Diamond^r t,\ t\Diamond'^{r'} s' \overset{\text{trans}}{\Longrightarrow} s(\Diamond \star \Diamond')^{r(t)r'} s'$$

$$T(s_1 \ldots s_n)\Diamond^r T(t_1 \ldots t_n) \overset{\text{decomp}}{\Longrightarrow} \left\{ s_i \Diamond^{\uparrow^{i,+}(T(s_1 \ldots s_n), r, T(t_1 \ldots t_n))} t_i \right\}_{i=1}^n \qquad T \neq\ \to$$

$$s \to s' \Diamond^r t \to t' \overset{\text{decomp}\to}{\Longrightarrow} s\overline{\Diamond}^{\uparrow^{1,-}(s\to s', r, t\to t')} t,\ s'\Diamond^{\uparrow^{2,+}(s\to s', r, t\to t')} t'$$

$$s\Diamond^r t \overset{\text{reverse}}{\Longrightarrow} t\overleftarrow{\Diamond}^{\overleftarrow{r}} s$$

Correctness and Completeness. Comparing C^U with standard unification closure [2–Definition 2.11, Theorem 2.15] directly yields the following result.

Proposition 2. Let $C = \{s_i \leq^{I_i} t_i\}_{i=1}^n$ be subtyping constraints. C^U is consistent iff unification of $\{s_i = t_i\}_{i=1}^n$ does not fail with a symbol clash.

3 Explanations by Unification

The closure process in Section 2 formally links the explanations sought in Section 1.3 to type inference with subtyping. However, it is too inefficient [14] to be executed in the type checker for every program. We therefore augment unification to maintain *paths* from which reasons can be reconstructed in case of a type error. Their addition requires constant cost per unification step, such that type-correct programs incur only a marginal overhead.

3.1   Paths and Constraint Reconstruction

A *path* is a sequence of types and relations. As will be made precise below, it represents a chain of constraints that are combined by transitivity, where the common type in the transitivity rule is shared between two subsequent constraints. A path thus resembles our casual abbreviation for a sequence of constraints used in Section 1.3.

Paths are defined by the following grammar, where t is a type and I, i, v are as in the definition of reasons (Section 2.2). We will write $t \Diamond p$ to abstract over the relation.

$$p ::= t \mid t \downarrow^{i,v} p \mid t \uparrow^{i,v} p \mid t \leq^I p \mid t \geq^I p$$

There is a side condition on paths of the form $t \uparrow^{i,v} t' \Diamond p$ and $t' \downarrow^{i,v} t \Diamond p$. Here t' must be constructed and its ith argument must be t. Furthermore, t''s constructor must covariant in this argument iff $v = +$ and contravariant for $v = -$. We say that p *links* s *to* t (written $s \overset{p}{=\!=} t$) if s is the first and t is the last type in p. By abuse of notation, $s \overset{p}{=\!=} t \in P$ means $p \in P$ with $s \overset{p}{=\!=} t$. The *concatenation* $p \circ q$ of two paths p, q is the partial function defined inductively on the path structure by

$$t \circ (t \Diamond q) = t \Diamond q \qquad (t \Diamond p) \circ q = t \Diamond (p \circ q)$$

For a set P of paths, P^* is the closure of P under concatenation of elements.

A path p with $s \overset{p}{=\!=} t$ contains enough information to reconstruct a constraint $s \Diamond^r t$. The main idea is to "parse" p with a stack automaton to identify pairs of $\uparrow^{i,v}$ and $\downarrow^{i,v}$. The relation $\Diamond$ is computed by the operations from Section 2.2.

Let p be a path, S a stack $\langle s_j \Diamond_j^{r_j} t_j, \uparrow^{(i_j, v_j)} \rangle_{j=1}^n$, C a partial constraint $s \Diamond^r$ (without the final type). Then $\mathcal{C}(S, C, P)$ is a partial function defined recursively on the structure of p with base $\mathcal{C}(\varepsilon, s \Diamond^r, t) = s \Diamond^r t$. The recursion step $\mathcal{C}(S, C, P) = \mathcal{C}(S', C', P')$ does a case analysis on the first relation of P and the top of S; it is given by the following table to highlight the parsing analogy.

S	C	P	S'	C'	P'
S	$s \Diamond^r$	$t \leq^I p$	S	$s(\Diamond^\star \leq)^{r(t)I}$	p
S	$s \Diamond^r$	$t \geq^I p$	S	$s(\Diamond^\star \geq)^{r(t)I}$	p
S	$s \Diamond^r$	$t \uparrow^{i,v} t' \Diamond^r p$	$(s \Diamond^r t, \uparrow^{i,v}) S$	$t' \Diamond^r$	p
$(s' \Diamond'^r t', \uparrow^{i,+}) S$	$s \Diamond^r$	$t \downarrow^{i,+} p$	S	$s'(\Diamond' \star \Diamond)^{r'(t') \uparrow^{i,+}(s,r,t)}$	p
$(s' \Diamond'^r t', \uparrow^{i,-}) S$	$s \Diamond^r$	$t \downarrow^{i,-} p$	S	$s'(\Diamond' \star \overline{\Diamond})^{r'(t') \uparrow^{i,-}(s,r,t)}$	p

Define $\mathcal{C}(t \Diamond^r q) := \mathcal{C}(\varepsilon, t \Diamond^r, q)$. A path p is *balanced* if $\mathcal{C}(p)$ is defined.

Reconstruction proceeds by nesting levels of $\uparrow^{i,v}$ / $\downarrow^{i,v}$. As usual in parsing, the stack S contains the currently open $\uparrow^{i,v}$-levels. The top level is represented by the partial constraint $s \Diamond^r$, whose right-hand side is implicitly the first type in the remaining path. Let us focus on the treatment of relations, the reasons are then straightforward. The first line extends the top level. Suppose the first type in p is t'. Then implicitly, the top level is $s \Diamond t$, the next constraint is $t \leq t'$. By transitivity, this yields the result $s(\Diamond \star \leq)t'$, but t' is kept implicit. The second line is analogous. The third line starts a new $\uparrow^{i,v}$-level, saving the already seen constraint for the current level on the stack and opening up a new top level. The fourth line extends the second level $s'\Diamond't'$ with the top level $s\Diamond t$. By the side condition on paths, t' is ith argument of s. Decomposition of $s\Diamond t$ at the ith argument thus yields $t'\Diamond s''$ and transitivity yields $s'(\Diamond' \circ \Diamond)s''$ as the new top level constraint. Again by the side condition, s'' occurs at the start of p and is kept implicit. The fifth line does the same for contravariant positions.

Remark 2. The reasons reconstructed by $\mathcal{C}$ have a special form: Reversal $\overleftarrow{}$ appears only at initial reasons, and transitivity is always left-associative, that is $r(t)(r'(t')r'')$ is replaced by $(r(t)r')(t')r''$. Using Proposition 1, and by analogy with negation normal form in classical logic [9], we call this class of reasons the *normal reasons*. For the programmer, the normal reasons are desirable: Reversal of initial reasons is intuitively clear, and the left-associative transitivity yields a linear structure on program locations within one explanation.

3.2   Unification with Paths

We use a variant of the Martelli-Montanari unification algorithm [15] for the main reason that it does not perform substitutions. The algorithm works on multiequations $\{\tilde{\alpha}\} = \{\tilde{t}\}$ where $\tilde{\alpha}$ is a set of type variables and $\tilde{t}$ is a multiset of non-variable types. A set of multiequations is *compact* if their left-hand sides are disjoint. The function $\mathrm{ME}(T) := \big(\{\tilde{\alpha}\} = \{\tilde{t}\}\big)$ splits up a set of types $T = \{\tilde{\alpha}\} \cup \{\tilde{t}\}$ to a multiequation. We add to this standard data structure a set of paths P. A *unification problem* is either $\bot$ *(failure)* or $\mathcal{U} = (E, S, P)$ where E (equations) and S (solved) are sets of multiequations. The notions of unifier and most general unifier are defined as usual [15,2]. We present the algorithm as rewrite rules on unification problems in Figure 3. We set $\mathcal{U} \implies \bot$ if no rule applies. Apart from the treatment of reasons, the repeated application of the first possible rule is equivalent to Algorithm 3 of [15]. Writing $\implies_{MM}$ for this repeated application, we thus have immediately:

Theorem 1. *Let $\mathcal{U}$ be a unification problem. Then σ is a unifier of $\mathcal{U}$ iff for some S, P we have $\mathcal{U} \implies_{MM} (\{\,\}, S, P)$ and σ is a unifier of S. Furthermore, a most general unifier for $\mathcal{U}$ can be obtained from S [15].*

Remark 3. The proviso $\forall e \in E, k \in 1..n : \alpha_k \notin \mathrm{FV}(e)$ of *Decomposition* replaces the occurs-check. It also entails that the left-hand-side variables need not be substituted for, because they do not occur in E. Any solvable, compact E contains a multiequation satisfying the proviso [15–Theorem 3.3 and Corollary].

Remark 4 (Efficiency). The only addition to the original algorithm is the construction of new path elements for the arguments in the decomposition step. Therefore, the algorithmic complexity of unification does not change.

Trivial

$$(\{\ \{\alpha_1 \ldots \alpha_n\} = \{\}\ \} \cup E, S, P) \Longrightarrow (E, \{\ \{\alpha_1 \ldots \alpha_n\} = \{\}\ \} \cup S, P)$$

where E is compact

Decomposition

$$(\{\ \{\alpha_1 \ldots \alpha_l\} = \{f(t_{11} \ldots t_{1m}) \ldots f(t_{n1} \ldots t_{nm})\}\ \} \cup E, S, P)$$
$$\Longrightarrow (\{\ \mathrm{ME}(\{t_{ij}\}_{i=1}^n)\}_{j=1}^m \cup E,$$
$$\{\ \{\alpha_1 \ldots \alpha_l\} = \{f(t_{11} \ldots t_{1m}) \ldots f(t_{n1} \ldots t_{nm})\}\ \} \cup S,$$
$$P \cup \{t_{ij} \uparrow^{j,v_j} f(t_{i1} \ldots t_{im}), f(t_{i1} \ldots t_{im}) \downarrow^{j,v_j} t_{ij}\}_{i=1}^n)$$

where $\forall k \in 1..l : \alpha_k \notin \mathrm{FV}(t_{ij}), \forall e \in E : \alpha_k \notin \mathrm{FV}(e)$,

E is compact, $v_j = \mathrm{variance}(f, j)$

Compactification

$$(\{\{\tilde{\alpha}, \tilde{\beta}\} = \{\tilde{s}\}, \{\tilde{\alpha}, \tilde{\gamma}\} = \{\tilde{t}\}\} \cup E, S, P)$$
$$\Longrightarrow \{\{\tilde{\alpha}, \tilde{\beta}, \tilde{\gamma}\} = \{\tilde{s}, \tilde{t}\}\} \cup E, S, P)$$

Fig. 3. Martelli-Montanari Unification

3.3 Type Inference with Explanations

Let C be a set of subtyping constraints with (initial) reasons. Define

$$(C)^= := (\{\mathrm{ME}(\{s, t\}) \mid s \leq^I t \in C\}, \{\}, \{s \leq^I t, t \overset{\leftarrow}{\leq^I} s \mid s \leq^I t \in C\})$$

Type inference of expression e in context Γ proceeds as follows:

1. Compute e's type and subtyping constraints C by $\Gamma \vdash e : t \mid C$.
2. Unify the set $(C)^=$ with the algorithm of Section 3.2.
3. If a clash occurs in a multiequation $\{\tilde{\alpha}\} = \{t_1 \ldots t_n\} \in (E, S, P)$
   (a) Compute P^* to obtain for $i \neq j \in \{1..n\}$ the balanced paths $t_i \overset{p_{ij}}{=\!=\!=} t_j$.
   (b) Reconstruct reasons $\mathcal{C}(p_{ij}) = t_i \Diamond^{r_{ij}} t_j$.
   (c) Produce explanations for the reasons r_{ij}.

Remark 5. The set P is implemented by a graph structure on types, where annotated references between types represent the relations of paths. Steps 3a and 3b then become a depth-first graph traversal of P, whose size if obviously linear in the number of unification steps and the program size. Note that $\mathcal{C}$ can be applied incrementally to prefixes of paths, with constant cost per step, such that unbalanced paths can be filtered immediately.

3.4 Soundness and Completeness

By Theorem 1, the type inference algorithm in Section 3.3 yields the same typings as the usual ML inference . More importantly for the current paper, the explanations generated in Step 3c correspond to those analyzed in Sections 1.3 and 2. The following theorem is shown by induction on $\mathrm{depth}(\mathcal{C}(p))$ in a straightforward manner.

Theorem 2 (Soundness). *Let C be subtyping constraints and $(C)^= \Longrightarrow_{MM}$ (E, S, P). If $p \in P^*$ with $\mathcal{C}(p) = c$ then $c \in C^U$.*

We have only partially investigated the matter of completeness, but in experiments we have never encountered an example where an expected explanation was missing. There are two immediate obstacles to completeness: First, according to Remark 2, only normal reasons will be constructed. This restriction seems rather beneficial, because two reasons that have the same normal form are equally useful to the programmer. Second, unification from Section 3.2 may fail to discover all reasons that C^U detects, because decomposition requires all top level constructors of the multiequation to agree before proceeding. However, as we explain type errors in the unification process, this restriction appears sensible as well.

Our algorithm does have a weaker completeness property: For any failure of unification, at least one reason can be reconstructed. Let us call a unification problem $\mathcal{U} = (E, S, P)$ *connected* iff for every multiequation $\{\tilde{\alpha}\} = \{\tilde{t}\} \in E$ and each pair $s, s' \in \{\tilde{\alpha}, \tilde{t}\}$ we have a balanced $p \in P^*$ with $s \overset{p}{=\!=} s'$. By induction on the number of unification steps, each unification problem arising in type inference is connected. For the initial problem, inspect the definition of $(\cdot)^=$; for the unification steps, the only interesting case is *Decomposition*, which adds just the $\uparrow/\downarrow$ elements to P that keep the new multiequations connected.

Theorem 3 (Weak Completeness). *Let $(C)^= \Longrightarrow_{MM} (E, S, P)$. For any $e \in E$, $s, t \in e$ there is a reason r and a path $s \overset{p}{=\!=} t \in P^*$ with $\mathcal{C}(p) = s \Diamond^r t$.*

3.5   Occurs Checks

The method proposed in this paper accommodates the occurs-check as well: Unification fails if ever an equation $\alpha = t$ must be solved where α occurs in t. By Theorem 3, there is then at least one path between α and t, and a reason for the occurs check can be reconstructed.

As a technical complication, the Martelli-Montanari algorithm does not apply substitutions (Remark 3), thus the offending α may not appear in t immediately. Instead, for a multiequation $e = (\{\tilde{\alpha}\} = \{\tilde{t}\})$, the substitution for a variable β in t_i must be retrieved in the multiequation $\{\ldots \beta \ldots\} = \{\tilde{t'}\}$ of the unification problem. By recursion, the original multiequation e will eventually be reached and a cycle is established.

4   Future Work

Polymorphic Let. **Let** and **letrec** are currently supported in a minimal fashion: Each binding (-group) is type checked separately, and standard generalization [17] is applied. The polymorphic value can be used according to Remark 1, but the explanations do not refer back to the value's definition. The solution is conceptually simple (but it could not be integrated smoothly with the data structures of the prototype implementation): After solving a unification problem for a binding group, we keep its set of paths P_0. Whenever the result type is involved in a type error, we add P_0 to the current paths P before graph traversal. As the type t of a polymorphic value is (partially) copied as t' for each reference, we add new path elements $t' \mapsto^i t$ and $t \leftarrow^i t'$ to allow the traversal to proceed from P to P_0 and vice versa. These elements are handled as parentheses in reconstruction (Section 3.1), and the unique *instance identifier* i permits sharing of the path graph P_0 between instances. Now data flows are traced through the definition, because if a polymorphic variable occurs several times in t, then P_0^* includes paths between the occurrences (Theorem 3).

Graph-Based Unification. We have used Martelli-Montanari unification for ease of stating invariants in Section 3, in particular because it never applies substitutions (Remark 3). We hope to integrate the method with the DAG-based OCaml implementation [20] by augmenting the record of type nodes with a field `paths` containing all the outgoing edges of the path graph. However, the well-known problem of greedy, left-to-right constraint solution must be tackled [5, 26, 21, 10, 19, 13].

5   Related Work

Starting from the intentions, our work is most closely related to the static debugger MrSpidey [8], which presents a data flow analysis to the programmer by an interactive arrow overlay mechanism; clearly, the inspiration for the form of desirable explanations stems from the screenshots of [8]. Similarly, Hansen and Shafarenko [11] report type errors in a subtyping discipline by listing the intermediate program points that lead to a given type conflict. Their type language is restricted to zero-ary constructors, hence they do not require decomposition. Both approaches do not include the reversal operation shown to be essential for ML typing in Section 1.3.

Neubauer and Thiemann [19] present a conservative extension of the ML type system by recursive types, based on Wright's [25] discriminative unions. Like in the original application of soft typing, unification can proceed after clashes to obtain unbiased explanations. Every type carries a *flow set* annotation, a slice in which each location is additionally flagged as a source or sink of the type. Symmetry of equality is accounted for by *flow classes* of equivalent locations, which are listed in type errors involving one type in the class.

Chitil [5] and Beaven and Stansifer [3] propose that understanding a type error is enabled by a detailed understanding of the inferred types. Chitil [5] generates compositional type deductions. His type inference computes a principal typing for each subexpression separately and unifies types and environments at application nodes. The user can interactively browse the resulting type deduction to explore type errors. Beaven and Stansifer [3] generate detailed explanations of inferred types by printing the entire type deduction. They include program fragments that necessitate the bindings of type variables, which they achieve by annotating the type graph, similarly to [23, 6] below.

Another group of approaches focuses on the explanation of the unification steps that have led to the error. They annotate the respective unification data structures by program locations (or slices) that induced the bindings. Wand [23] modifies the unification algorithm to keep track of the source locations that correspond to each variable binding. Duggan and Bent [6] instrument unification to decorate the type graph with the program locations that lead to equality constraints. Haack and Wells [10] use a constraint-based formulation. They annotate the generated equality constraints with the introducing program location and unification propagates this information. The resulting slice at an inconsistent constraint is minimized for error reporting, where a slice is minimal if no constraint can be removed without removing the inconsistency. Unfortunately, minimization is not unique and it is not clear which solution is chosen by the presented greedy algorithm. Stuckey et al. [21] augment the approach of Haack and Wells by an explanation of Haskell's type class constraints. Report generation involves three steps, each of which is based on heuristics: Selection of error location, of the relevant types and of the source for each relevant type. Yang et al. [26, 27] aim at imitating type explanations given by human experts. Their algorithm $\mathcal{H}$ types subexpressions independently by unifying assumption environments (similar to [5]). They annotate the AST nodes with their inferred types, and types with the AST nodes responsible for the their introduction. Unlike slicing approaches, they also record justifications similar to our initial reasons, but without the data flow interpretation. McAdam [16–Chapter 5] generalizes previous techniques for explanations. He constructs a graph with program locations, type constructors and type variables as nodes and establishes required equalities by inserting edges. The result of ML type inference, as well as several earlier forms of explanation can be read from the graph structure.

Heeren et al. [13, 12] aim at specialized typing rules for libraries. The aspect that is akin to our work is their *type graphs* [12–Section 6]. These graphs include auxiliary links for *derived* or *implicit* equalities (see Section 2.2) that directly connect all types within one equivalence class. Unlike our work, the derived equivalences arise from tracing unification instead of the directed data flow reasons, thus the classes can be reported only as sets, not as linear chains.

The work by Braßel [4] and Tip and Dinesh [22] also aims at reporting program slices that are responsible for the error, yet their means are different: Braßel [4] replaces selected parts of the erroneous program with an expression of most general type; if the error disappears, he concludes that the replaced part must be responsible for the error. He then proceeds by several heuristics to refine the set of replaced program parts. Tip and Dinesh [22] implement their type checker by term rewriting; whenever a type checking judgement, expressed as a redex, fails, *dependence tracking* reveals those subterms of the input program that have led to the failing redex.

6   Conclusion

We have presented an efficient method to generate comprehensible explanations for ML type errors based on elementary data flow reasoning. The explanations have a linear structure that can be visualized in an interactive environment and they carry sufficient information to enable a judicious filtering before output. They provide both a detailed textual description and a high-level arrow overlay to the source code that are closely related: Each arrow in the overlay represents one or more elementary data flows mentioned in the description. The notorious backflows, which are artifacts that propagate type information against the direction of data flows, are indicated to the programmer.

The language under consideration includes higher-order functions, compound data structures and matching. Data flow reasoning is maintained in a natural fashion through all of these constructs by introducing implicit flows and taking variance of type constructors into account (Section 1.3). A full treatment of polymorphic let has been deferred to a graph-based implementation (Section 4).

The method integrates well with a unification-based type checker (Section 3). The overhead for type-correct programs is modest (Remark 4) and the generation of explanations is no more complex than the preceding type check (Remark 5).

Acknowledgment

I am greatly indebted to Martin Gasbichler, Dorothea Flothow and Mandeep Singh for helping me improve both language and presentation of the material. I thank the reviewers and the program committee, in particular Frank Huch, for their extensive and helpful comments on the submitted version of the paper.

References

1. Alexander Aiken and Edward L. Wimmers. Type inclusion constraints and type inference. In *Conference on Functional Programming Languages and Computer Architecture*, pages 31–41. ACM press, 1993.
2. Franz Baader and Wayne Snyder. Unification theory. In Alan Robinson and Andrei Voronkov, editors, *Handbook of automated reasoning*, volume I, chapter 8, pages 445–533. Elsevier Science, Amsterdam, The Netherlands, 2001.
3. Mike Beaven and Ryan Stansifer. Explaining type errors in polymorphic languages. *ACM Letters on Programming Languages and Systems*, 2(1–4):17–30, 1993.
4. Bernd Braßel. TypeHope: There is hope for your type errors. In *16th International Workshop on Implementation and Application of Functional Languages (IFL'04)*, Lübeck, Germany, September 8–10 2004. University of Kiel. Report 0408.
5. Olaf Chitil. Compositional explanation of types and algorithmic debugging of type errors. In *Proceedings of the Sixth ACM SIGPLAN International Conference on Functional Programming (ICFP'01)*, pages 193–204, Florence, Italy, 2001.
6. Dominic Duggan and Frederick Bent. Explaining type inference. *Science of Computer Programming*, 27(1):37–83, 1996.
7. Jonathan Eifrig, Scott Smith, and Valery Trifonov. Type inference for recursively constrained types and its application to OOP. *Electronic Notes in Theoretical Computer Science*, 1, 1995.
8. Cormac Flanagan, Matthew Flatt, Shriram Krishnamurthi, Stephanie Weirich, and Matthias Felleisen. Catching bugs in the web of program invariants. *ACM SIGPLAN Notices*, 31(5):23–32, 1996.

9. Jean H. Gallier. *Logic for Computer Science – Foundations of Automatic Theorem Proving.* Harper & Row Publishers, 1986.
10. Christian Haack and J. B. Wells. Type error slicing in implicitly typed higher-order languages. *Science of Computer Programming*, 50(1–3):189–224, March 2004. Special issue on 12th European symposium on programming (ESOP 2003).
11. James Hansen and Alex Shafarenko. Type error reporting in a single-assignment language with homomorphic overloading. In *International Workshop on the Implementation of Functional Languages*, Edinburgh, Schottland, September 2003.
12. Bastiaan Heeren, Jurriaan Hage, and Doaitse Swierstra. Generalizing Hindley-Milner type-inference algorithms. Technical Report UU-CS-2002-031, Institute of Information and Computing Sciences, Utrecht University, 2002.
13. Bastiaan Heeren, Jurriaan Hage, and S. Doaitse Swierstra. Scripting the type inference process. *ACM SIGPLAN Notices*, 38(9), September 2003.
14. My Hoang and John C. Mitchell. Lower bounds on type inference with subtypes. In *Conference Record of POPL'95: 22nd ACM SIGPLAN-SIGACT Symposium on Principles of Programming Languages*, San Francisco, California, January 23-25 1995. ACM Press.
15. Alberto Martelli and Ugo Montanari. An efficient unification algorithm. *ACM Transactions on Programming Languages and Systems*, 4(2):258–282, April 1982.
16. Bruce James McAdam. *Repairing Type Errors in Functional Programs.* PhD thesis, Division of Informatics, University of Edinburgh, 2002.
17. Robin Milner. A theory of type polymorphism in programming. *Journal of Computer and System Sciences*, 17:348–375, 1978.
18. John C. Mitchell. Type inference with simple subtypes. *Journal of Functional Programming*, 1(3):245–285, July 1991.
19. Matthias Neubauer and Peter Thiemann. Discriminative sum types locate the source of type errors. In *Proceedings of the 8th ACM SIGPLAN International Conference on Functional Programming*, pages 15–26, Uppsala, Sweden, 2003. ACM.
20. Objective Caml 3.08. http://caml.inria.fr, July 2004.
21. Peter J. Stuckey, Martin Sulzmann, and Jeremy Wazny. Improving type error diagnosis. In *Proceedings of Haskell Workshop (Haskell'04)*, May 2004. To appear.
22. F. Tip and T.B. Dinesh. A slicing-based approach for locating type errors. *ACM Transactions on Software Engineering and Methodology*, 10(1):5–55, January 2001.
23. Mitchell Wand. Finding the source of type errors. In *Proceedings of the 13th ACM SIGACT-SIGPLAN Symposium on Principles of Programming Languages*, pages 38–43. ACM Press, 1986.
24. Mitchell Wand. A simple algorithm and proof for type inference. *Fundamenta Informaticae*, 10:115–122, 1987.
25. Andrew K. Wright. *Practical Soft Typing.* PhD thesis, Rice University, Houston,Texas, August 1994.
26. Jun Yang. *Improving polymorphic type explanations.* PhD thesis, Department of Computing and Electrical Engineering, Heriot-Watt University, October 2001.
27. Jun Yang, Greg Michaelson, and Phil Trinder. Explaining polymorphic types. *The Computer Journal*, 45(4):436–452, 2002.

V→M: A Virtual Machine for Strict Evaluation of (Co)Recursive Functions

Baltasar Trancón y Widemann

Fakultät für Elektrotechnik und Informatik
Technische Universität Berlin
bt@cs.tu-berlin.de

Abstract. Corecursive definitions are usually only meaningful in functional languages with lazy evaluation semantics, because their domain and range may contain cyclic data graphs. By inspection of the call stack, it is possible in a strict evaluation environment to detect cycles in a computation, and thus transform finite input graphs in finite time. This paper presents a virtual machine with suitable cycle handling primitives and operational semantics to implement strict evaluation of corecursive functions. We discuss the impact on calling conventions and definition constructs, and demonstrate the relevance of the introduced features by application to the domain of infinite precision decimal arithmetics.

1   Introduction

Corecursion is an alternative interpretation of functions defined in terms of themselves. It is more powerful than recursion in the sense that domain and range sets are not assumed to be well-founded. Corecursion can be formulated in terms of either non-well-founded algebra or coalgebra. Whereas non-well-founded algebra is quite popular in the context of lazy functional programming, coalgebra is a promising, but rather exotic meta-theory.

For an advanced treatment of constructive corecursion in a non-well-founded setting, see [14]. We shall focus on a coalgebraic setting in this article, instead. It is of course not possible to give a self-contained account of coalgebra or corecursive function theory within a couple of pages. But some intuition can be gained by starting with a classical remark about recursion cited by WIKIPEDIA[18]:

> If you already know what recursion is, just remember the answer. Otherwise, find someone who is standing closer to DOUGLAS HOFSTADTER than you are; then ask him or her what recursion is.
>
> ANDREW PLOTKIN

This interesting algorithm can be dualized as follows:

> Try as hard as you can to understand what corecursion is; then find someone who might do better and send him or her to acquire more knowledge. Meanwhile, do not hesitate to tell everybody what you think that corecursion is.

C. Grelck et al. (Eds.): IFL 2004, LNCS 3474, pp. 90–107, 2005.
© Springer-Verlag Berlin Heidelberg 2005

Any reader with a firm algebraic background is likely to feel uneasy about this strategy, suspecting fearsome things such as *infinite regression* and *vicious circles*. But corecursion can be perfectly sound and productive.

Example 1 (Exact Division). Consider the calculation of a rational number by division of two naturals, carried out using an algorithm that dates back to the 16th century:

$$19 : 33 = 0.57$$

$$\underline{0}$$
$$19$$
$$\underline{165}$$
$$25$$
$$\underline{231}$$
$$19$$

There are two ways to proceed from the depicted state of calculation.

1. More digits can be obtained by iterated subtraction, yielding arbitrarily precise approximations $0.57575757\ldots$. This is what a lazy functional program would do.
2. A cycle can be detected, in this case by the repetition of the remainder 19, yielding the exact, periodic value $0.\overline{57}$. This behavior is closer to the spirit of coalgebra. All further examples in this article shall be elaborations of the same idea.

   This kind of "termination without base case" magic does not work for all problems, however: there is no such shortcut for calculating an irrational number such as π or $\sqrt{2}$. $\qquad\qquad\square$

1.1   Strict Corecursion

Corecursion is a powerful definition technique for functions working on potentially infinite data. Corecursive computation is commonly associated with lazy evaluation, because a corecursively defined function does not terminate when evaluated naïvely with strict algebraic semantics.

Categorial languages such as Charity[5] introduce final coalgebra semantics as a sound theoretical basis for primitive corecursion. Starting from the observation that traditional implementations of strict functional languages with heap cells and references to encode data graphs are semantically non-final coalgebras that may well serve as approximations of a final coalgebra, it is possible to develop a technique of strict evaluation of corecursive functions. This technique, its encoding and optimization have been presented in [15], and its proof in [16].

Example 2 (Primitive Corecursion in a Nutshell). Consider the following well-known type definitions:

type $list[\alpha] == nil \mid cons(\alpha, list[\alpha])$
type $nat == zero \mid succ(nat)$
type $maybe[\alpha] == nothing \mid just(\alpha)$

The goal of defining the function **fun** $length : list[\alpha] \to nat$ can be achieved in two ways. The first (and much more popular) way is induction on the algebraic structure of the domain type,[1] which we shall call the *recursive* form:

$$\textbf{def } length(\underline{nil}) == 0$$
$$\textbf{def } length(\underline{cons}(hd, tl)) == succ(length(tl))$$

Note that there is a single *algebra* function that implements all constructor operations of nat, and its inverse is a *coalgebra* function implementing the deconstructors:

fun $cnat : maybe[nat] \to nat$ **fun** $dnat : nat \to maybe[nat]$

def $cnat(nothing) == 0$ **def** $dnat(0) == nothing$

def $cnat(just(n)) == succ(n)$ **def** $dnat(succ(n)) == just(n)$

The *length* function can be redefined by coinduction on the coalgebraic structure of its codomain type. This *corecursive* form is obtained from the recursive form simply by left composition with $dnat$:

$$\textbf{def } \underline{dnat}(length(nil)) == nothing$$
$$\textbf{def } \underline{dnat}(length(cons(hd, tl))) == just(length(tl))$$

To understand this definition, consider that $dnat$ implements the totalized *predecessor* function. In a lazy setting, both forms are equivalent and determine full evaluation for finite list arguments, and arbitrarily deep approximation for infinite list arguments.

In a strict setting however, the second form is more powerful, because it defines also the full normal form of *provably infinite* lists, by establishing a relation between the *tail* observation on a list and the *predecessor* observation on its length. Observations are defined as the following partial functions:

def $tail(cons(hd, tl)) == tl$ **def** $pred(succ(n)) == n$

A list l is provably infinite, iff there is some $n > 0$ such that $tail^n(l)$ is defined and the same object as l, i.e., if l is represented by a finite cycle. An example with $n = 4$ looks like this:

If a cycle of the same size is produced as the result, i.e., if $pred^n(length(l))$ is defined and the same object as $length(l)$, one can easily verify that this satisfies the corecursive definition of $length$. Finally, a number that is its own (transitive) predecessor must be ω, which is the expected result. $\square$

---

[1] Induction patterns are underlined.

In a purely functional context, identical function incarnations will yield identical results. What may seem trivial leads to the conclusion that computations on cyclical data need traverse each cycle only once, as long as the result can be reused upon reentry to the cycle. An effective implementation requires early assignment of return values, leaving uninitialized "holes" in data structures to be filled at arbitrarily deeply nested points of program execution. This is combined with online *stack inspection* to detect cyclical reincarnation. The concept of stack inspection is better known from the area of security (see [6]), but it is naturally well-suited to the task of cycle detection, as well.

Basing an evaluation technique on stack inspection causes some practical problems. Stack inspection, as a very low-level operation, is

1. hardly portable, and
2. reserved to privileged code in many "secure" environments.

Therefore, a prototypic implementation of strict corecursion will not be given as a coding scheme targeting an existing platform, but as a dedicated operational model, the virtual machine V→M.[2]

1.2   Scope and Structure of This Paper

This paper outlines the design of a virtual machine dedicated to the strict evaluation of both recursive and corecursive functions. It does not give a complete specification. Rather, the principal features are introduced and motivated alongside a series of small, but nontrivial application examples. The examples are presented in first-order functional pseudocode. The semantics of this language and its mapping to V→M code are only explained in instructive cases; the rest is left as an exercise to the reader. The complete, executable code for the examples in this paper is roughly 500 lines in "assembly language" format, and too redundant to justify a full listing.

The focus of this paper lies on the vocabulary and operation of the V→M itself, discussed at a fairly high level of abstraction. Peripheral topics such as compilation from a functional front-end language to V→M code, verification of V→M code, or (just-in-time/offline) compilation from V→M to microprocessor code are not covered.

1.3   Application Domain: Exact Rational Decimal Arithmetics

Fractional numbers of infinite precision have succeeded as an instructive example of lazy evaluation: in [8], lazy coding techniques are presented for handling infinite sequences of digits, and for carry propagation in infinite precision decimal arithmetics. We shall adopt the problem, and propose a strict counterpart of the lazy solution. Comparing the elegance of the two solutions is more a mat-

---

[2] The arrow in V→M is meant to denote a function arrow, as well as a graph edge, as well as a pointer.

ter of taste than a scientific topic, but the strict technique has some objective advantages:

1. It has no pathological unproductive cases, and
2. because results are fully evaluated to normal form, numbers may not only be *computed*, but also *compared* and *printed* with infinite precision.

Of course, the price to be paid is the exclusion of irrational numbers, since only periodic sequences of digits can have a finite normal form.

To our best knowledge, the generalization of the arithmetical standard algorithms from finite to periodical decimal fractions has not been subject of any publication before, so these algorithms can be considered as a contribution in the area of applied functional programming on their own, in isolation from the V⊸M machinery that implements them.

1.4   Expressive Power

The techniques of strict corecursion and lazy recursion extend the simple functional paradigm of strict recursion in complementary ways:

1. Lazy recursion is elegant at the construction of infinite objects, but fails at their analysis. Example problems that exceed the power of lazy recursion are comparison and pretty-printing of cyclic data.
2. Strict corecursion is elegant at the construction and analysis of cyclic objects, but fails at non-periodic generation. Example problems that exceed the power of strict corecursion are unbounded enumeration algorithms such as the sieve of ERATOSTHENES or the HAMMING problem.

2   Virtual Machine Basics

2.1   Architecture and Status

The virtual machine V⊸M presented in this paper resembles the design (but not the complexity) of imperative machines such as the Java VM[9], or the .NET CLR[4], rather than that of functional machines such as the spineless, tagless G-Machine[12] of Haskell or the Charity[5] machine. The main design differences to the mentioned object-oriented environments are:

1. *Higher-order* functions and *closures* instead of *virtual methods* as the paradigm for dynamic dispatching. These are not implemented in the current prototype, however.
2. A collection of *referential transparency* invariants to regulate the side effects of write accesses to memory, especially for the remote filling of holes in partially initialized data. These invariants arise naturally from the use of a purely functional front-end language (and a conservative compiler), or can be enforced by V⊸M code verification.

   If this restriction is loosened, it should be possible for imperative and corecursive code to coexists and interoperate on a V⊸M.

There is a running implementation of the central tools, the V→M toolkit. All V→M toolkit components are written in Java. The interfaces between the components are fully abstract to enable the integration of alternative implementations of all following subsystems.

Interpreter. This is the heart of the toolkit. It manipulates three abstract, pluggable interfaces: the *heap*, *type* and *code* models. There is a *visual* extension (subclass) of the interpreter with useful tracing and inspection facilities.

Heap Model. The one implementation available so far relies on the hosting Java garbage collector for memory management. A reference counting implementation using a tagged cyclic algorithm (see [7, 3, 13, 11]) is under development.

Type and Code Models. Both a bootstrapping implementation as Java classes and a heap-based reflexive embedding, suitable for dynamic generative programming, are available.

Loader. Code can be loaded into the interpreter either by direct access to the code model's API, or from textual input by the provided *assembler*.

2.2   State Space

A state of the V→M comprises:

1. a *heap*,
2. a *stack*,
3. a set of *function* implementations, and
4. a set of *constant* values

The former two components are obviously dynamic. The latter can be considered static for most applications. It is possible, however, to use the reflexive type and code models mentioned in the previous section for dynamic code generation.

Heap. The heap space of the V→M contains the currently allocated memory cells, which come in several variants:

1. *tuples* of n field slots,
2. *cotuples* of a tag·symbol and an optional body slot,
3. *closures* of a function and argument slots (currently not implemented).

Passing data *by value* means passing a reference to a whole cell, whereas passing *by reference* means passing a reference to a slot within a cell.

The V→M provides operations to *create* cells, and to *read*, *write* and *reference* slots. For referentially transparent code, writing is supposed to happen exactly once. Additional memory management primitives will be introduced for use with the reference counting heap model.

The structure of the data graphs formed by cells and references is specified by a simple (co)algebraic type system, consisting of the following (potentially recursive) constructs:

1. *products* of either labeled or anonymous (0, 1, 2, ...) components,
2. *coproducts* of constants and parametric variants,
3. higher-order *function* types (currently not implemented).

The following two type definitions will be used in the further examples of corecursive functions.

Example 3 (Infinite Digit Sequences). The digits representing a fractional number (ignoring the position of the decimal point) may be represented by the following recursive product, defining a cofree datatype of infinite streams of integers (we assume a restriction to the range $0 \dots 9$ for the following examples):

$$\textbf{type } digits == (int, digits)$$

Note that, in a strict implementation, only finitely representable, i.e., periodic values (the rational subset of the final coalgebra) are included in the cofree datatype, which causes exactly the restriction from real to rational numbers (see [10]).

Note also that, since there is no base case to the type definition,

1. the associated free datatype (with initial algebra semantics) is empty, and
2. a recursive function consuming such a stream digit-wise has infinite recursion depth for *any* algebraic evaluation strategy. Only cycle detection enables termination.   □

Example 4 (Bool). The type of boolean values need not be built into the V→M, but can be defined as a coproduct of two constants (body-less cotuples):

$$\textbf{type } bool == false \mid true \qquad \qquad □$$

Stack. The stack is segmented into a *frame* for each function incarnation, providing space for the following data:

1. the *identity* of the incarnated function,
2. *input* and *output* parameters,
3. local *variables*, and
4. an *operand* stack for inter-operation data flow.

The V→M provides operations to *read*, *write* and *reference* some of these stack slots. Input parameters are read-only, whereas output parameters may be written or referenced (passed on), but not read. Early writing to output parameters is essential for the stack-efficient tail-corecursive evaluation of corecursive functions, and for effective cycle detection.

The order of parameters for a nested call on the operand stack is defined as follows: The output parameters are pushed first, in ascending order, followed by the input parameters. The inner order of each of the two parameter blocks is arbitrary and could be reversed without problems, but having input parameters on top of the stack has some advantages (see figure 2, section 3.2).

Functions. A function may have m input and n output parameters. Input parameters are passed by value, output parameters by reference to an uninitialized memory slot, either a stack slot or a heap cell field. A function may reference another function by a *proper call* (always creating a new stack frame), or itself by a *tail call* (reusing the most recent stack frame, if safe; see section 3.4).

The passing of result values by output parameters allows every primitively corecursive function to execute one of its corecursive calls as a tail call, because they appear as constructor arguments only. For example, if the domain type of the function is linear, then only tail calls are needed. In the case that the function arguments are cycle-free, the function will *de facto* execute as a loop on constant stack space.

Note that there may be either one or two blocks of code associated with each function definition (see section 3.1).

Constants. Constants are evaluated eagerly at machine startup time. A constant definition is given as a function with zero input and one output parameter, which is called with a reference to the (otherwise read-only) constant value slot.

Note that, unlike in other strict, purely functional environments, there is no problem with (mutually) recursive constants; provided there is a finite-space corecursive definition (see example 5).

3   Special Features

3.1   Cycle Detection

Strict corecursion is implemented in V→M by standard strict recursion, combined with the detection of cycles by inspecting the call stack: If a function definition has a second body (the *recycle* body), it is capable of cycle handling. Then perform stack inspection when the function is called. If an enclosing frame for the same function with identical input parameters is detected, execute the recycle body instead of the normal one. In the case of primitive corecursion, it consists of a single `ditto` operation that copies the output parameters from the enclosing to the inner frame, yielding a cycle in the output graph.[3] Other code may be useful for cycle handling as well (see [16] and example 6 for further applications). But some caution must be exercised to prevent the result of a computation from depending on the details of cycle detection, which would ruin final coalgebraic semantics.

Example 5 (Trailing Zero). Figure 1 shows the primitively corecursive definition of an infinite sequence of zeroes, and the corresponding V→M code for both initialization function bodies.[4]   □

Since stack inspection incurs a runtime overhead at least linear in stack depth, it is worthwhile to

---

[3] `ditto` is the only operation that may read an output parameter.

[4] The `tail` operation actually creates a new stack frame in this case, see section 3.4.

---

def *all0* == (*0*, *all0*)

recycle ditto

`tuple    digits`	// *create new tuple cell C, push reference to C*
`dup`	// *copy reference to C*
`setparam 0`	// *write C to output parameter*
`dup`	
`getconst int0`	// *push value 0*
`setfield digits.0`	// *init first field of C with 0*
`reffield digits.1`	// *replace last reference to C by its second field C.1*
`tail`	// *C.1 becomes corecursive output parameter*

`ditto`	// *copy output of enclosing incarnation; creates a cycle*

Fig. 1. Corecursive Constant Initialization (Example)

1. distinguish between recursive and corecursive function definitions, and ignore cycles when evaluating the former, and
2. optimize away as many inspections as possible (see section 3.4).

As we already pointed out in [15], cycle detection is completely orthogonal to *memoization*. The result of a function incarnation is relevant for cycle detection only while it is pending, and for memoization only after it has completed. This orthogonality has two remarkable effects:

1. Both techniques may be combined, with harmless interactions (see [15]).
2. Memoization has to use heap space. Cycle detection, on the other hand, relies on stack only, and consequently has no memory management penalties.

3.2   In-situ Evaluation

The convention of passing function results by having the callee write to (dereferenced) output parameters is different from the most common model of strict function evaluation, where function results are passed back by value onto the caller's operand stack. Because the latter convention is more natural for function composition, there is an emulation feature called *insitu* output parameter:

By an *insitu* operation a stack slot is allocated and initialized with a reference to itself. This slot behaves like a regular output parameter for the callee, and like a stack-held result slot for the caller. When the parameter is written to for the first time, the reference is destroyed. It is therefore safe only in referentially transparent code.

A subsequent *insitu call* simply leaves the output parameters on the stack after the function call. It requires all output parameters to be *insitu*.

3.3   Control Flow

The only intra-function control flow operation provided by the V→M is a categorial *cotupling* construct. It takes a cotuple value off the operand stack, and

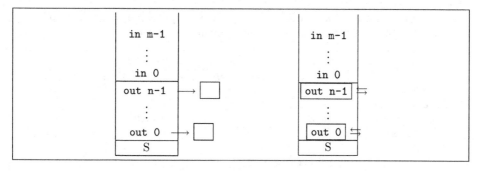

Fig. 2. Standard and *Insitu* Calling Convention

branches to a continuation block with matching label. If the cotuple had a body, that is pushed back onto the operand stack before the continuation is executed. This operation subsumes *if, case,* and one-level pattern matching.

Example 6 (Infinite Order). All relevant ordering relations on digits can be defined by slight variations of the following code, as shown on the right:

$$\textbf{def } (x, xs) =^{(a)} (y, ys) ==$$

$$\textbf{if } x < y \textbf{ then } \textit{false}^{(b)}$$

$$\textbf{if } y < x \textbf{ then } \textit{false}$$

$$\textbf{else } xs =^{(a)} ys$$

$$\textbf{recycle } \textit{true}^{(c)}$$

	(a)	(b)	(c)
$=$		*false*	*true*
$\leq$		*true*	*true*
$<$		*true*	*false*

Figure 3 shows the code for $=$, excluding pattern matching. Assume that values x, xs, y, ys are in local variables 0 to 3, respectively.

The upper bound for the recursion depth of $x = y$ until the cycle is detected is in the order of the least common multiple of the period lengths of x and y, and thus linear in the size of any argument. □

Note that **recycle** *false* yields an inductive predicate, whereas **recycle** *true* yields a coinductive predicate! The complete formalization of these issues is lengthy, but the essence can be given in a few paragraphs. Consider a predicate definition in the form of HILBERT-style deduction rules:

$$\frac{A_1 \cdots A_n}{B}$$

In the presence of circular data, there coexist two semantics: the inductive (least-fixpoint) and the coinductive (greatest-fixpoint) semantics. The former yields a predicate that holds only for the finitely derivable cases, whereas the latter yields a predicate that holds for all but the finitely refutable cases. The same definition can be transformed into an equivalent sequent calculus with the standard meta-rule for axioms:

$$\frac{\Delta \vdash A_1 \quad \cdots \quad \Delta \vdash A_n}{\Delta \vdash B} \qquad \qquad \overline{\Delta, A \vdash A}$$

Computing the least fixpoint of such a system requires **recycle** *false*, because any cycle yields an infinite and therefore invalid derivation.

```
insitu                          // leave space for result of x < y
getvar          0               // push x
getvar          2               // push y
call insitu     intLT           // test x < y; leave result on the stack
cotupling       bool            // if x < y
  true:                         // then
    cotuple     bool.false      // push false
    setparam    0               // write false to output parameter
  false:                        // else
    ...                         // repeat with x and y swapped
    cotupling   bool            // if y < x
      true:                     // then
        cotuple bool.false      // push false
        setparam 0              // write false to output parameter
      false:                    // else
        refparam 0              // delegate computation of output
        getvar   1              // push xs
        getvar   3              // push ys
        tail
cotuple         bool.true       // push true
setparam 0                      // write true to output parameter
```

Fig. 3. Digit Sequence Equality

Instead of computing the greatest fixpoint of the same system, we can equivalently compute the least fixpoint of a *cycle-detecting* system, where the conclusion B of each rule is added to the axioms of its premises A_i, which corresponds exactly to **recycle** *true*:

$$\frac{\Delta, B \vdash A_1 \quad \cdots \quad \Delta, B \vdash A_n}{\Delta \vdash B}$$

This kind of cycle detection and handling is not new; it has been used for decades for implementing numerous variants of graph traversal.

3.4 Optimized Cycle Detection

The overhead incurred by inspecting the whole call stack on every function call is too high for any serious implementation. In [15], we presented a number of substantial optimizations. They are based on a heap invariant that requires every cycle in memory to contain at least one tagged edge (but as few as possible). In purely functional code, cycles may only be caused by ditto operations, therefore tagging exactly the ditto edges is a safe and simple strategy. We have also argued in [15] that the resulting tag placement is minimal and optimal for subsequent traversal.

In a lazy setting, the usefulness of a corecursive definition is determined by its *productivity*: Every finite evaluation depth of the *result* must be reachable in finite time (for a formalization, see [14]). Primitive corecursion is productive by construction. This fact has been exploited, e.g., for the strong termination properties of Charity.

In a strict setting, there is the additional requirement that cycle detection be effective and efficient. We shall call a function *consumptive*, if its corecursive input parameters are either constant or obtained by following references, i.e., the function does not call itself on newly created objects. If the function fulfills the stronger property that its corecursive input parameters are obtained by following exactly one reference edge, then it is called *thoroughly consumptive*. The class of thoroughly consumptive functions comprises all catamorphisms and their extensions to cofree domain types. The following examples will demonstrate that many practical function definitions belong to this class.

For thoroughly consumptive functions, the overhead of cycle detection can be reduced greatly: If all parameters of such a corecursive call are untagged edges, then stack inspection can be omitted for this call, without compromising termination: If there is a cycle, then it will eventually be reached by traversal of a tagged edge.

The same optimization approach also makes tail call elimination possible: If any parameter of a call to a thoroughly consumptive function refers to a cell that is not pointed to by any tagged edge, then this incarnation will never be subject to (successful) cycle detection, and the corresponding stack frame can be reused immediately.

Note that both optimizations always apply to *all* cells of cycle-free data (free terms). Consider, e.g., the domain of finite lists. Any function that is a catamorphism on this domain and an anamorphism on its codomain[5] will execute as a true loop.

Example 7 (Normalizing Digits). The inherent redundancy of the decimal representation (e.g., $099\ldots = 100\ldots$) can be eliminated by the following normalization function:

$$\textbf{def } norm(x, xs) ==$$
$$\textbf{if } x = 0 \textbf{ then } (x, norm\ xs)$$
$$\textbf{else if } xs = all0 \textbf{ then } (x - 1, all9)$$
$$\textbf{else } (x, norm\ xs)$$
$$\textbf{recycle ditto}$$

The corecursion $norm(x, xs) \rightsquigarrow (x, norm\ xs)$ is thoroughly consumptive. Therefore, all stack frames except the one for the first periodical digit can be omitted. See figure 4 for the V→M code corresponding to $(x, norm\ xs)$.   □

―――――――――

[5] This includes *map*, *length*, and many others; but not *filter*.

```
tuple    digits   // create new tuple cell C, push C
dup
setparam 0         // write C to output parameter
dup
getvar   0         // push x
setfield digits.0  // write x to field C.0
reffield digits.1  // obtain reference to field C.1
getvar   1         // push xs
tail               // corecursively write (norm xs) to C.1
```

Fig. 4. Tail Corecursion (Example)

4 Advanced Application: Arithmetics

4.1 Subtraction

Infinite precision arithmetics exhibit quite tricky data flow: Because computation has to progress left-to-right (there is no right end to start with), carry digits have to propagate at least one step *back in time*. [8] developed an intricate lazy computation scheme to "borrow carry digits from the future", or rather have lazy evaluation of the carry sequence probe ahead as needed (incurring some caveats and pathological cases where nothing useful happens).

The following diagram illustrates the situation $x - y = z$, where c is the carry sequence:

$$
\begin{array}{llllll}
 & x_1 & x_2 & x_3 & x_4 & x_5 & \cdots \\
- & y_1 & y_2 & y_3 & y_4 & y_5 & \cdots \\
\hline
 & c_1 & c_2 & c_3 & c_4 & c_5 & \cdots \\
\hline
= & z_1 & z_2 & z_3 & z_4 & z_5 & \cdots \\
\end{array}
$$
$$\longrightarrow t$$

In a strict setting, where we can easily rewind to the left end *after* the computation, things are much easier. We start with digit-wise half-subtraction:

$$
\begin{array}{llllll}
 & x_1 & x_2 & x_3 & x_4 & x_5 & \cdots \\
- & y_1 & y_2 & y_3 & y_4 & y_5 & \cdots \\
\hline
= & z'_1 & z'_2 & z'_3 & z'_4 & z'_5 & \qquad z'_i = (x_i - y_i) \bmod 10 \\
 & c'_1 & c'_2 & c'_3 & c'_4 & c'_5 & \qquad c'_i = (x_i - y_i) \operatorname{div} 10 \\
\end{array}
$$

Example 8 (Half-Subtraction). The following function computes one digit of local result and local carry value on each corecursive call:

$$
\begin{aligned}
\textbf{def } & subaux\big((x, xs), (y, ys)\big) == \\
& \textbf{let} \qquad z' == x - y \\
& \qquad\quad (zs', cs') == subaux(xs, ys) \\
& \quad \textbf{in if } 0 \le z' \textbf{ then } \big((z', zs'), (0, cs')\big) \\
& \qquad\qquad\quad \textbf{else } \big((z' + 10, zs'), (1, cs')\big) \\
& \textbf{recycle ditto}
\end{aligned}
$$

$$\textbf{let } (zs', cs') == subaux(xs, ys) \textbf{ in } ((z', zs'), (0, cs'))$$

```
tuple    digits    // create new tuple cell C, push C
dup
setparam 0          // write C to first output parameter
dup
getvar   4          // push z'
setfield digits.0 // write z' to field C.0
reffield digits.1 // obtain reference to field C.1

tuple    digits    // create new tuple cell D, push D
dup
setparam 1          // write D to second output parameter
dup
getconst int0       // push value 0
setfield digits.0 // write 0 to field D.0
reffield digits.1 // obtain reference to field D.1

getvar   1          // push xs
getvar   3          // push ys
tail                // corecursively write subaux(xs, ys) to (C.1, D.1)
```

Fig. 5. Half-Subtraction (Excerpt)

This definition is thoroughly consumptive and can be transformed into tail-corecursion by distributing the second *let*-equation. Figure 5 gives the code for the first branch. $\square$

If underflow is excluded, then $c_1' = 0$. One step of carry propagation is performed by iterated subtraction $z' - \bar{c}$ (where $c' = c_1'\bar{c}$). Eventually, when $c' = 00\ldots$, a fixpoint is reached and $z' = z$. Because each digit can underflow at most once, this process converges in a finite number of iteration steps. The same bounds as for the relations (see example 6) apply.

Example 9 (Subtraction).

$$\textbf{def } x - y ==$$
$$\textbf{if } y = all0 \textbf{ then } x$$
$$\textbf{else let } (z', (\_, c')) == subaux(x, y)$$
$$\textbf{in } z' - c'$$

Note that this definition has no *recycle* block, since it is recursive, not corecursive.
$\square$

4.2   Addition and Multiplication

With subtraction given, addition can be implemented immediately via the equation $x + y = x - (0 - y)$. A more efficient algorithm can be obtained by dualising the subtraction algorithm.

The relation of multiplication and division is not equally symmetric: division subsumes multiplication by $x * y = x/(1/y)$, but it is not obvious how to come up with a corecursive multiplication algorithm. In the next section, we will show that division is conceptually more straightforward, yet exhibits some technically interesting problems.

4.3   Division

Example 10 (Iterated Subtraction). The heart of the division algorithm is a recursive function that performs iterated subtraction, and thus computes the first digit of the quotient and the complete remainder.

$$\textbf{def } divaux(xs, ys) ==$$
$$\textbf{if } xs < ys \textbf{ then } (0, xs)$$
$$\textbf{else let } (z, xs') == divaux(xs - ys, ys)$$
$$\textbf{in } (z + 1, xs')$$

□

Example 11 (Naïve Division). The process is then iterated by dividing through the tenth part of the remainder to obtain the next digit, and so on until a cycle is detected.

$$\textbf{def } x/y ==$$
$$\textbf{let } (z, r) == divaux(x, y)$$
$$\textbf{in } (z, r/(0, y))$$
$$\textbf{recycle ditto}$$

Unfortunately, this function is not likely to terminate! An obvious hint of the problem is the constructor call $(0, y)$ occurring as corecursion argument. It may yield a fresh object on every call, and thus will not result in a cycle. The actual problem is of even more general nature; see the next section for a detailed explanation. □

5   Quasicycles

As in every TURING-complete computation formalism, there are both plain and subtle causes for non-termination. In order to reason about termination of strict corecursive functions, one must keep in mind that the implementation is often an approximation.

The semantics of corecursion are defined in terms of a final coalgebra. The heap of a machine with cells and references naturally is a coalgebra, but clearly a non-final one: the duplication of bisimilar (structurally equivalent) objects is generally perfectly legal. There are environments that employ a technique called *hash-consing* for algebraic terms to maintain uniqueness, but this pays off only in special applications (see [17]). Besides, bisimilarity is more effort to decide than algebraic equivalence (see [1] and example 6).[6] For efficiency reasons, the uniqueness of constructed objects should therefore not be relied upon.

In this setting, it is possible for the *specification* of a function (working on a final coalgebra) to corecur in a finite graph of objects, while the *implementation* (working on a non-final coalgebra) results in traversal of a dynamically expanding, infinite graph:

$$
\begin{array}{ccc}
A & \longrightarrow & B \\
\uparrow & & \downarrow \\
D & \longleftarrow & C
\end{array}
\qquad\qquad
A \to B \to C \to D \to A \to B \to \cdots
$$

In general, unification of bisimilar objects is impossible *a priori* (because of the late initialization of fields) and infeasible *a posteriori* (because of the relatively high cost for comparing and hashing cyclic data). Instead, we have chosen to provide an alternative technique of cycle detection. For a function marked as *quasicyclical*, the matching of enclosing stack frames is not exact, but modulo bisimilarity. Runtimes for calls to this function are increased (where the inspection phase cannot be optimized away), but not for other parts of the program. This way, the gap between theory and practice can be closed.

Example 12 (Corrected Division). The cancellation of $0xs/0ys$ to xs/ys is sufficient to detect the period of the quotient modulo bisimilarity.

$$
\begin{aligned}
&\textbf{def } (x, xs)/(y, ys) \; == \\
&\qquad \textbf{if } x = 0 \wedge y = 0 \textbf{ then } xs/ys \\
&\qquad \textbf{else let } (z, r) == divaux\big((x, xs), (y, ys)\big) \\
&\qquad\qquad \textbf{in } \big(z, r/(0, (y, ys))\big) \\
&\textbf{recycle quasi ditto}
\end{aligned}
$$

$\square$

6   Conclusion

We have outlined the architectural design of the V→M, a virtual machine for strict function evaluation that supports corecursion by a small set of special primitives. Its operation principles have been introduced and motivated by examples from the domain of infinite precision decimal arithmetics.

The working implementation of the V→M core components, including a GUI visualization of the interpreter, and some example programs, are available from `http://uebb.cs.tu-berlin.de/v2m`.

---

[6] Surprisingly, bisimilarity is not as hard as general graph isomorphy, and requires linear time.

6.1   Related Work

The correspondences with and differences from related designs have been stated in various sections of this paper. To summarize: the design of V→M and its satellite formalisms is an attempt to combine the elegance and symmetry of coalgebra-enabled systems, such as Charity, with the elaborate and interoperation-friendly implementation techniques for strict languages (see, e.g. [2]). The examples that govern the structure of this paper have been inspired by philosophical works on numbers and computational (co)algebra, most notably [8, 10].

6.2   Future Work

Many typical components of virtual machine platform toolkits remain to be implemented:

Front-End Compilers. A fully formal extension of the functional pseudocode used in this paper is currently under development as the primary front-end language for V→M.

Also, a major subset of Charity (excluding only truly infinite data) could be compiled to V→M. We would be most interested in a comparing evaluation of the two platforms.

Back-End Compilers. Both offline compilation to some other platform and just-in-time compilation in order to speed up the interpreter would be useful tools for creating real applications in V→M code.

Just-in-time compilation is not very attractive for the Java-based interpreter, however, because the Java VM lacks primitives for referencing subfields of objects in memory as required by V→M.

An offline translation to C and subsequent compilation with an optimizing C compiler, on the other hand, seems a promising strategy for obtaining competitive performance of V→M programs with moderate effort.

The verification of code integrity and static type safety is a standard problem of program analysis, much simplified in the V→M context by the rigidly restricted control flow. A more challenging task is the verification of referential transparency, as required by a purely functional front-end language.

We envision that an axiomatic specification for this verification process might also serve as a contribution to the formalization of the (somewhat fuzzy) notion of referential transparency itself.

Acknowledgments

Thanks to Markus Lepper, formerly at Technische Universität Berlin, for helpful discussions on coalgebra and the V→M design, and to the anonymous referees for their comments.

References

1. S. Abiteboul and J. van den Bussche. Deep equality revisited. In *Deductive and Object-Oriented Databases*, 1995.
2. A.V. Aho, R. Sethi, and J.D. Ullman. *Compilers: Principles, Techniques, and Tools*. Addison-Wesley, 1986.
3. D.R. Brownbridge. Cyclic reference counting for combinator machines. volume 201 of *LNCS*. Springer, 1985.
4. Common language infrastructure. Standard 23271, ISO/IEC, 2003.
5. R. Cockett and T. Fukushima. About Charity. Technical Report 92/480/18, University of Calgary, 1992.
6. C. Fournet and A.D. Gordon. Stack inspection: Theory and variants. *ACM Trans. Program. Lang. Syst.*, 25(3):360–399, 2003.
7. R. Jones and R. Lins. *Garbage Collection*. Wiley, Chichester, 1996.
8. J. Karczmarczuk. The most unreliable technique in the world to compute π, 1998. http://users.info.unicaen.fr/~karczma/arpap/lazypi.ps.gz.
9. T. Lindholm and F. Yellin. *The Java Virtual Machine Specification (Second Edition)*, 1999.
10. D. Pavlovic and V. Pratt. On coalgebra of real numbers. In B. Jacobs and J.J.M.M. Rutten, editors, *Coalgebraic Methods in Computer Science*, volume 19 of *Electronic Notes in Computer Science*. Elsevier, 2000.
11. E.J.H. Pepels, M.C.J.D. van Eekelen, and M.J. Plasmeijer. A cyclic reference counting algorithm and its proof. Technical Report 88-10, Computing Science Department, University of Nijmegen, 1988.
12. S.L. Peyton Jones. Implementing lazy functional languages on stock hardware: The spineless tagless g-machine. *Journal of Functional Programming*, 2(2):127–202, 1992.
13. J.D. Salkild. Implementation and analysis of two reference counting algorithms. Master's thesis, University College, London, 1987.
14. A. Telford and D. Turner. Ensuring streams flow. In M. Johnson, editor, *Algebraic Methodology and Software Technology (AMAST)*, volume 1349 of *LNCS*, pages 509–523, 1997.
15. B. Trancón y Widemann. Stacking cycles: Functional transformation of circular data. In *Implementation of Functional Languages*, volume 2670 of *LNCS*. Springer, 2002.
16. B. Trancón y Widemann. Advanced strict corecursion. In *Draft Proceedings of the IFL 2003*. Department of Computer Science, Heriot-Watt University, Edinburgh, 2003.
17. M. G. J. Van Den Brand, J. Heering, P. Klint, and P. A. Olivier. Compiling language definitions: the asf+sdf compiler. *ACM Trans. Program. Lang. Syst.*, 24(4):334–368, 2002.
18. Wikipedia: Recursion, 2005. http://en.wikipedia.org/wiki/Recursion.

A Virtual Machine
for Functional Logic Computations[*]

Sergio Antoy[1], Michael Hanus[2], Jimeng Liu[1], and Andrew Tolmach[1]

[1] Portland State University, Computer Science Dept.,
P.O. Box 751, Portland, OR 97207, U.S.A.
{antoy, jimeng, apt}@cs.pdx.edu
[2] Christian-Albrechts-Universität Kiel, Institut für Informatik,
Olshausenstr. 40, D-24098 Kiel, Germany
mh@informatik.uni-kiel.de

Abstract. We describe the architecture of a virtual machine for executing functional logic programming languages. A distinguishing feature of our machine is that it preserves the operational completeness of non-deterministic programs by concurrently executing a pool of independent computations. Each computation executes only root-needed sequential narrowing steps. We describe the machine's architecture and instruction set, and show how to compile overlapping inductively sequential programs to sequences of machine instructions. The machine has been implemented in Java and in Standard ML.

1   Introduction

Functional logic programming aims at integrating the characteristic features of functional and logic programming into a single paradigm. In the last decade, the theory of functional logic computations has made substantial progress. Significant milestones include a model that integrates narrowing and residuation [13], narrowing strategies for several classes of programs suitable for functional logic languages [5], a functional-like model for non-deterministic computations [3], and well-defined semantics for programming languages of this kind [1, 11].

These results have been influential in the design and implementations of functional logic programming languages, e.g., Curry [18] and $\mathcal{TOY}$ [19]. Most existing implementations of these languages are based on a translation of source code to Prolog code (e.g., [7]), which can be executed by existing standard Prolog engines. This approach simplifies the task of implementing functional logic language features: e.g., source language variables can be implemented by Prolog variables and narrowing can be simulated by resolution. But some problems arise; most notably, the depth-first evaluation strategy of the Prolog system causes the loss of the operational completeness of functional logic computations and inhibits the implementation of advanced search strategies [17].

---

[*] This work was supported in part by the National Science Foundation under grants CCR-0110496 and CCR-0218224 and by the German Research Council (DFG) under grants Ha 2457/1-2 and Ha 2457/5-1.

C. Grelck et al. (Eds.): IFL 2004, LNCS 3474, pp. 108–125, 2005.
© Springer-Verlag Berlin Heidelberg 2005

This paper describes a fundamentally different approach to the implementation of a functional logic language, namely a virtual machine for functional logic computations. Section 2 sketches the key features of functional logic languages. Section 3 describes the architecture of the virtual machine. In particular, we describe how functional logic features influence several key decisions, e.g., non-determinism and the desire for operational completeness suggest an architecture that executes a pool of independent computations concurrently. We describe the kind of steps executed by each computation in the pool. By choosing a specific class of source programs, we can arrange that the machine only needs to execute root-needed steps sequentially, a characteristic that promotes both simplicity and efficiency. We describe the registers of the machine, the information they contain, and how the machine instructions control the flow of information between these registers. Finally, we sketch how a program can be compiled into machine instructions. Examples are provided throughout the discussion. Section 4 describes on-going efforts at implementing the virtual machine in both Java and Standard ML. The Java implementation, which is the more highly developed, is mainly intended as a compiler/interpreter for Curry, but it could be used to interpret compiled functional logic programs coded in other languages. Section 5 contains the conclusion and a brief discussion of related work.

2   Functional Logic Computations

Functional logic computations generalize functional computations by adding three specific features: non-determinism, narrowing and residuation (see [12] for a survey). Our machine is not designed for a specific programming language. The examples in this paper are in Curry, but the details of the source language are largely irrelevant. Our only assumption is that source programs can be converted to a particular variety of first-order term rewriting systems. The requirements on these rewriting systems are described in more detail below.

2.1   Functional Logic Features

Non-determinism is the feature that allows an expression to have multiple distinct values. Non-determinism broadens the class of programs that can be coded using functional composition [3]. For example, a program that solves a *cryptarithm* must assign digits to each letters. This can be expressed as "let s = digit in..." where digit is defined by the rules

```
digit = 0
digit = 1
...
digit = 9
```
(1)

The rules of digit are *not* mutually exclusive, i.e., the expression digit has 10 distinct values. The value eventually chosen for a given letter is constrained, according to a cryptarithm, by some other part of the program. All the rewrite rules of function digit have the same left-hand side. (In Sections 3.6 and 3.7, we will consider these 10 rules as a single rule where the right-hand side is non-deterministically chosen among

10 possibilities. A justification of this viewpoint and the opportunity to exploit it for an efficient evaluation strategy are in [3].)

Narrowing is the glue between functional and logic computations. The execution of a functional logic program may lead to the evaluation of an expression containing an uninstantiated variable. Narrowing "guesses" a value for the variable when this is necessary to keep the computation going. For example, the function that returns the last element of a list can be coded as follows ("++" is the list concatenation function):

$$\texttt{last l | l =:= x++[e] = e   where x,e free} \qquad (2)$$

The evaluation of `last [1,2,3]` prompts the evaluation of `[1,2,3] =:= x++[e]`, the rule's condition (e_1 =:= e_2 denotes the equality constraint that is satisfied if e_1 and e_2 are evaluable to unifiable data terms). The variables `x` and `e` are uninstantiated. Narrowing finds values for these variables that satisfy the condition; this is all it takes to compute the last element of the input list.

Residuation is an alternative mechanism for handling evaluation of an expression containing an uninstantiated variable. In this case, the evaluation suspends, and control is transferred to the evaluation of another expression in hopes that the latter will instantiate the variable so that the former can resume execution. (Evidently this only makes sense when more than one subexpression is available to be evaluated, e.g., the conjuncts of a "parallel and" operation.) The decision of whether to narrow or residuate is specified by the programmer on a per-function basis. Generally, primitive arithmetic operations and I/O functions residuate, since it seems impractical to guess values in these cases, whereas most other functions narrow.

2.2   Overlapping Inductively Sequential Rewrite Systems

Our abstract machine is intended to evaluate programs that can be expressed as *overlapping inductively sequential term rewriting systems* [3]. Roughly speaking, this means that pattern matching can be represented by (nested) case expressions with multiple right-hand sides for a single pattern. More precisely, every function of an overlapping inductively sequential system can be represented by a particular variety of *definitional tree* [2, 3], which we specify in Section 3.7.

It is shown in [4] that every functional logic program defined by constructor-based rewrite rules, including programs in the functional logic languages Curry and $\mathcal{TOY}$, can be transformed into an overlapping inductively sequential system. This class properly includes the first-order programs of the functional languages ML and Haskell. Higher-order features, i.e., applications of a functional expression to an argument, can be represented as an application of a specific first-order function *apply* (where partial applications are considered as data terms)—a standard technique to extend first-order languages with higher-order features [23]. (Additional preliminary compiler transformations, e.g., name resolution, lambda lifting, etc., are typically needed to turn source programs into rewrite system form; we do not discuss these further here.)

3   Virtual Machine

In this section we describe how the features of functional logic computations, in particular non-determinism and narrowing, shape the architecture of our virtual machine. We only sketch the machine's support for residuation; full details of this are beyond the scope of this paper.

3.1   Pool of Computations

A fundamental aspect of functional logic computations is non-determinism—both in its ordinary form, as in example (1), and through narrowing, as in example (2). The execution of a non-deterministic step involves one of several choices in the replacement of a redex—or, to use a more appropriate term in our environment, a *narrex*. (In the remainder of the paper, we use "narrowing" to refer to either narrowing or rewriting, which is a special case of narrowing.) For example, in the cryptarithm solver mentioned earlier, the evaluation of digit leads to 10 possible replacements.

One of our main goals is to ensure the operational completeness of computations. For instance, consider the following function to reverse the elements in a list:

$$\begin{aligned} &\texttt{rev (x:xs) = rev xs ++ [x]} \\ &\texttt{rev []   = []} \end{aligned} \qquad (3)$$

A complete computation mechanism will be able to compute a solution to the equation rev l =:= [1,2], namely {l=[2,1]}. A conventional backtracking policy that tries each clause of rev in order will loop forever on the first clause, and hence is not complete. The simplest policy to ensure completeness is to execute any non-deterministic choice fairly, independently of the other choices. In our virtual machine, this is achieved by concurrently computing the outcome of each replacement. In our machine, a *computation* is explicitly represented by a data structure, which holds the term being evaluated, a substitution, and a state indicator with values such as *active, complete,* or *residuating*.

The machine maintains a *pool* of computations. Initially, there is only one active computation in the pool, containing the initial *base term*. Computations change state depending on events or conditions resulting from the execution of machine instructions. For example, when a computation makes a non-deterministic step, the computation is *abandoned*; new computations, one for each possible step, are created, added to the pool, and become *active*. When a computation obtains a normal form or a head normal form (we have a different kind of computation for each task), the computation state is set to *complete*.

The core of the machine is an engine to perform head normal form computations, by executing sequences of machine instructions. There is one such sequence associated with each function of the source program, which we call the *code* of the function. The purpose of a function's code is to perform a narrowing step of an application of the function to a set of arguments, or to create the conditions that lead to a narrowing step (details are given in Section 3.3). The instructions operate on an internal *context* consisting of several registers and stacks (described in Section 3.5). The instruction sequence is always statically bounded in length, and contains no loops. For the simplest functions, it is just a few instructions long. For more complicated functions, the number of instructions goes up to a few dozen, but seldom more than that. When the virtual machine completes the execution of a function's code, most of the context information become irrelevant.

To manage the pool of computations fairly, the machine must share the processor among active computations so that they make some "progress" toward a result over time. We considered several strategies to ensure fair sharing. For example, a fixed amount of time could be allocated to each computation. If a computation C ends before the expiration of its time, a different computation is executed. Otherwise, C is interrupted. When all the other computations existing in the pool at the time of the interruption of C have received their fair share of time, the execution of C resumes. A similar strategy would be to allocate a fixed number of virtual machine instructions.

A drawback of the above strategies is that when a computation is interrupted, the instruction execution context must be saved, and subsequently restored when the computation resumes. In order to minimize the overhead of switching contexts, we have adopted a simpler strategy that never interrupts instruction sequences. This remains fair because the length of each instruction sequence is bounded. When the machine selects a computation from the pool, it executes the entire code of some function for that computation, and then returns the computation to the pool. It then repeats this process fairly for every other computation of the pool.

3.2   Terms and Computations

In the model for functional logic programming described in [13], a computation is the process of evaluating an expression by narrowing. The expression is a term of the rewrite system modeling the program. A *term* t is a *variable* v or a *symbol* s of fixed arity $n \geqslant 0$ applied to m terms $t_1, \ldots, t_m$, $m \leq n$, written as $s(t_1, \ldots, t_m)$. Symbols are partitioned into data *constructors* c and *functions* or *operations* f. A *data term* is a term without defined functions, a *pattern* is a function applied to data terms, and a *head normal form* is a term without a defined function at the root, i.e., a variable or a constructor-rooted term. In examples, we often write terms using infix notation for symbols. A position *pos* in a term is represented by a sequence of positive integers representing subterm choices, beginning at the root. For example, the position of x in f(y,b(x,z)) is the sequence 2·1. We write $t|_{pos}$ for the subterm at position *pos* in t.

Evaluating a term results in both a *computed value*, as in functional programming, and a *computed answer*, as in logic programming. The computed value is a data term, and the computed answer is a substitution, possibly the identity, from some free variables of the term being evaluated to data terms. In Example (2), the evaluation of [1,2,3] =:= x++[e] returns the computed value Success, a predefined constant for constraints, and the computed answer $\{x \mapsto [1,2], e \mapsto 3\}$.

Thus, the state of a computation includes both a term and a substitution. Initially, the computation data structure for a term t holds t itself and the identity substitution. As narrowing steps are executed, both the term and the substitution fields of the computation structure are updated. A computation is *complete* when the machine cannot perform a step in the term being evaluated.

The machine supports three kinds of computations. **Normal form computations** attempt to narrow terms all the way to data terms. The virtual machine is intended to be used within a host program that provides the read-eval-print loop typical of many functional and logic interpreters. The host program provides the initial base term for the machine to evaluate to normal form, and waits for the computed values and answers to be returned (if the program narrows variables or executes non-deterministic steps, multiple value/answer results are possible).

Head normal form computations try to evaluate terms to constructor-rooted terms or variables. Executing these computations is the core activity of the machine, during which the definitions of functions are applied. Since normal form computations can be modeled by head normal form computations using auxiliary operations (see, e.g., [15]), we concentrate on head normal form computations in this paper; they are described in more detail in Section 3.3.

Parallel-and computations handle the evaluation of a conjunction of two terms. Residuation is only meaningful in the presence of these computations. Each conjunct is evaluated by a different computation. For each conjunction, the computation of one and only one of the two conjuncts is active at any one time (implementing an interleaving semantics for concurrency [13]). If the computation of the first conjunct residuates, the computation of the second one becomes active. The second computation may "unblock" the first one, thus becoming *waiting* itself, or may residuate as well. In this case, the entire computation blocks. If all the parallel-and computations derived from a given base term are blocked, the base term computation *flounders*. Since we are omitting details of residuation support in this paper, we ignore parallel-and computations in subsequent sections.

The computations in the machine's pool are conceptually independent of each other. In our implementation, the evaluation of some subterms common to two independent computations may be shared, but this is only for the sake of efficiency. Thus, we describe the execution of a computation disregarding the fact that other computations may be present in the pool.

3.3   Head Normal Form Computations

The execution of a head normal form computation attempts to rewrite an *operation*-rooted term into a *constructor*-rooted term or variable. The evaluation strategy executed by our machine is *root-needed* reduction [21] with the addition of narrowing and non-deterministic steps. Simply put, the strategy repeatedly attempts to apply rewrite rules at the top of an operation-rooted term until a constructor-rooted term or variable is obtained.

The implementation of this strategy for a given function depends only on the forms of the left-hand sides of that function's defining rules. In fact, the definitional trees that our system uses to represent programs already implicitly encode the strategy. The next needed step in the evaluation of a term $f(t_1, \ldots, t_n)$ can be obtained by comparing the symbols at certain positions in the arguments of f with corresponding symbols in f's definitional tree. A sequence of comparisons determines which rule to apply, or which subterm to evaluate. To implement these tree-based operations, we compile the definitional tree for each function f to a code sequence of virtual machine instructions, as described in Section 3.7. The instructions themselves are described in Section 3.6.

The code for a function effectively chooses which rule to apply to a term. But it is also possible that *no* rule can be applied at the top of an operation-rooted term. This can occur for one of only two reasons: (1) an operation-rooted argument of a function application must be evaluated to a head normal form before any rule can be applied, or (2) the function is incompletely defined. An example of each condition follows. Consider the definitions of the usual functions that compute the head of a list and the concatenation of lists, denoted by the infix operator "++".

$$
\begin{aligned}
&\texttt{head (x:\_) = x}\\
&\texttt{[]}\quad\ \ \texttt{++ y = y}\\
&\texttt{(x:xs) ++ y = x : xs ++ y}
\end{aligned}
\tag{4}
$$

The term $t = \texttt{head}\,(u \mathbin{+\!\!+} v)$, for any u and v, is an example of the first condition. To evaluate t, it is necessary to evaluate $(u \mathbin{+\!\!+} v)$ which is a recursive instance of the original problem, i.e., to evaluate an operation-rooted term to a head normal form.

The term $t = \texttt{head []}$ is an example of the second condition. In a deterministic language, where the execution of a program consists of a single computation, this condition is usually treated as an error. In a non-deterministic language, where the execution of a program may consist of several independent computations, this condition is often benign. The machine uses a distinguished symbol, which we denote by $\texttt{fail}$, to replace terms that have no value. Since for every computation of the pool the machine executes exclusively needed steps, the reduction of any subterm to $\texttt{fail}$ implies that the entire computation should fail.

3.4   Data Representation

We now describe the virtual machine more formally. The terms manipulated by the machine are represented by acyclic directed graphs stored in heaps. This graph-based representation of terms is necessary to capture the intended sharing semantics of the language, and also allows us to express important optimizations when manipulating and replacing subterms. Formally, a *heap* is a finite map $\Gamma : H \to P + V$, where H is an abstract set of *handles* (e.g., heap addresses), P is a set of pairs of the form $\langle s, (h_1, \ldots, h_n)\rangle$, where s is a program symbol of arity $m \geqslant 0$, $n \leqslant m$, and $h_1, \ldots, h_n$ are handles, and V is a set of program variables v. (We distinguish elements of P from those of V by always writing the former using pair notation.) The term *represented* by handle h in heap Γ is given by

$$
trm_\Gamma(h) = \begin{cases} s(trm_\Gamma(h_1), \ldots, trm_\Gamma(h_n)) & \text{if } \Gamma(h) = \langle s, (h_1, \ldots, h_n)\rangle \\ v & \text{if } \Gamma(h) = v \end{cases}
$$

We make extensive use of finite maps in what follows, so we fix some general notation for these here. If M is a finite map, then $M[u := v]$ is the result of extending or updating M with a mapping from u to v. We write $\emptyset$ for an empty map, and $[u := v]$ as shorthand for the singleton map $\emptyset[u := v]$. We write $Dom(M)$ for the domain of M.

The storage areas of the machine (described in Section 3.5) hold handles for terms; more loosely, we sometimes just say they hold terms and we extend some standard term rewriting notations to handles. For example, if h is handle and $p = p_1 \cdot p_2 \cdots p_n$ is a position, then we define

$$h|_{p_1 \cdots p_n} = h_{p_1}|_{p_2 \cdots p_n} \text{ where } \Gamma(h) = \langle \_, (h_1, \ldots, h_n) \rangle$$

It follows immediately that $trm_\Gamma(h|_p) = trm_\Gamma(h)|_p$. We also define the set of *subhandles* of a handle in the obvious way:

$$shs_\Gamma(h) = \begin{cases} \{h\} \cup shs_\Gamma(h_1) \cup \ldots \cup shs_\Gamma(h_n) & \text{if } \Gamma(h) = \langle s, (h_1, \ldots, h_n) \rangle \\ \{h\} & \text{if } \Gamma(h) = v \end{cases}$$

For any handle h, the terms represented by the handles in $shs_\Gamma(h)$ are just the subterms of $trm_\Gamma(h)$.

Substitutions σ are finite maps from handles to handles, where the handles of the domain typically (but not necessarily) represent variables. Substitutions are never applied destructively to change a term in-place, since different computations might need to apply different substitutions to a same term. Instead, they are applied to handles representing terms by making a clone (deep copy) of the term. More precisely, we define a "clone with substitution" operator as follows:

$$clone_\sigma(\Gamma_0, h) = \begin{cases} (\Gamma_0, \sigma(h)) & \text{if } h \in Dom(\sigma) \\ (\Gamma_0, h) & \text{if } shs_\Gamma(h) \cap Dom(\sigma) = \emptyset \\ (\Gamma', h') & \text{otherwise, where} \\ & \Gamma_0(h) = \langle s, (h_1, \ldots, h_n) \rangle \\ & (\Gamma_i, h_i') = clone_\sigma(\Gamma_{i-1}, h_i) \quad (1 \leq i \leq n) \\ & \Gamma' = \Gamma_n[h' := \langle s, (h_1', \ldots, h_n') \rangle] \quad (h' \notin Dom(\Gamma_n)) \end{cases}$$

This *clone* operator is quite efficient since it copies (only) the spines of the term above any substituted variables; any parts of the source term remaining unaffected by the substitution are shared by the result term. For cloning to have the expected substitution semantics on the represented terms, it is important that no variable appears more than once in the heap; i.e., if $trm_\Gamma(h_1) = v$ and $trm_\Gamma(h_2) = v$, then $h_1 = h_2$. We call heaps having this property *well-formed*, and we take care to start the machine with a well-formed heap and maintain the well-formedness invariant during execution. Suppose Γ is well-formed, $trm_\Gamma(h) = t$ and $trm_\Gamma(j) = u$ for some terms t and u, and $trm_\Gamma(k) = v$ for some variable v. If $(\Gamma', h') = clone_{[k:=j]}(\Gamma, h)$, then $trm_{\Gamma'}(h') = t[u/v]$, i.e., the usual term substitution of u for v in t.

3.5   Storage Areas

As discussed in the previous sections, our machine fairly executes a pool of independent computations. The context of each computation includes a heap and four separate *storage areas*, a generic name for stacks and registers.

Suppose that t is the term to evaluate in a head normal form computation. We recall that initially t is operation-rooted; the computation completes successfully when t is evaluated to a constructor-rooted term or variable. The computation begins by executing the code associated with the function at the root of t. In the course of executing this code, it may become necessary to recursively evaluate operation-rooted subterms of t. The **pre-narrex stack** keeps track of these recursive computations. It is a stack containing handles $h_n, \ldots, h_2, h_1$ of a heap Γ, with h_n the top, having the following properties.

1. At the beginning of the computation, $n = 1$ and $trm_\Gamma(h_1) = t$.
2. Every term represented by a handle in the stack, with the possible exception of h_n, the top of the stack, is operation-rooted and it is not a narrex.
3. For all $i > 1$, h_i is a subhandle of h_{i-1} with the property that $trm_\Gamma(h_i)$ must be evaluated to a head normal form before $trm_\Gamma(h_{i-1})$ can be evaluated to a head normal form.

The top of the pre-narrex stack contains the term handle currently being evaluated. Referring to example (4), if head $(u + v)$ is on the pre-narrex stack, then $u + v$ will be pushed on the stack, too, because the former cannot be evaluated to a head normal form unless the latter is evaluated to a head normal form. The machine allocates a separate pre-narrex stack to each head normal form computation.

The other three storage areas are local to the execution of a single function code sequence.

Current Register. This is a simple register containing a term handle. Many of the machine's instructions implicitly reference this register. For example, to apply a rewrite rule of the function "++" defined in (4) to the term $u + v$, one must check whether the term u is rooted by [] or ":" or some function symbol. The BRANCH instruction that performs the test expects to find the term to be tested in the current register.

Pre-term Stack. This is a stack for constructing narrex replacements. These are always term handles instantiating a right-hand side of a rule. The arguments of a symbol application are first pushed on the stack in reverse order. The MAKETERM instruction, which is parameterized by the symbol being applied, replaces these arguments with the application term. For example, the term [1,2]++[3,4], which is a narrex, is replaced by 1:([2]++[3,4]) which is constructed as follows. First, the handles for the terms [3,4] and [2] are pushed on the pre-term stack. Executing "MAKETERM ++" replaces them with a handle to the new term [2]++[3,4]. Then, the handle for the term 1 is pushed on the stack as well and executing "MAKETERM :" replaces the two topmost elements with a handle for 1:([2]++[3,4]).

Free variable registers. The rewrite rules that define the functions of the program can contain free (extra) variables. Several occurrences of a same free variable may be needed to construct the narrex replacement. Therefore, when a free variable is created, its handle is stored in a register (using instruction STOREVAR) to be retrieved later (using instruction MAKEVAR) if it occurs again. For example, consider the following rule that tells whether a string of odd length is a palindrome:

$$\texttt{palind s = s =:= x ++ (y : reverse x)   where x,y free} \qquad (5)$$

The construction of an instance of the right-side of this rule begins with pushing x, for the right-most occurrence of the right-hand side, on the pre-term stack. Later on, another occurrence of x is to be pushed on the stack. Thus, a handle to x must be kept around so that it can be retrieved later and pushed again. The machine maintains the set of free variables as a finite map from variable index numbers (which are parameters to the STOREVAR and MAKEVAR instructions) to variable handles. The content of these local storage areas can be discarded at the end of the execution of the function code. Since computations are never interrupted in the middle of an instruction sequence, there need only be one instance of these areas, which can be shared by all computations.

3.6   Machine Instructions

The virtual machine evaluates terms by executing sequences of instructions. Each instruction acts on the heap and the current computation to produces a (possibly) altered heap and zero or more new or changed computations. Thus, the behavior of a computation C in the current heap Γ will be specified as a transition $\Gamma, C \implies \Gamma', \{C_1, \ldots, C_n\}$ ($n \geq 0$) where Γ' is a modified heap and $C_1, \ldots, C_n$ are the new or changed computations. Some instructions move information between the various storage areas. Others build or take apart terms. Building a term extends the heap; some other operations update it. Figure 1 gives transition rules for the instructions.

The machine begins a head normal form evaluation with a single active computation, containing a single term handle on the pre-narrex stack, and a well-formed heap. (The information in all the other storage areas is irrelevant.) The machine then repeats the following cycle. A computation is chosen (fairly) for execution from the active computation pool. If the top of the pre-narrex stack represents an operation-rooted term, the machine retrieves the code for the operation and begins to execute it. If the top of the pre-narrex stack represents a constructor-rooted term or a variable, the stack is simply popped; in this case an appropriate handle in the heap will already have been updated with that term. If the pre-narrex stack is empty, the computation is completed and is removed from the pool of active computations; the computed value can be read from the heap by the host program.

The code for a function is a sequence of instructions I. (In fact, because BRANCH instructions may contain multiple sub-sequences of instructions, the code really forms a tree.) The LOAD and BRANCH instructions deal with fetching and testing (handles of) existing terms. LOAD p extracts the subhandle at position p from the handle on top of the pre-narrex stack and puts it in the current register. BRANCH $I_0, \ldots, I_n$ tests and dispatches on the form of the term represented by the handle in the current register. If the head of this term is a function symbol, the term is pushed on the pre-narrex stack to be eventually narrowed to a head normal form. If it is the special constant fail, the current computation is abandoned (see below). If it is a logic variable, control is dispatched to the instruction sub-sequence I_0, which ordinarily arranges to narrow or residuate. Otherwise, the term must be rooted by some constructor c from some datatype t; control is dispatched to instruction sequence I_j, where j is the index of c in the canonical ordering of constructors for t. Note that BRANCH can only occur at the end of an instruction sequence.

$$\Gamma, ([], h{:}N, \_, \_, \_) \implies \Gamma, \{(code(f), h{:}N, \_, [], \emptyset)\}$$
$$(\Gamma(h) = \langle f, \_\rangle)$$

$$\Gamma, ([], h{:}N, \_, \_, \_) \implies \Gamma, \{([], N, \_, [], [])\}$$
$$(\Gamma(h) = \langle c, \_\rangle \text{ or } \Gamma(h) = v)$$

$$\Gamma, ([], [], \_, \_, \_) \implies \Gamma, \emptyset$$

$$\Gamma, (\text{LOAD } p_1 \cdots p_n : I, [t_m, \ldots, t_1], \_, T, F) \implies \Gamma, \{(I, [t_m, \ldots, t_1], t_m|_{p_1 \cdots p_n}, T, F)\}$$

$$\Gamma, (\text{BRANCH } \ldots : [], N, h, \_, \_) \implies \Gamma, \{([], h{:}N, \_, [], \emptyset)\} \quad (\Gamma(h) = \langle f, \_\rangle)$$

$$\Gamma, (\text{BRANCH } \ldots : [], \_, h, \_, \_) \implies \Gamma, \emptyset \quad (\Gamma(h) = \langle \mathtt{fail}, ()\rangle)$$

$$\Gamma, (\text{BRANCH } I_0, \ldots : [], N, h, T, F) \implies \Gamma, \{(I_0, N, h, T, F)\} \quad (\Gamma(h) = v)$$

$$\Gamma, (\text{BRANCH } I_0, \ldots, I_n : [], N, h, T, F) \implies \Gamma, \{(I_j, N, h, T, F)\}$$
$$(\Gamma(h) = \langle c, \_\rangle, c \; j\text{-th constructor})$$

$$\Gamma, (\text{PUSH} : I, N, R, T, F) \implies \Gamma, \{(I, N, R, R{:}T, F)\}$$

$$\Gamma, (\text{POP} : I, N, \_, t{:}ts, F) \implies \Gamma, \{(I, N, t, ts, F)\}$$

$$\Gamma, (\text{MAKEANON} : I, N, R, T, F) \implies \Gamma[h := v], \{(I, N, R, h{:}T, F)\}$$
$$(h \notin Dom(\Gamma), v \text{ fresh})$$

$$\Gamma, (\text{STOREVAR } n : I, N, R, T, F) \implies \Gamma[h := v], \{(I, N, R, T, F[n := h])\}$$
$$(h \notin Dom(\Gamma), v \text{ fresh})$$

$$\Gamma, (\text{MAKEVAR } n : I, N, R, T, F) \implies \Gamma, \{(I, N, R, F(n){:}T, F)\}$$

$$\Gamma, (\text{MAKETERM } s : I, N, R, [t_m, \ldots, t_1], F) \implies$$
$$\Gamma[h := s(t_m, \ldots, t_{m-n+1})], \{(I, N, R, [h, t_{m-n}, \ldots, t_1], F)\}$$
$$(h \notin Dom(\Gamma), arity(s) = n \leqslant m)$$

$$\Gamma, (\text{REPLACE} : [], h{:}N, R, [], \_) \implies \Gamma[h := R], \{([], h{:}N, \_, [], \emptyset)\}$$

$$\Gamma_0, (\text{NARROW} : [], [t_m, \ldots, t_1], h, [c_1, \ldots, c_k], \_) \implies \Gamma_k, \{([], [h_i], \_, [], \emptyset) \mid 1 \leq i \leq k\}$$
$$\text{where } \sigma_i = [h := c_i] \text{ and } (\Gamma_i, h_i) = clone_{\sigma_i}(\Gamma_{i-1}, t_1) \quad (1 \leq i \leq k)$$

$$\Gamma_0, (\text{CHOICE} : [], [t_m, \ldots, t_1], \_, [c_1, \ldots, c_k], \_) \implies \Gamma_k, \{([], [h_i], \_, [], \emptyset) \mid 1 \leq i \leq k\}$$
$$\text{where } \sigma_i = [t_m := c_i] \text{ and } (\Gamma_i, h_i) = clone_{\sigma_i}(\Gamma_{i-1}, t_1) \quad (1 \leq i \leq k)$$

Fig. 1. Machine instruction set. Instructions map a heap and an active computation to a revised heap and a set of result computations. Computations are described by tuples of the form (I, N, R, T, F), where I is an instruction sequence, N is the pre-narrex stack, R is the current register, T is the pre-term stack, and F is the free variable map. $code(f)$ denotes the sequence of virtual machine instructions associated to function f as described in Section 3.7. Standard Haskell-style list notation is used for stacks and sequences. An underscore ($\_$) denotes a field whose contents don't matter

A number of instructions manipulate the pre-term stack. PUSH and POP move handles between the current register and the stack. MAKEANON creates a fresh, independent free variable in the heap and pushes its handle. MAKEVAR pushes the handle of a (potentially) shared free variable (previously created by STOREVAR) from the shared free-variable map. MAKETERM s constructs a new term representation in the heap with root symbol s and the top $arity(s)$ elements of the stack as arguments, and pushes its handle in place of the arguments. Finally, REPLACE updates the handle on the top of *pre-narrex* stack to have the same contents as the handle in the current register.

1	LOAD	1	load u in the current register
2	BRANCH		
	[		u is an uninstantiated variable
3	MAKETERM	[]	pre-term stack contains [ ]
4	MAKEANON		push _
5	MAKEANON		push _
6	MAKETERM	:	pre-term stack contains [ ] and _:_
7	NARROW		
	]		
	[		u is [ ]
8	LOAD	2	load v
9	REPLACE		
	]		
	[		u is $u_0 : u_s$
10	LOAD	2	load v
11	PUSH		
12	LOAD	1·2	load u_s
13	PUSH		
14	MAKETERM	++	pre-term stack contains $u_s {+}{+} v$
15	LOAD	1·1	load u_0
16	PUSH		
17	MAKETERM	:	pre-term stack contains $u_0 : u_s {+}{+} v$
18	POP		
19	REPLACE		
	]		

Fig. 2. Compilation of the definition of the function "++". This code is executed to evaluate a term of the form $u{+}{+}v$. The instruction numbers at the left and the comments at the right are not part of the code itself

The remaining instructions, which only appear at the end of an instruction sequence, place multiple, non-deterministic alternative computations into the active pool. NARROW executes a narrowing step. When this instruction is executed, the current register holds the handle for a variable v and and the pre-term stack holds handles for the instantiations $c_1, \ldots, c_k$, $k > 0$, of this variable. For each instantiation c_i, the root term of the computation t_1 is cloned under the substitution $[h := c_i]$. The computation executing the non-deterministic step is abandoned and a new computation corresponding to each clone is added to the pool. Note that each new computation starts from the root term and an empty pre-narrex stack; this stack gets rebuilt independently in each computation. CHOICE is similar, except that it executes a non-deterministic reduction step. When this instruction is executed, the top of the pre-narrex stack holds a narrex t_m and the pre-term stack holds the replacements $c_1, \ldots, c_k$, $k > 1$, of this narrex. For each replacement c_i, the root term of the computation t_1 is cloned under the substitution $[t_m := c_i]$.

There is one further instruction, RESIDUATE, which moves a computation from the active pool to a waiting pool pending the instantiation of a logic variable. A precise description of this instruction and of the remainder of the residuation mechanism are beyond the scope of this paper.

In addition to these instructions, some activities of the machine are performed by built-in functions. Generally, these are library functions that could not be defined by ordinary rewrite rules. An example of a built-in function is *apply*, which takes two terms as arguments and applies the first to the second. For correctly-typed programs, the first argument of *apply* evaluates to a term of the form $f(x_1, \ldots, x_n)$ where the arity of f is greater than n, i.e., f is a partial application. The function *apply* performs a simple manipulation of the representation of terms. It would be easy to replace the built-in function *apply* with a machine instruction. However, built-in functions are preferable to machine instructions because they keep the machine simpler and they are loaded only when needed.

Figure 2 shows the code for the list concatenation function "++" defined in (4). This code is executed when the top of the pre-narrex stack contains a term of the form u++v.

3.7   Compilation

Every function of an overlapping inductively sequential program has a *definitional tree* [2, 3], which is a hierarchical representation of the rewrite rules of a function that has become the standard device for the implementation of narrowing computations. We compile each definitional tree into a sequence of virtual machine instructions. Because a definitional tree is a high-level abstraction for the definition of a sound, complete and theoretically efficient narrowing strategy [6], mapping this strategy into virtual machine instructions increases our confidence in both the correctness and the efficiency of the execution. The notation for the variant of definitional trees we use is summarized in Figure 3.

(definitional tree) $\mathcal{T} = Branch(p, pos, flex?, [\mathcal{T}_1, \ldots, \mathcal{T}_n])$
$\qquad\qquad | \ Rule(p, [r_1, \ldots, r_n])$

(right-hand side) $r = ([v_1, \ldots, v_n], t)$

Fig. 3. Notation for definitional trees

A trees consist of internal *Branch* nodes, which encode choices between left-hand-side patterns of rewrite rules, and leaf *Rule* nodes, which correspond to the right-hand sides of rewrite rules. *Branch* nodes contain a pattern p to match, a position *pos* within the term to be matched, a flag *flex?* indicating whether or not the branch is *flexible* or *rigid*, i.e., whether to narrow or residuate if the corresponding position of a term being processed is a variable. In the node *Rule(p,rs)*, *rs* is a list of non-deterministic alternative right-hand sides for the rule. Each right-hand side (vs, t) consists of a term t and a list of free variables *vs* that appear in t but not in p.

As examples, the definitional tree for the function (++) defined in (4) is:

$Branch(\texttt{x++y}, 1, True, [Rule(\texttt{[]++y}, [([], \texttt{y})]),$
$\qquad\qquad\qquad\qquad Rule((\texttt{x:xs})\texttt{++y}, [([], \texttt{x:(xs++y)})])]),$

the tree for `palind` (5) is:

$Rule(\texttt{palind s}, [([x, y], s \texttt{ =:= x++(y:reverse x)})]),$

and the tree for $\texttt{digit}$ (1) is:

$Rule(\texttt{digit}, [([], 0), ([], 1), \ldots, ([], 9)]),$

where, for readability, we write terms and patterns using infix notation.

Figure 4 gives an algorithm for compiling definitional trees to sequences of abstract machine instructions. For simplicity, we assume all definitional trees are canonical, in the sense that every *Branch* node corresponding to a position of type τ has a child for each data constructor of τ, and the children are in the canonical order for data constructors. (In reality, the compiler would use auxiliary type information to determine the full set of possible children, and generate code to produce $\texttt{fail}$ for the missing ones.) We assume the existence of a function *posOf* v p that returns the position (if any) of variable v in pattern p (assuming v appears at most once in p). Various optimizations on the resulting code are possible; for example, the sequence of instructions [PUSH,POP] can be omitted, as illustrated by the code in Figure 2, or the instructions STOREVAR n and MAKEVAR n can be replaced by a single MAKEANON instruction for free variables that occur only once in the right-hand side.

compileTree $(Branch(p, pos, flex?, [T_1, \ldots, T_n])) =$
  [LOAD *pos*,
   BRANCH [*handleVariable*,
          compileTree T_1,
          $\ldots$,
          compileTree T_n]]
  where handleVariable =
       if flex? then
            $buildChoice_1$ ++ $\cdots$ ++ $buildChoice_n$ ++ [NARROW]
                where $buildChoice_i$ = [MAKEANON$_1$, ..., MAKEANON$_{n_i}$,
                                       MAKETERM c_i]
                    where $c_i(d_1, \ldots, d_{n_i})$ = $(patternOf\ T_i)\,|pos$
       else [RESIDUATE]

compileTree $(Rule(p, [rhs_1, \ldots, rhs_n]) =$
  if n = 1 then
       $(compileRhs\ rhs_1)$ ++ [POP, REPLACE]
  else $(compileRhs\ rhs_1)$ ++ $\ldots$ ++ $(compileRhs\ rhs_n)$ ++ [CHOICE]
  where compileRhs $([v_1, \ldots, v_n], t)$ =
                    [STOREVAR 1, ..., STOREVAR n] ++ $(compileTerm\ t)$
       where compileTerm (v) = *if* $\exists j$ *with* $v = v_j$ *then*
                                       [MAKEVAR j]
                                   else [LOAD $(posOf\ v\ p)$, PUSH]
            compileTerm $(s(t_1, \ldots, t_n))$ =
            $(compileTerm\ t_n)$ ++ $\cdots$ ++ $(compileTerm\ t_1)$ ++
            [MAKETERM s]

Fig. 4. Pseudo-code for compilation of definitional trees to sequences of virtual machine instructions. Standard Haskell-style notation is used for lists

Some practical adjustments to the pseudo-code of Figure 4 are necessary to accommodate built-in types, such as integers and characters. There are a few additional machine instructions, e.g., MAKEINT and MAKECHAR, for this purpose.

4   Implementation

We have two prototype implementations of the virtual machine described in this paper. One implementation, in Java, is currently our main development avenue. A second implementation, in Standard ML, is being used mostly as a proof of concept. Since the code is not optimized because it is still evolving, we do not present a detailed benchmark suite here. Nevertheless, the initial performance results appear to be promising. A computationally intensive test computes Fibonacci numbers with an intentionally inefficient program. This test shows that the machine executes approximately 0.5 million reductions (i.e., function calls) per second on a 2.0 Ghz Linux-PC (with AMD Athlon XP 2600). On the same benchmark, the PAKCS [14] implementation of Curry, which compiles Curry programs into Prolog using the scheme in [7], runs about twice as fast. PAKCS is one of the most efficient Curry implementations, apart from MCC [20], which produces native code. However, neither of these implementations is operationally complete. For example, neither produces a solution to example (3).

We have used Java and ML due to their built-in support for automatic memory management and appropriate programming abstractions which simplified the development of our prototypes. The same approach has been taken in [16], which describes an abstract machine for Curry and its implementation in Java. On the negative side, the use of Java limits the speed of the execution—the Java implementation in [16] is more than an order of magnitude slower than PAKCS [7]. On the positive side, our machine can be also implemented in C/C++ from which we can expect a considerable efficiency improvement.[1] A possible strategy is to integrate a C-based execution engine into the Java support framework.

Non-deterministic computations are executed independently. However, because of the use of term handles, a common deterministic term of two independent computations is evaluated only once. For example, consider the term $digit + t$, where $digit$ is defined in (1). A distinct computation is executed for each replacement of $digit$, but t is evaluated only once for all these computations. In situations of this kind, our machine is faster than PAKCS.

In our implementations, a narrex is replaced in place (with a destructive update) whenever possible. Non-deterministic steps prevent replacement in place, since several replacements should update a single term. Currently, the machine constructs not only the replacement of a narrex, but also the spine of the entire term in which the narrex occurs. This is unnecessarily inefficient and we plan to improve the situation in the future together with other optimizations of the machine architecture and code.

---

[1] [16] compares the speed of the same virtual machine for Curry coded in Java vs. in C/C++. The latter is more than one order of magnitude faster compared to a Java implementation with a Just-In-Time compiler.

Our virtual machine is intended for the execution of functional logic programs in a variety of source languages. Our immediate choice of source language is Curry [18]. For this application, we have a complete compiler (written in Curry) into our virtual machine but several other non-trivial software components, such as a command line parser, a loader, a debugger and a run-time library, are necessary as well. The virtual machine has good built-in capabilities for tracing and debugging. A specific problem of an operationally complete implementation of non-deterministic computations is that steps of different computations are interleaved. Presenting steps in the order in which they are executed produces traces which are hard to read. An external debugger with a suitable interface for non-deterministic computations is described in [9]. Finally, we have implemented a handful of modules for built-in types, such as the integers, that cannot be compiled from source programs.

To conclude, we have a solid, though preliminary, implementation of the virtual machine. Several key software components of an interactive development environment need further work. The Java implementation of the machine is available for download from http://redstar.cs.pdx.edu/~antoy/flp/vm. The distribution also links a tutorial description of the machine including an animation of the behavior of the instructions.

5   Conclusion and Related Work

We have described the architecture of a virtual machine for the execution of functional logic computations. The machine's design is based on solid theoretical results. In particular, the machine is intended for overlapping inductively sequential programs and computes only root-needed steps (modulo non-deterministic choices). Larger classes of programs, up to those modeled by the whole class of constructor-based conditional rewrite systems, can be executed after initial transformation.

A small set of machine instructions performs pattern matching and narrex replacement, two key activities of the machine. Both narrowing and non-deterministic steps are executed by a single instruction since the machine is specifically designed for functional logic computations. The machine is also designed to execute several computations concurrently to ensure the operational completeness. Implementations of the machine in Java and ML are complete and fairly efficient, through not yet optimized.

The implementation of functional logic languages is an active area of research. A common approach is the translation of functional logic source programs into Prolog programs, where Prolog has the role of a portable, specialized machine language, e.g., [7]. Another approach relies on an abstract machine. The machine presented here is only one of several alternatives the authors have considered. In [8], Antoy, Hanus, et al. describe a virtual machine with many similarities to that described in this paper, but a major difference. Functions are compiled into Java objects rather than sequences of virtual machine instruction as in the example of Figure 2, i.e., the target language is Java rather than an instruction set of a virtual machine. In [16] Hanus and Sadre presented also a virtual machine for compiling Curry programs that exploits Java threads to implement the concurrent features of Curry and ensures the operational completeness of non-deterministic computations. To manage the bindings of logical variables caused by different non-deterministic computations, they used bindings tables that are partially shared between computations. The resulting architecture is more complex than the machine presented in this paper and has fewer possibilities for optimization, e.g., the sharing of deterministic evaluations between non-deterministic computations discussed in Section 4. Thus, this implementation is no longer supported.

In [22], Tolmach, Antoy, and Nita describe a definitional interpreter for Curry-like languages based on the semantics of Albert, *et al.* [1]. The primary contrast with the present work is in the treatment of the heap. Rather than conceiving of the system as a graph rewriting engine that generates modified copies of the source term as it runs, [22] treats the program as fixed, read-only code that operates on multiple variant *versions* of the heap. A direct performance comparison between these two approaches remains to be made.

Among related work by others, Chakravarty and Lock [10] proposed a virtual machine for functional logic languages that combines implementation techniques from functional and logic programming in an orthogonal way. To implement logic language features, they used traditional logic programming implementation techniques based on backtracking so that the operational completeness is not ensured. The same is true for the virtual machine used in the Curry implementation MCC [20]. Due to the native code compilation used in MCC, the implementation is quite efficient but not operational complete due to the use of a backtracking strategy.

A minimal comparison of efficiency was addressed earlier. However, our effort is mainly characterized by the simplicity of both the instruction set and the storage areas and by the rigorous theoretical results on which the machine is founded.

Acknowledgments

Pravin Damle made extensive contributions to the implementation. Marius Nita and the anonymous reviewers gave helpful suggestions on the presentation of the paper.

References

1. E. Albert, M. Hanus, F. Huch, J. Oliver, and G. Vidal. Operational semantics for declarative multi-paradigm languages. *Journal of Symbolic Computation (to appear)*, 2005.
2. S. Antoy. Definitional trees. In *Proc. 3rd International Conference on Algebraic and Logic Programming (ALP'92)*, pages 143–157. Springer LNCS 632, 1992.
3. S. Antoy. Optimal non-deterministic functional logic computations. In *Proc. Int. Conf. on Algebraic and Logic Programming (ALP'97)*, pages 16–30. Springer LNCS 1298, 1997.
4. S. Antoy. Constructor-based conditional narrowing. In *Proc. of the 3rd International Conference on Principles and Practice of Declarative Programming (PPDP'01)*, pages 199–206, Florence, Italy, Sept. 2001. ACM.
5. S. Antoy. Evaluation strategies for functional logic programming. *Journal of Symbolic Computation*, 2005. To appear.
6. S. Antoy, R. Echahed, and M. Hanus. A needed narrowing strategy. *Journal of the ACM*, 47(4):776–822, 2000.
7. S. Antoy and M. Hanus. Compiling multi-paradigm declarative programs into Prolog. In *Proc. of the 3rd International Workshop on Frontiers of Combining Systems (FroCoS 2000)*, pages 171–185, Nancy, France, March 2000. Springer LNCS 1794.

8. S. Antoy, M. Hanus, B. Massey, and F. Steiner. An implementation of narrowing strategies. In *Proc. of the 3rd International ACM SIGPLAN Conference on Principles and Practice of Declarative Programming (PPDP 2001)*, pages 207–217. ACM Press, 2001.

9. S. Antoy and S. Johnson. TeaBag: A functional logic language debugger. In *Proc. 13th International Workshop on Functional and (Constraint) Logic Programming (WFLP 2004)*, pages 4–18, Aachen (Germany), 2004. Technical Report AIB-2004-05, RWTH Aachen.

10. M.M.T. Chakravarty and H.C.R. Lock. Towards the uniform implementation of declarative languages. *Computer Languages*, 23(2-4):121–160, 1997.

11. J. C. González Moreno, F. J. López Fraguas, M. T. Hortalá González, and M. Rodríguez Artalejo. An approach to declarative programming based on a rewriting logic. *The Journal of Logic Programming*, 40:47–87, 1999.

12. M. Hanus. The integration of functions into logic programming: From theory to practice. *Journal of Logic Programming*, 19&20:583–628, 1994.

13. M. Hanus. A unified computation model for functional and logic programming. In *Proc. 24st ACM Symposium on Principles of Programming Languages (POPL'97)*, pages 80–93, 1997.

14. M. Hanus, S. Antoy, M. Engelke, K. Höppner, J. Koj, P. Niederau, R. Sadre, and F. Steiner. PAKCS: The Portland Aachen Kiel Curry System. Available at http://www.informatik.uni-kiel.de/~pakcs/, 2004.

15. M. Hanus and C. Prehofer. Higher-order narrowing with definitional trees. *Journal of Functional Programming*, 9(1):33–75, 1999.

16. M. Hanus and R. Sadre. An abstract machine for Curry and its concurrent implementation in Java. *Journal of Functional and Logic Programming*, 1999(6), 1999.

17. M. Hanus and F. Steiner. Controlling search in declarative programs. In *Principles of Declarative Programming (Proc. Joint International Symposium PLILP/ALP'98)*, pages 374–390. Springer LNCS 1490, 1998.

18. M. Hanus (ed.). Curry: An integrated functional logic language (vers. 0.8). Available at http://www.informatik.uni-kiel.de/~curry, 2003.

19. F. López-Fraguas and J. Sánchez-Hernández. TOY: A Multiparadigm Declarative System. In *Proc. of RTA'99*, pages 244–247. Springer LNCS 1631, 1999.

20. W. Lux and H. Kuchen. An efficient abstract machine for Curry. In K. Beiersdörfer, G. Engels, and W. Schäfer, editors, *Informatik '99 — Annual meeting of the German Computer Science Society (GI)*, pages 390–399. Springer Verlag, 1999.

21. A. Middeldorp. Call by need computations to root-stable form. In *Proc. 24th ACM Symposium on Principles of Programming Languages*, pages 94–105, Paris, 1997.

22. A. Tolmach, S. Antoy, and M. Nita. Implementing functional logic languages using multiple threads and stores. In *Proc. of the Ninth International Conference on Functional Programming (ICFP 2004)*, pages 90–102, Snowbird, Utah, USA, Sept. 2004. ACM Press.

23. D.H.D. Warren. Higher-order extensions to PROLOG: are they needed? In *Machine Intelligence 10*, pages 441–454, 1982.

Source-Based Trace Exploration

Olaf Chitil

University of Kent, UK

Abstract. Tracing a computation is a key method for program compre-
hension and debugging. HAT is a tracing system for Haskell 98 programs.
During a computation a trace is recorded in a file; then the user studies
the trace with a collection of viewing tools. Different views are complementary and can productively be used together. Experience shows that
users of the viewing tools find it hard to keep orientation and navigate to
a point of interest in the trace. Hence this paper describes a new viewing tool where navigation through the trace is based on the program
source. The tool combines ideas from algorithmic debugging, traditional
stepping debuggers and dynamic program slicing.

1   Hat and Its Views

A tracer gives us access to otherwise invisible information about a computation.
It is a tool for understanding how a program works and for locating the source
of runtime errors in a program. HAT is a tracer for the lazy functional language
Haskell 98. HAT combines the tracing methods of several preceding systems [13,
3, 4]. Tracing a computation with HAT consists of two phases, trace generation
and trace viewing:

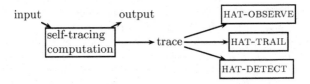

First, a special version of the program runs. In addition to its normal in-
put/output behaviour it writes a trace into a file. Second, after the program has
terminated, we study the trace with a collection of viewing tools:

- HAT-DETECT provides algorithmic debugging, that is, semi-automatic local-
  isation of program faults. Trace viewing consists of the system asking questions about the computation such as "Should `factorial 3 = 42`?" which we
  have to answer with "yes" or "no". After a series of questions and answers
  the debugger gives the location of a fault in the program.
- HAT-TRAIL enables us to follow redex trails; we explore a computation backwards, from an effect — such as output or a runtime error — to its cause.

C. Grelck et al. (Eds.): IFL 2004, LNCS 3474, pp. 126–141, 2005.
© Springer-Verlag Berlin Heidelberg 2005

Trace viewing consists of us selecting expressions whose parent, the function call that generated the expression, is then displayed. An example with selected expressions underlined: <u>42</u> → 3*<u>14</u> → <u>2*7</u> → <u>factorial 2</u> → factorial 3.

– HAT-OBSERVE allows the observation of functions. A functional value is displayed as a finite mapping from all the arguments the function was called with in the computation to the respective results, for example: {factorial 0 = 7, factorial 1 = 7, factorial 2 = 14, factorial 3 = 42}.

Each viewing tool gives a different view of a computation; in practice, the views are complementary and can productively be used together [2]. The trace as concrete data structure liberates the views from the time arrow of the computation. Hat provides valuable insights into long computations of real-world programs

Nonetheless, HAT still has a number of shortcomings. One of these is that it is often hard to navigate through large computations. By using the existing viewing tools together and calling one tool from the other we can in principle quickly reach any point in the trace. However, the questions: "where am I in the trace?" and "how do I get to the point I want to see in the trace?" often occur. We require orientation guides.

One candidate for an orientation structure immediately springs to mind: the program source. We are likely to be familiar with the source, because we wrote it, read it beforehand and/or will have to modify it. All expressions in the trace originate from the source. Usually the source is far shorter than the huge computation trace.

Surprisingly, none of the existing viewing tools take advantage of the source. All HAT viewing tools display only expressions and equations of the traced computation. The tools just allow opening a source browser with the cursor positioned at the redex or at the definition of the function of current interest.

This paper describes a new HAT viewing tool, HAT-EXPLORE, that allows simple, free navigation through a trace while providing orientation based on the program source. HAT-EXPLORE combines ideas from algorithmic debugging, traditional stepping debuggers and dynamic program slicing. The following sections describe in several steps the design of HAT-EXPLORE and some implementation issues. HAT-EXPLORE is part of the HAT distribution which is available from http://haskell.org/hat.

2   Algorithmic Debugging

Algorithmic debugging is based on the representation of a computation as an Evaluation Dependency Tree (EDT) [6, 5]. Each node of the tree is labelled with an equation, which is a reduction of a redex to a value. The tree is basically the proof tree of a natural semantics for a call-by-value evaluation with 'miraculous' stops where arguments are not needed for the final result value. The call-by-value structure ensures that arguments are values, not complex unevaluated expressions. Figure 2 shows the EDT of the sorting program given in Figure 1. Note

```
main = putStrLn (sort "sort")

sort :: Ord a => [a] -> [a]
sort []     = []
sort (x:xs) = insert x (sort xs)

insert :: Ord a => a -> [a] -> [a]
insert x [] = [x]
insert x (y:ys) = if x <= y then x : ys else y : insert x ys
```

Fig. 1. A faulty insertion sort program

that {IO} denotes an IO-action value for which no informative representation is available.

In algorithmic debugging an oracle decides which nodes of the EDT are correct and which are incorrect. A node is correct if and only if its reduction of a function agrees with the semantics we as programmers *intend* the function to have. A node that is incorrect but whose children are all correct is faulty. The definition of the function reduced in this node is faulty and needs to be modified. Hence the aim of algorithmic debugging is to find a faulty node. The definition of a faulty node is intuitive: if a function call yields an incorrect result, but all the calls made from this function call are correct, then the definition body must be faulty. In the EDT of Figure 2 all nodes except the IO-related ones have been declared as correct ($\sqrt{}$) or incorrect ($\times$). The double framed nodes are faulty. Both faulty nodes are caused by the same faulty part of the definition of `insert`.

A formal specification can be the basis of the oracle and the correctness of nodes can be considered in any order. However, most algorithmic debugging systems assume that the user is the oracle and implicitly traverses the EDT

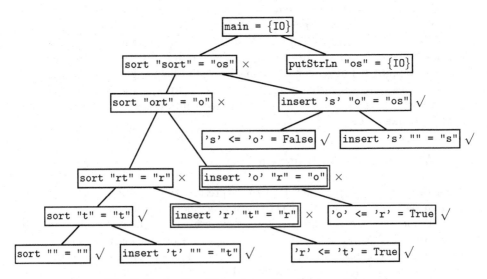

Fig. 2. Evaluation Dependency Tree for insertion sort

while answering questions about correctness with "yes" or "no". Entering "no" makes a child of the current node the new current node (If the node has no children, the aim of debugging has been reached, because the current node is faulty). Entering "yes" makes the next yet unvisited sibling of the current node the new current node (if all siblings have been visited, then the next yet unvisited sibling of the parent is chosen, and so on). Usually, the user of an algorithmic debugging tool is not meant to be aware of these non-trivial navigation steps, but shall just answer the questions.

3 Source-Based Free Navigation Through the Evaluation Dependency Tree

Basically HAT-EXPLORE is a tool for free navigation through an EDT. The EDT is a complete representation of a computation. While navigation via "yes"/"no" answers is fairly complex, it is straightforward to provide simple navigation through the tree via the cursor keys: up to the parent, down to the first child, and left and right to siblings. Most importantly, however, the program source can provide good orientation while traversing the EDT. The call-by-value structure of the EDT ensures that the EDT reflects the program structure. If $f \ldots = \ldots$ is the reduction of a node, then the redexes of its children are all instances of the definition body of the function f. Figure 3 demonstrates this property.

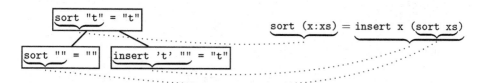

Fig. 3. Relationship between parent and children in EDT and program source

The display of HAT-EXPLORE is divided into two parts: the current reduction and the source. In the source the *call site* of the redex of the current reduction is underlined.

```
==== Hat-Explore 0.3 ==== Call 2/2 ==============================
sort "t" = "t"
---- Insert.hs ---- line 1 to 9 -------------------------------
main = putStrLn (sort "sort")

sort :: Ord a => [a] -> [a]
sort [] = []
sort (x:xs) = insert x ( sort xs )

insert :: Ord a => a -> [a] -> [a]
insert x [] = [x]
insert x (y:ys) = if x <= y then x : ys else y : (insert x ys)
```

Optionally the *definition site* of the function of the redex can also be high-lighted, but usually definition site and call site are far apart in the source and having more than one source window would be confusing. The call site is a smaller, more specific fragment of the source than the definition site. Additionally, this fragment is directly surrounded by the call sites of the redexes of the siblings of the current reduction. The call sites of the siblings are also highlighted but not underlined like the current redex. When we change the current reduction via left or right cursor keys, only underlining changes in the source. So, given the state of the last screenshot, pressing the left cursor key yields (display shortened):

```
==== Hat-Explore 0.3 ==== Call 1/2 ==============================
insert 'r' "t" = "r"
---- Insert.hs ---- line 1 to 5 ----------------------------------
main = putStrLn (sort "sort")

sort :: Ord a => [a] -> [a]
sort [] = []
sort (x:xs) = insert x (sort xs)
```

In contrast, a move to the parent via cursor key up or to a child via cursor key down usually requires a complete change of the displayed source, because parents and children are further away. So pressing cursor key down yields:

```
==== Hat-Explore 0.3 ==== Call 1/1 ==============================
'o' <= 'r' = True
---- Insert.hs ---- line 6 to 9 ----------------------------------

insert :: Ord a => a -> [a] -> [a]
insert x [] = [x]
insert x (y:ys) = if x <= y then x : ys else y : (insert x ys)
```

Pressing cursor key up once returns to the last but one screen. Pressing cursor key up again yields:

```
==== Hat-Explore 0.3 ==== Call 1/2 ==============================
sort "ort" = "o"
---- Insert.hs ---- line 4 to 7 ----------------------------------
sort [] = []
sort (x:xs) = insert x (sort xs)

insert :: Ord a => a -> [a] -> [a]
```

The call site of a parent or child can be in a different module. HAT-EXPLORE lazily loads a module source when it is needed and displays it.

4   A Stack for Context

Experience shows that after some navigation we still often lose orientation. We know the call site of the current reduction, but a single call site is possibly used very often in a computation. More contextual information about the current reduction is needed. So a stack of parents is added to the display of HAT-EXPLORE. It shows the descendants chain of reductions from `main = {IO}` down to the current reduction as last element. Every time we move down to a child, this child is pushed on the stack; every time we move up to a parent, an element is popped from the stack. Hence the stack is displayed upside down, with the top element in the bottom line.

```
==== Hat-Explore 1.0 ==== Call 1/2 =============================
  1. main = {IO}
  2. sort "sort" = "os"
  3. sort "ort" = "o"
  4. insert 'o' "r" = "o"
---- Insert.hs ---- line 3 to 9 -----------------------------------
sort :: Ord a => [a] -> [a]
sort [] = []
sort (x:xs) = insert x (sort xs)

insert :: Ord a => a -> [a] -> [a]
insert x [] = [x]
insert x (y:ys) = if x <= y then x : ys else y : (insert x ys)
```

In practice reductions are much larger than in the small sorting example; a single reduction may cover several lines. Hence only a small number of reductions can be shown at a time. Experience shows that in most cases the last few reductions are sufficient for orientation in the EDT.

5 Source-Based Algorithmic Debugging

HAT-EXPLORE still supports algorithmic debugging. We can declare if the current reduction is correct or incorrect with respect to our intentions and also change and take back any previous such declaration. The tool uses several colours for highlighting: correct reductions are green, incorrect ones are yellow, unknown/undeclared ones are blue. When the tool identifies a reduction as faulty, it is highlighted in red.

Let us work step by step through an example session for the faulty insertion sort program. The tool starts with the reduction of `main`.

```
==== Hat-Explore 2.00 ==== Call 1/1 ============================
  1. main = {IO}


---- Insert.hs ---- lines 1 to 3 ---------------------------------
main = putStrLn (sort "sort")

sort :: Ord a => [a] -> [a]
```

We cannot say if this reduction is correct, but only press cursor down to look at the children:

```
==== Hat-Explore 2.00 ==== Call 1/2 =============================
  1. main = {IO}
  2. putStrLn "os" = {IO}

---- Insert.hs ---- lines 1 to 3 --------------------------------
main = putStrLn ( sort "sort" )

sort :: Ord a => [a] -> [a]
```

The first child is a reduction of a trusted function and hence assumed to be correct. So we press cursor right to look at the second child:

```
==== Hat-Explore 2.00 ==== Call 2/2 =============================
  1. main = {IO}
  2. sort "sort" = "os"

---- Insert.hs ---- lines 1 to 3 --------------------------------
main = putStrLn ( sort "sort" )

sort :: Ord a => [a] -> [a]
```

This reduction disagrees with our intentions and hence we press 'w' to declare the reduction as wrong:

```
==== Hat-Explore 2.00 ==== Call 2/2 =============================
  1. main = {IO}
  2. sort "sort" = "os"

---- Insert.hs ---- lines 1 to 3 --------------------------------
main = putStrLn ( sort "sort" )

sort :: Ord a => [a] -> [a]
```

To find out why the reduction is wrong we have to look at the children, so we press cursor down:

```
==== Hat-Explore 2.00 ==== Call 1/2 =============================
  1. main = {IO}
  2. sort "sort" = "os"
  3. insert 's' "o" = "os"
---- Insert.hs ---- lines 3 to 5 --------------------------------
sort :: Ord a => [a] -> [a]
sort [] = []
sort (x:xs) = insert x (sort xs)
```

We press 'c' to declare the reduction as correct and then press cursor right to look at the second child:

```
==== Hat-Explore 2.00 ==== Call 2/2 =============================
  1. main = {IO}
  2. sort "sort" = "os"
  3. sort "ort" = "o"
---- Insert.hs ---- lines 3 to 5 --------------------------------
sort :: Ord a => [a] -> [a]
sort [] = []
sort (x:xs) = insert x ( sort xs )
```

We press 'w' to declare the reduction as wrong and then press cursor down to inquire further:

```
==== Hat-Explore 2.00 ==== Call 1/2 =============================
  2. sort "sort" = "os"
  3. sort "ort" = "o"
  4. insert 'o' "r" = "o"
---- Insert.hs ---- lines 3 to 5 --------------------------------
sort :: Ord a => [a] -> [a]
sort [] = []
sort (x:xs) = insert x (sort xs)
```

We press 'w' to declare the reduction as wrong:

```
==== Hat-Explore 2.00 ==== Call 1/2 =============================
  2. sort "sort" = "os"
  3. sort "ort" = "o"
  4. insert 'o' "r" = "o"
---- Insert.hs ---- lines 3 to 5 --------------------------------
sort :: Ord a => [a] -> [a]
sort [] = []
sort (x:xs) = insert x ( sort xs )
```

So the reduction `insert 'o' "r" = "o"` is faulty. We have located the fault, it must be in the definition of `insert`. If we are not convinced, we can still press cursor down to see that `insert 'o' "r" = "o"` has only a single child, a reduction of a trusted function, which is assumed to be correct:

```
==== Hat-Explore 2.00 ==== Call 1/1 =============================
  3. sort "ort" = "o"
  4. insert 'o' "r" = "o"
  5. 'o' <= 'r' = True
---- Insert.hs ---- lines 7 to 9 --------------------------------
insert :: Ord a => a -> [a] -> [a]
insert x [] = [x]
insert x (y:ys) = if x <= y then x : ys else y : (insert x ys)
```

Declaring the (in)correctness of the current reduction is separate from navigation; it does not automatically navigate to a new reduction. Thus we are free to declare (in)correctness of reductions in any order. In practice it is often much easier to recognise an incorrect reduction than being sure that a reduction is correct. HAT-EXPLORE allows us to look at all children of a redex, determine that one of them is incorrect, and continue exploring that reduction, without having to consider the correctness of its siblings. We might not even rely on algorithmic debugging at all but just use declarations of (in)correctness as memory hints.

6   Program Slicing

Algorithmic debugging is based on the principle that if a node of the EDT is incorrect, then a faulty node must be amongst this node and its descendants, that is, the bug is in that sub-EDT of the EDT. If a sub-EDT of this sub-EDT has a correct node as root, that sub-EDT can be subtracted, the faulty node must be in the remaining sub-EDT. During algorithmic debugging the faulty sub-EDT is cut smaller and smaller, until it is reduced to a single node, the faulty node. HAT-EXPLORE marks the definition of the function reduced in the faulty node. However, that happens only rather late, after the faulty node has been identified. So in addition, HAT-EXPLORE can mark the definitions of all functions that are reduced in the nodes of the current faulty sub-EDT. These definitions comprise the faulty slice.

In the example session of the previous section a faulty slices is marked in *italics*. When sort "sort" = "os" is declared as wrong, the definition of sort and insert become the faulty slice. When insert 'o' "r" = "o" is declared as wrong, the definition of sort is subtracted from the faulty slice, leaving only the definition of insert.

While we declare nodes as correct or incorrect, the faulty sub-EDT and thus the slice of definitions that must contain a fault keep shrinking. The shrinking of the faulty slice shows us that we are making progress, it may quickly exclude large parts of the program, possibly parts that had been wrongly suspected, and when the faulty slice has become small we may spot the fault straight away without even having to continue algorithmic debugging to its end. While traversing an EDT we often skip declaring the correctness of a node; for example, because it might be hard (large input or output) or impossible (values of abstract data types) to determine. Figure 4 shows a partially annotated EDT where the nodes of the faulty sub-EDT are marked.

A faulty sub-EDT of a partially annotated EDT is defined as a minimal connected subgraph such that for any completion of the annotation the sub-EDT contains a faulty node. So an unannotated EDT has no faulty sub-EDT, because all nodes might be correct. In general an annotated EDT can have several (disjoint) faulty sub-EDTs. HAT-EXPLORE marks the faulty sub-EDT that contains the currently viewed node or, if the current node is outside of any faulty sub-EDT, the next faulty sub-EDT above the current node.

7   Smaller Faulty Slices and Code Coverage

The faulty slice can be made smaller without additional input from us. Keeping the faulty sub-EDT unchanged, we can determine a smaller faulty slice. When

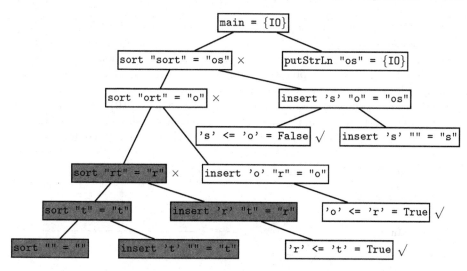

Fig. 4. A Faulty Sub-EDT

the faulty sub-EDT contains a reduction $f \dots = \dots$, it is not necessary to add the whole definition of function f to the faulty slice. For a specific reduction usually only parts of the definition body of the reduced function are evaluated because of pattern matching, conditionals and lazy evaluation. The fault can only be in that part of the definition that was actually evaluated for that particular reduction. Evaluated parts of the definition are the call sites of the children of the node plus demanded constants, data constructor applications and literals.[1] HAT-EXPLORE optionally only shows this smaller faulty slice. In our example program the "else" branch was never evaluated for the current, incorrect reduction.

```
==== Hat-Explore 2.03 ==== Call 2/2 | faulty slice | executed ===
1. main = {IO}
2. sort "sort" = "os"
3. sort "ort" = "o"
---- Insert.hs ---- line 3 to 9 -----------------------------------
sort :: Ord a => [a] -> [a]
sort [] = []
sort (x:xs) = insert x ( sort xs )

insert :: Ord a => a -> [a] -> [a]
insert x [] = [x]
insert x (y:ys) = if x <= y then x : ys else y : (insert x ys)
```

---

[1] If a constant is evaluated, it is impossible to determine if it was demanded for the currently considered reduction or a different part of the computation, because constants are shared. For most data constructor applications and literals, the entry in the HAT trace contains no indication if they were ever demanded in the computation. To be on the safe side, in all such cases the expression has to be included in the slice, if the surrounding expression construct is included.

Unfortunately it is no longer true that the fault has to be within the faulty slice. The fault may also be within the patterns on the left-hand-sides of the defining equations. [2] The fault might even be that an equation that should be there is missing. This last possibility cannot be expressed well by marking any slice at all.

By declaring the root reduction of the EDT, `main = {IO}`, as incorrect and asking HAT-EXPLORE to mark only the evaluated faulty slice, we can obtain the slice of the program that was evaluated at all during the whole computation:

```
==== Hat-Explore 2.03 ==== Call 1/1 | faulty slice | executed ===
  1. main = {IO}


---- Insert.hs ---- line 1 to 9 ----------------------------------
main = putStrLn (sort "sort")

sort :: Ord a => [a] -> [a]
sort [] = []
sort (x:xs) = insert x (sort xs)

insert :: Ord a => a -> [a] -> [a]
insert x [] = [x]
insert x (y:ys) = if x <= y then x : ys else y : (insert x ys)
```

So HAT-EXPLORE can serve as a code coverage tool.

8   Trusting

HAT supports a notion of trusting modules. The computation of these modules is not traced [3]. By default all Haskell standard libraries are trusted. The reduction of a trusted function is still recorded in the trace. For example, `length "hi" = 2` may be recorded, but not its recursive call `length "i" = 1`. So leafs of the EDT can be reductions of trusted functions. HAT-EXPLORE assumes by default that these reductions are correct.

Trusted functions can be higher-order and the functional arguments may be normal untrusted functions [10, 5], for example `map myInc [1,2,3] = [2,3,4]`. In that case the reduction of the trusted function can have children, namely the reductions of the passed untrusted functions. So `map myInc [1,2,3] = [2,3,4]` has the children `myInc 1 = 2, myInc 2 = 3` and `myInc 3 = 4`. In general, trusting causes parts of an EDT to be "cut out", even out of the middle of

---
[2] The Hat trace does not include any information on the pattern matching process. For an unsuccessful match it cannot be determined which parts of a pattern were used and exactly where matching failed. The trace has no information on locations of patterns in the source. Nonetheless, HAT works fine for computations that abort with a pattern match failure, as Section 10 demonstrates.

the tree. If a trusted reduction has children, it cannot assumed to be correct by default.

The children of trusted higher-order functions have call sites within trusted modules. Displaying these call sites would contradict the idea of a trusted module whose implementation is irrelevant.[3] So when the current reduction is the child of a trusted reduction, HAT-EXPLORE highlights the call site of the trusted parent instead of the child; it does so in a different style to indicate the different situation. The children of such a reduction without call site are again reductions with call site. So there is no danger of us losing orientation because we might have to make a long sequence of navigation steps without highlighting of call sites.

```
==== Hat-Explore 2.03 ==== Call 2/4 | faulty slice | executed ===
 1. main = {IO}
 2. sort "sort" = "os"
 3. foldr insert [] "sort" = "os"
 4. insert 'r' "t" = "r"

---- FoldrInsert.hs ---- line 3 to 9 -----------------------------
sort :: Ord a => [a] -> [a]
sort xs = foldr insert [] xs

insert :: Ord a => a -> [a] -> [a]
insert x [] = [x]
insert x (y:ys) = if x <= y then x : ys else y : (insert x ys)
```

9   Constants

A constant definition, such as `nats = [0..]`, has to be handled specially in the construction of an EDT. In a computation the definition body is only evaluated once and the value is shared by all calls (i.e. uses) of the constant in the program. The algorithmic debugger Freja [5] does not include the reduction of a constant at its call site, but produces a forest of EDTs, one EDT per constant definition (the definition of `main` is a constant definition). This approach would complicate free navigation. Hence in HAT-EXPLORE there is only a single EDT with the EDT of a constant inserted at its call sites. The EDT of the constant is shared by all call sites, so that the EDT is no longer a tree but a directed graph. Navigation into the EDT of a constant is natural. Where to go back up is also uniquely identified by the information in the stack.

Because constant definitions may be (mutually) recursive, the EDT may be cyclic. Algorithmic debugging only works for trees or acyclic graphs. It is currently the responsibility of the user to be aware that algorithmic debugging may not be able to locate a faulty reduction within the computation of mutually recursive functions. The faulty slice is still correct, but it may never shrink further than a set of mutually recursive definitions.

---

[3] Hence the HAT trace also does not contain any such source location information.

10   Other Starting Points

Normally HAT-EXPLORE starts with the reduction of `main`. Although paths through the EDT are only logarithmic in the size of the tree, a reduction of interest may still be far away from the root.

Other viewing tools such as HAT-TRAIL and HAT-OBSERVE may give quicker access to a reduction of interest. It was simple to extend these tools so that we can directly switch from one of them to HAT-EXPLORE, starting at the reduction that we just investigated in the other tool.

Experience shows that faults are often not far (within the EDT) from the observed error. Hence the feature of HAT-TRAIL, to start directly at the reduction that raised a runtime error, has been added to HAT-EXPLORE. A slightly modified version of our insertion sort causes a pattern match failure. HAT-EXPLORE starts as follows, displaying the error value as _|_ (bottom):

```
==== Hat-Explore 2.03 ==== Call 1/2 | faulty slice | complete ===
 4. sort "rt" = _|_
 5. sort "t" = _|_
 6. insert 't' [] = _|_
---- Insert.hs ---- line 1 to 9 --------------------------------
sort :: Ord a => [a] -> [a]
sort [] = []
sort (x:xs) = insert x (sort xs)

insert :: Ord a => a -> [a] -> [a]
insert x (y:ys) = if x <= y then x : ys else y : (insert x ys)
```

11   Implementation

HAT-EXPLORE has been implemented in about 1000 lines of Haskell. It also uses a library for accessing the trace that is shared with other viewing tools.

The Hat trace is a complex graph of expression components. The reconstruction of an EDT from this structure is described in [13]. For the efficiency of HAT-EXPLORE it is important that a small part of an EDT can be constructed easily from reading only a small part of the trace. So both memory and time costs for the construction of the small part of an EDT that is demanded by the user in a single interaction step is independent of the generally huge size of the trace. Only determining the faulty slice is expensive. It requires traversing the whole faulty sub-EDT in the trace. Hence the user can turn off this feature.

The algorithmically most complex part of HAT-EXPLORE is the handling of source slices. A slice is a set of source locations, where a location consists of start line and column and end line and column. HAT-EXPLORE comprises an abstract data type of slices with several functions for combining and subtracting slices. Slices are used to highlight parts of the source while excluding subexpressions. In an extreme case an application has to be highlighted, without highlighting its function and arguments. The slice for highlighting can be obtained by subtracting the locations of the subexpressions from the location of the whole application. In the case of an application only the space between the function and the arguments may remain in the slice.

To support HAT-EXPLORE, HAT required two extensions: Originally the trace contained for each recorded expression and each defined function the filename, line and column where it starts in the source. Now HAT records a full location that also includes the line and column at which such an expression or definition ends. The lexer and parser had to be modified and the abstract syntax tree slightly extended. Second, now a trusted reduction in the trace has an explicit list of pointers to its children. In the past, HAT-DETECT used an incomplete approximation algorithm to determine children; to find all children for certain, a time consuming search through most of the trace would have been required. Only the definition of a single combinator in the HAT library of tracing combinators [3] had to be modified. Both extensions slightly changed the trace file format, but only few changes in a library for accessing the trace were needed to make all previously existing HAT viewers work with the file format. Overall, both extensions only needed a small number of changes to HAT and benefit other viewing tools besides HAT-EXPLORE.

HAT-EXPLORE has a simple textual user interface based on text interleaved with ANSI escape sequences for various forms of highlighting. This user interface is portable and was easy to implement. Nonetheless it has its limitations; in particular, different highlighting of nested expressions yields output that is hard to read. For this purpose multiple underlining similar to the old redex trail browser [11] would be more suitable.

12   Related Work

Using HAT-EXPLORE reminds one of using a *classical stepping debugger* for an imperative programming language, such as DDD[3]. The debugger highlights the current execution line. The user can perform one execution step, moving to a line which was called from the previous line. Alternatively, the user can go to the next line, skipping the execution of all function calls. So the source-based navigation model of HAT-EXPLORE has already been proven useful for imperative languages. Users of these stepping debuggers can build on previous experience when moving to HAT-EXPLORE. While the user steps through the computation HAT-EXPLORE also provides with each function call its result. In a side-effect free functional language the result fully describes the semantics of the function call. Thus it is far easier to locate the faulty program part than it is in a stepping debugger for an imperative language.

Algorithmic debugging [9] has been the starting point for HAT-EXPLORE. There exist several algorithmic debuggers for lazy functional languages [5, 13, 8]. They all allow more direct navigation through the EDT then via "yes"/"no" an-

---

[3] http://www.gnu.org/software/ddd/

swers but they do not encourage free navigation. They do not use the source.

Program slicing is a well-known technique for analysing and particularly debugging programs [12]. The faulty slice of HAT-EXPLORE (both with full definitions and with evaluated expressions only) is a dynamic slice in that sense, with the reduction of the root node as *slicing criterion*. However, whereas program slicing is based on the control and data flow of a computation, the EDT expresses the control and data flow of a computation only in a limited form.

In [7] a slicing method for a core of the Haskell-like functional logic language Curry is described. Although the slicing criterion is also based on a reduction, these slices are not related to EDTs and the authors do not claim that a fault has to be within a slice. Their trace structure [1], although also called redex trail, differs in several points from the HAT trace. In particular, parent pointers have a different meaning; they do not point to an EDT parent and hence it is doubtful that an EDT can be reconstructed from this trace structure.

13   Conclusions and Future Work

HAT-EXPLORE is a new trace viewing tool for the HAT system that enables us to navigate freely and intuitively through the trace of a Haskell 98 program. The display of the source together with a stack of reductions for the context give good orientation. The tool combines algorithmic debugging with program slicing and the user interface of a traditional stepping debugger. Initial informal feedback from users has been positive.

The HAT system gives important insights into the internals of computations of Haskell programs. Nonetheless there is still much work to do. Features of several existing HAT viewers could be combined. In particular, it is possible to merge HAT-TRAIL and HAT-EXPLORE. However, the resulting tool might be too complex to use. Alternatively, HAT-TRAIL could be extended by source-based orientation facilities. HAT does not support all types of programs well. For example, tracing of IO intensive programs is limited because the IO monad is just treated as an abstract data type with unknown values; some higher-order programs rely on a complex control flow that is hard to visualise adequately.

This paper demonstrates that it is relatively easy to extend the HAT system by a new viewing tool for which it was not designed originally. HAT provides a modular framework for further exploration of tracing systems.

Acknowledgements

This work relies heavily on previous work on the Haskell tracer HAT by Colin Runciman, Malcolm Wallace and Thorsten Brehm. I also thank the four referees for their constructive comments.

References

1. Bernd Braßel, Michael Hanus, Frank Huch, and German Vidal. A semantics for tracing declarative multi-paradigm programs. In *Proceedings of the 6th ACM-SIGPLAN International Conference on Principles and Practice of Declarative Programming*, pages 179–190. ACM Press, 2004.
2. Olaf Chitil, Colin Runciman, and Malcolm Wallace. Freja, Hat and Hood — A comparative evaluation of three systems for tracing and debugging lazy functional programs. In Markus Mohnen and Pieter Koopman, editors, *Implementation of Functional Languages, 12th International Workshop, IFL 2000*, LNCS 2011, pages 176–193. Springer, 2001.
3. Olaf Chitil, Colin Runciman, and Malcolm Wallace. Transforming Haskell for tracing. In *Proceedings of the 14th International Workshop on Implementation of Functional Languages (IFL 2002)*, LNCS 2670, pages 165–181, 2003.
4. Koen Claessen, Colin Runciman, Olaf Chitil, John Hughes, and Malcolm Wallace. Testing and tracing lazy functional programs using QuickCheck and Hat. In *4th Summer School in Advanced Functional Programming*, LNCS 2638, pages 59–99, August 2003.
5. Henrik Nilsson. *Declarative Debugging for Lazy Functional Languages*. PhD thesis, Linköping, Sweden, May 1998.
6. Henrik Nilsson and Jan Sparud. The evaluation dependence tree as a basis for lazy functional debugging. *Automated Software Engineering: An International Journal*, 4(2):121–150, April 1997.
7. C. Ochoa, J. Silva, and G. Vidal. Dynamic Slicing Based on Redex Trails. In *Proc. of the ACM SIGPLAN 2004 Symposium on Partial Evaluation and Program Manipulation (PEPM'04)*, pages 123–134. ACM Press, 2004.
8. B. Pope and Lee Naish. Practical aspects of declarative debugging in Haskell-98. In *Fifth ACM SIGPLAN Conference on Principles and Practice of Declarative Programming*, pages 230–240, 2003.
9. E. Y. Shapiro. *Algorithmic Program Debugging*. MIT Press, 1983.
10. Jan Sparud and Colin Runciman. Complete and partial redex trails of functional computations. In C. Clack, K. Hammond, and T. Davie, editors, *Selected papers from 9th Intl. Workshop on the Implementation of Functional Languages (IFL'97)*, pages 160–177. Springer LNCS Vol. 1467, September 1997.
11. Jan Sparud and Colin Runciman. Tracing lazy functional computations using redex trails. In H. Glaser, P. Hartel, and H. Kuchen, editors, *Proc. 9th Intl. Symposium on Programming Languages, Implementations, Logics and Programs (PLILP'97)*, pages 291–308. Springer LNCS Vol. 1292, September 1997.
12. Frank Tip. A survey of program slicing techniques. *Journal of programming languages*, 3:121–189, 1995.
13. Malcolm Wallace, Olaf Chitil, Thorsten Brehm, and Colin Runciman. Multiple-view tracing for Haskell: a new Hat. In *Preliminary Proceedings of the 2001 ACM SIGPLAN Haskell Workshop*, UU-CS-2001-23. Universiteit Utrecht, 2001. Final proceedings to appear in ENTCS 59(2).

Shrinking Reductions in SML.NET

Nick Benton[1], Andrew Kennedy[1], Sam Lindley[2], and Claudio Russo[1]

[1] Microsoft Research, Cambridge
{nick, akenn, crusso}@microsoft.com
[2] LFCS, University of Edinburgh
Sam.Lindley@ed.ac.uk

Abstract. One performance-critical phase in the SML.NET compiler involves rewriting intermediate terms to monadic normal form and performing non-duplicating β-reductions. We present an imperative algorithm for this simplification phase, working with a mutable, pointer-based term representation, which significantly outperforms our existing functional algorithm. This is the first implementation and evaluation of a linear-time rewriting algorithm proposed by Appel and Jim.

1   Introduction

SML.NET [3,4] is a compiler for Standard ML that targets the .NET Common Language Runtime [7]. Like most other compilers for functional languages (e.g. GHC [10]), SML.NET is structured as the composition of a number of transformation phases on an intermediate representation of the user program. As SML.NET is a whole program compiler, the intermediate terms are typically rather large and good performance of the transformations is critical for usability.

Like MLj [5], SML.NET uses a monadic intermediate language (MIL) [2] that is similar to Moggi's computational metalanguage. Most of the phases in SML.NET perform specific transformations, such as closure conversion, arity raising or monomorphisation, and are run only once. In between several of these phases, however, is a general-purpose 'clean-up' pass called *simplify*. Running *simplify* puts the term into *monadic normal form* [6,8], which we have previously called *cc-normal form* and is essentially the same as *A normal form* or *administrative normal form* for CPS [8]. The *simplify* pass also performs *shrinking reductions*: β-reductions for functions, computations, products that always reduce the size of the term.

Appel and Jim [1] describe three algorithms for shrinking reductions. The first 'naïve' and second 'improved' algorithms both have quadratic worst-case time complexity, and the third 'imperative' algorithm is linear, but requires a mutable representation of terms. Appel and Jim did not implement the third algorithm, which does not integrate easily in a mainly-functional compiler. Both SML/NJ and SML.NET use the 'improved' algorithm, which is reasonably efficient in practice. Nevertheless, SML.NET spends a significant amount of time performing shrinking reductions. We have now implemented a variant of the imperative algorithm in SML.NET, and achieved significant speedups.

C. Grelck et al. (Eds.): IFL 2004, LNCS 3474, pp. 142–159, 2005.
© Springer-Verlag Berlin Heidelberg 2005

This paper makes several contributions. It gives the first implementation and benchmarks of the imperative algorithm in a real compiler. It extends the imperative algorithm to a richer language than considered by Appel and Jim. It introduces a 'one-pass' traversal strategy, giving a weak form of compositionality. An extended version of this work appears in the third author's PhD thesis [9].

2 Simplified MIL

For purposes of exposition we present a simplified version of MIL:

Atoms	$a, b ::= x \mid c$
Values	$v, w ::= a \mid \mathsf{pair}(a, b) \mid \mathsf{proj}_1(a) \mid \mathsf{proj}_2(a) \mid \mathsf{inj}_1(a) \mid \mathsf{inj}_2(a)$
Computations	$m, n, p ::= \mathsf{app}(a, b) \mid \mathsf{letfun}\ f(x)\ \mathsf{be}\ m\ \mathsf{in}\ n$
	$\mid \mathsf{val}(v) \mid \mathsf{let}\ x\ \mathsf{be}\ m\ \mathsf{in}\ n \mid \mathsf{case}\ a\ \mathsf{of}\ (x_1)n_1\ ;\ (x_2)n_2$

where variables are ranged over by f, g, x, y, z, and constants are ranged over by c. Note that the letfun construct binds a possibly recursive function.

We say that a reduction is a *shrinking* reduction if it always reduces the size of terms (counting the number of nodes). The most important reductions are given by the shrinking β-rules:

$(\to .\beta_0)$ $\mathsf{letfun}\ f(x)\ \mathsf{be}\ n\ \mathsf{in}\ m\ \longrightarrow\ m,$ $\qquad\qquad\qquad f \notin fv(m)$

$(\to .\beta_1)$ $\mathsf{letfun}\ f(x)\ \mathsf{be}\ m\ \mathsf{in}\ C[\mathsf{app}(f, a)]\ \longrightarrow\ C[m[x := a]],\ \ f \notin fv(C[\cdot], m, a)$

$(T.\beta_0)$ $\mathsf{let}\ x\ \mathsf{be}\ \mathsf{val}(v)\ \mathsf{in}\ m\ \longrightarrow\ m,$ $\qquad\qquad\qquad\quad x \notin fv(m)$

$(T.\beta_a)$ $\mathsf{let}\ x\ \mathsf{be}\ \mathsf{val}(a)\ \mathsf{in}\ m\ \longrightarrow\ m[x := a]$

$(\times.\beta)$ $\mathsf{let}\ y\ \mathsf{be}\ \mathsf{val}(\mathsf{pair}(a_1, a_2))\ \mathsf{in}\ C[\mathsf{proj}_i(y)]$
$\qquad\qquad \longrightarrow\ \mathsf{let}\ y\ \mathsf{be}\ \mathsf{val}(\mathsf{pair}(a_1, a_2))\ \mathsf{in}\ C[a_i]$

$(+.\beta)$ $\mathsf{let}\ y\ \mathsf{be}\ \mathsf{val}(\mathsf{inj}_i(a))$
$\qquad\ \ \mathsf{in}\ C[\mathsf{case}\ y\ \mathsf{of}\ (x_1)n_1\ ;\ (x_2)n_2]$
$\qquad\qquad \longrightarrow\ \mathsf{let}\ y\ \mathsf{be}\ \mathsf{val}(\mathsf{inj}_i(a))\ \mathsf{in}\ C[n_i[x_i := a]]$

We write R_β for the one-step reduction relation defined by the β-rules. The *simplify* transformation also performs commuting conversions. These ensure that bindings are explicitly sequenced, which enables further rewriting.

$(T.CC)$ $\mathsf{let}\ y\ \mathsf{be}\ (\mathsf{let}\ x\ \mathsf{be}\ m\ \mathsf{in}\ n)\ \mathsf{in}\ p$
$\qquad\qquad \longrightarrow\ \mathsf{let}\ x\ \mathsf{be}\ m\ \mathsf{in}\ \mathsf{let}\ y\ \mathsf{be}\ n\ \mathsf{in}\ p$

$(\to.CC)$ $\mathsf{let}\ y\ \mathsf{be}\ (\mathsf{letfun}\ f(x)\ \mathsf{be}\ m\ \mathsf{in}\ n)\ \mathsf{in}\ p$
$\qquad\qquad \longrightarrow\ \mathsf{letfun}\ f(x)\ \mathsf{be}\ m\ \mathsf{in}\ \mathsf{let}\ y\ \mathsf{be}\ n\ \mathsf{in}\ p$

$(+.CC)$ $\mathsf{let}\ y\ \mathsf{be}\ (\mathsf{case}\ a\ \mathsf{of}\ (x_1)n_1\ ;\ (x_2)n_1)\ \mathsf{in}\ m$
$\qquad\qquad \longrightarrow\ \mathsf{letfun}\ f(y)\ \mathsf{be}\ m\ \mathsf{in}\ \mathsf{case}\ a\ \mathsf{of}\ (x_1)\mathsf{let}\ y_1\ \mathsf{be}\ n_1\ \mathsf{in}\ \mathsf{app}(f, y_1)$
$\qquad\qquad\qquad\qquad\qquad\qquad\ ;\ (x_2)\mathsf{let}\ y_2\ \mathsf{be}\ n_2\ \mathsf{in}\ \mathsf{app}(f, y_2)$

We write R_{CC} for the one-step reduction relation defined by the CC-rules, and R for $R_\beta \cup R_{CC}$. Unlike the β rules, the commuting conversions are not actually shrinking reductions. However, $T.CC$ and $\rightarrow.CC$ do not change the size, whilst $+.CC$ gives only a constant increase in the size.

An alternative to the $+.CC$ rule is:

$(+.CC')$ let y be case a of $(x_1)n_1$; $(x_2)n_2$ in m

            $\longrightarrow$ case a of (x_1)let y_1 be n_1 in m_1 ; (x_2)let y_2 be n_2 in m_2

where y_1, y_2 are fresh, $m_i = m[y := y_i]$. This rule duplicates the term m and can exponentially increase the term's size. The $+.CC$ rule instead creates a single new abstraction, shared across both branches of the case, though this inhibits some further rewriting. We write R'_{CC} for the one-step relation defined by the CC-rules where $(+.CC)$ is replaced by $(+.CC')$, and R' for $R_\beta \cup R'_{CC}$.

Proposition 1. *R' is strongly-normalising.*

Proof. First, note that R_β is strongly-normalising as R_β-reduction strictly decreases the size of terms. We define two measures $|\cdot|_\beta$ and $|\cdot|_{cc}$ on terms:

$$|a|_\beta = 1 \qquad |\text{letfun } f(x) \text{ be } m \text{ in } n|_\beta = |m|_\beta + |n|_\beta + 1$$
$$|\text{proj}_i(a)|_\beta = |\text{inj}_i(a)|_\beta = 2 \qquad |\text{let } x \text{ be } m \text{ in } n|_\beta = |m|_\beta + |n|_\beta + 1$$
$$|\text{app}(a,b)|_\beta = |\text{pair}(a,b)|_\beta = 3 \qquad |\text{val}(v)|_\beta = |v|_\beta + 1$$
$$|\text{case } a \text{ of } (x_1)n_1 ; (x_2)n_2|_\beta = max(|n_1|_\beta, |n_2|_\beta) + 2$$

$$|a|_{cc} = 1 \qquad |\text{letfun } f(x) \text{ be } m \text{ in } n|_{cc} = |m|_{cc} + |n|_{cc} + 1$$
$$|\text{proj}_i(a)|_{cc} = |\text{inj}_i(a)|_{cc} = 2 \qquad |\text{let } x \text{ be } m \text{ in } n|_{cc} = |m|_{cc}^2 + |n|_{cc} + 1$$
$$|\text{app}(a,b)|_{cc} = |\text{pair}(a,b)|_{cc} = 3 \qquad |\text{val}(v)|_{cc} = |v|_{cc} + 1$$
$$|\text{case } a \text{ of } (x_1)n_1 ; (x_2)n_2|_{cc} = max(|n_1|_{cc}, |n_2|_{cc}) + 2$$

The lexicographic ordering $(|\cdot|_\beta, |\cdot|_{cc})$ is a measure for R'-reduction. Each shrinking β-reduction decreases $|.|_\beta$, whilst each CC-reduction decreases $|.|_{cc}$ and leaves $|.|_\beta$ unchanged. $\square$

Proposition 2. *R is strongly-normalising.*

The proof uses R'-reduction to simulate R-reduction. The full details are omitted, but the idea is that for any R-reduction a corresponding non-empty sequence of R'-reductions can be performed. Thus, given that all R'-reduction sequences are finite, all R-reduction sequences must also be finite. The proof is slightly complicated by the fact that no non-empty sequence of R'-reductions corresponds with the β-reduction of a function introduced by the $+.CC$ rule. A simple way of dealing with this is to count a $+.CC'$-reduction as two reductions.

Note that R-reductions are not confluent. The failure of confluence is due to the $(+.CC)$ rule. Replacing $(+.CC)$ with $(+.CC')$ does give a confluent system. Confluence can make reasoning about reductions easier, but we do not regard failure of confluence as a problem. In our case, preventing exponential growth in the size of terms is far more important.

3   Previous Work

Appel and Jim [1] considered a calculus which is equivalent to a sub-calculus of our simplified MIL. In our setting the reductions that their algorithms perform are equivalent to: $\rightarrow .\beta_1$-, $\times.\beta$-, $T.\beta_0$-, and a restriction of $\rightarrow .\beta_0$-reduction. Appel and Jim show that their calculus is confluent in the presence of these reductions, and other 'δ-rules' satisfying certain criteria.

The reductions rely on knowing the number of occurrences of a particular variable. The quadratic algorithms store this information in a table *Count* mapping variable names to their number of occurrences. Appel and Jim's naïve algorithm repeatedly (i) zeros the usage counts, (ii) performs a *census* pass over the whole term to update the usage counts and then (iii) traverses the term performing reductions on the basis of the information in *Count*, until there are no redexes remaining.

The improved algorithm, used in SML/NJ and SML.NET, dynamically updates the usage counts as reductions are performed. This allows more reductions to be performed on each pass, and only requires a full census to be performed once. The improved algorithm is better in practice, but both algorithms have worst-case time complexity $\Theta(n^2)$ where n is the size of the input term.

Appel and Jim's imperative algorithm runs in linear time and uses a pointer-based representation of terms which directly links all occurrences of a particular variable. This enables an efficient test to see if removing an occurrence will create any new redexes, and an efficient way of jumping to any such redexes. The algorithm first traverses the program tree collecting the set of all redexes. Then it repeatedly removes a redex from the set and reduces it in-place (possibly adding new redexes to the set), until none remain.

4   A Graph-Based Representation

Our imperative algorithm works with a mutable graph representation comprising a doubly-linked expression tree and a list of pairs of circular doubly-linked lists collecting all the recursive (respectively non-recursive) uses of each variable. Such graphs can naturally be presented pictorially as shown by the example in Fig. 1.

Figure 2 shows the β-reductions for functions in this pictorial form. We find the pictorial representation intuitively very useful, but awkward to reason with

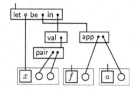

Fig. 1. Pictorial representation of let x be $\mathsf{app}(f, a)$ in $\mathsf{val}(\mathsf{pair}(x, x))$

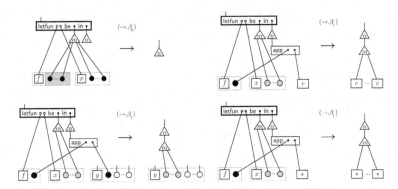

Fig. 2. Graph reductions

or use in presenting algorithms. Hence, like Appel and Jim, we will work with a more abstract structure comprising an expression tree and a collection of maps which capture the additional graphical structure between nodes of the tree.

The structure of expression trees is determined by the abstract syntax of simplified MIL. In order to capture mutability we use ML-style references. Each node of the expression tree is a reference cell. We call the entities which reference cells contain *objects*. Given a reference cell l, we write $!l$ to denote the object of l, and $l := u$ to denote the assignment of the object u to l.

Atoms	$!a, !b ::= r \mid c$
Values	$!v, !w ::= a \mid \mathsf{pair}(a, b) \mid \mathsf{proj}_1(a) \mid \mathsf{proj}_2(a) \mid \mathsf{inj}_1(a) \mid \mathsf{inj}_2(a)$
Computations	$!m, !n, !p ::= \mathsf{app}(a, b) \mid \mathsf{letfun}\ f(x)\ \mathsf{be}\ m\ \mathsf{in}\ n$
	$\mid \mathsf{val}(v) \mid \mathsf{let}\ x\ \mathsf{be}\ m\ \mathsf{in}\ n \mid \mathsf{case}\ a\ \mathsf{of}\ (x_1)n_1\ ;\ (x_2)n_2$
	$e ::= v \mid m \qquad d ::= e \mid x \mid r$

where f, g, x, y, z range over defining occurrences, and r, s, t over uses. We write $parent(e)$ for the parent of the node e. A distinguished sentinel node, *root*, marks the top of the expression tree. The object dead (omitted from the grammar) is used to indicate a *dead* node. If a node is dead then it has no parent. The *root* node is the parent of the proper expression tree and is always dead. We define $children(e)$ of an expression node to be the set of nodes appearing in $!e$.

Initially both *parent* and *children* are entirely determined by the expression tree. However, in our algorithm we take advantage of the *parent* map in order to classify expression nodes as active or inactive. We ensure that the following invariant is maintained: for all expression nodes e, either

- e is active: $parent(d) = e$, for all $d \in children(e)$;
- e is inactive: $!(parent(d)) = $ dead for all $d \in children(e)$; or
- e is dead: $!e = $ dead.

We define *splicing* as the operation which takes one subtree m and substitutes it in place of another subtree n. The subtree m is removed from the expression

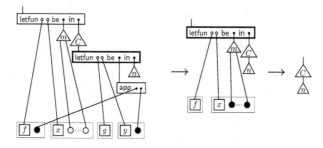

Fig. 3. Triggering non-local reductions

tree and then reintroduced in place of n. The parent map is adjusted accordingly for the children of m. We define *splicing a copy* as the corresponding operation which leaves the original copy of m in place. The operation $\lceil q \rceil$ returns a new node containing q, with parent *root*. When embedded in an enclosing node $e[\lceil q \rceil]$, the parent of $\lceil q \rceil$ is e. In patterns, $\lceil \cdot \rceil$ matches against the contents of a node.

The *def-use* maps abstract the structures used for representing occurrences:

- $def(r)$ gives the defining occurrence of the use r.
- $non\text{-}rec\text{-}uses(x)$ is the set of non-recursive uses of the defining occurrence x.
- $rec\text{-}uses(x)$ is the set of recursive uses of the defining occurrence x.

In the real implementation occurrences are held in a pair of doubly-linked circular lists, such that each pair of lists intersects at a defining occurrence. We find it convenient to overload the maps to be defined over all occurrences and also define some additional maps:

$$non\text{-}rec\text{-}uses(r) = non\text{-}rec\text{-}uses(def(r))$$

$$rec\text{-}uses(r) = rec\text{-}uses(def(r)) \qquad def(x) = x$$

$$occurrences(r) = uses(r) \cup \{def(r)\} \quad uses(r) = non\text{-}rec\text{-}uses(r) \cup rec\text{-}uses(r)$$

None of these additional definitions affects the implementation.

The graph structure allows constant time movement up and down the expression tree in the normal way, but also allows constant time non-local movement via the occurrence lists. For example, consider the dead-function eliminations:

$$\text{letfun } f(x) \text{ be } m \text{ in } C[\text{letfun } g(y) \text{ be app}(f, y) \text{ in } n]$$

$$\longrightarrow_{(\to.\beta_0)} \text{letfun } f(x) \text{ be } m \text{ in } C[n] \qquad \longrightarrow_{(\to.\beta_0)} \quad C[n]$$

where $f, g \notin fv(C, n)$, illustrated in Fig. 3. After one reduction, g is dead, so its definition can be deleted, removing the only use of f. Since this use is connected to its defining occurrence, we can detect that the definition of f is now dead. The defining occurrence is connected to its parent (*root*) so the new dead-function redex can be reduced under the parent.

5   A One-Pass Algorithm

In contrast to Appel and Jim's imperative algorithm, the algorithm we have implemented operates in one-pass. Essentially, the one-pass algorithm performs a depth-first traversal of the expression tree, reducing redexes on the way back up the tree. Of course, these reductions may trigger further reductions elsewhere in the tree. By carefully deactivating parts of the tree, we are able to control the reduction order and limit the testing required for new redexes. Here is an outline of our one-pass imperative algorithm:

$$
\begin{aligned}
contract(e) = \ & reduceCCs(e) \\
& deactivate(e) \\
& \text{apply } contract \text{ to children of } e \\
& reactivate(e) \\
& reduce(\text{true}, e) \\
reduce(initial, e) = \ & \text{if } e \text{ is a redex then} \\
& \quad \text{reduce } e \text{ in place} \\
& \quad \text{perform further reductions triggered by reducing } e
\end{aligned}
$$

The operation $reduceCCs(e)$ performs commuting conversions on the way down the tree. The order of commuting conversions can have a significant effect on code quality, a poor choice leading to many jumps to jumps. We have found that the approach of doing them on the way down works well in practice (although the contract algorithm would still be valid without the call to $reduceCCs$).

$reduceCCs(e) = $ case $!e$ of
    (let y be e' in p) $\Rightarrow$
            if $reduceCC(e, y, e', p) \neq \emptyset$ then $reduceCCs(e)$ else skip
    (_) $\Rightarrow$ skip

$reduceCC(e, y, e', p) = $ case $!e'$ of
    (letfun $f(x)$ be m in n) $\Rightarrow$
        splice $\lceil$let y be n in $p\rceil$ in place of e'
        splice $\lceil$letfun $f(x)$ be m in $e'\rceil$ in place of e
        return $\{e'\}$
    (let x be m in n) $\Rightarrow$
        splice $\lceil$let y be n in $p\rceil$ in place of e'
        splice $\lceil$let x be m in $e'\rceil$ in place of e
        return $\{e'\}$
    (case a of $(x_1)n_1 ; (x_2)n_2$) $\Rightarrow$
        splice $\lceil$let y_1 be n_1 in $\lceil$app$(f, y_1)\rceil\rceil$ in place of n_1
        splice $\lceil$let y_2 be n_2 in $\lceil$app$(f, y_2)\rceil\rceil$ in place of n_2
        splice $\lceil$letfun $f(y)$ be p in $\lceil$case a of $(x_1)n_1 ; (x_2)n_2\rceil\rceil$
        in place of e (where f is fresh)
        return $\{n_1, n_2\}$
    (_) $\Rightarrow$ return $\emptyset$

Note that commuting conversions can also be triggered by other reductions. The return value for *reduceCC* will be used in the definition of *reduce* in order to catch reductions which are triggered by applying commuting conversions.

deactivate(e) deactivates e: *parent*(d) is set to dead for every $d \in children(e)$.
reactivate(e) reactivates e: *parent*(d) is set to e for every $d \in children(e)$.

Deactivating nodes on the way down prevents reductions from being triggered above the current node in the tree. On the way back up the nodes are reactivated, allowing any new redexes to be reduced. Because subterms are known to be normalised, fewer tests are needed for new redexes. Consider, for example:

$$\text{let } y \text{ be (let } x \text{ be } m \text{ in } n) \text{ in } p \longrightarrow_{T.CC} \text{let } x \text{ be } m \text{ in let } y \text{ be } n \text{ in } p$$

Because we know that let x be m in n is in normal form, m cannot be of the form let($\ldots$), letfun($\ldots$), case($\ldots$) or val($\ldots$). Hence, it is not necessary to check whether let x be m in let y be n in p is a redex. (Of course, let y be n in p may still be a redex, and indeed exposing such redexes is one of the main purposes of performing CC-reduction.)

5.1   Reduction

The *reduce* function is the heart of the algorithm. Rather than maintaining a global 'work-list' of redexes, as Appel and Jim do, *reduce*(*initial*, e) reduces any new redexes created inside e (but none that are created above e in the expression tree). *initial* is boolean flag indicating whether this call to reduce originates from *contract* rather than some other recursive call. If *reduce*(*initial*, e) is invoked on an expression node which is not a redex, then no action is performed. The *reduce* function also returns a boolean to indicate whether a reduction took place. As we shall see, this is necessary in order to detect the triggering of new reductions. We now expand the definition of *reduce*.

$$reduce(initial, e) = \text{case } !e \text{ of}$$
$$(\text{letfun } f(x) \text{ be } m \text{ in } n) \Rightarrow$$
$$\quad \text{if } non\text{-}rec\text{-}uses(f) = \emptyset \text{ then}$$
$$\quad\quad \text{splice } n \text{ in place of } e$$
$$\quad\quad reduceOccs(cleanExp(m))$$
$$\quad\quad \text{return true}$$
$$\quad \text{else if } rec\text{-}uses(f) = \emptyset \text{ and } non\text{-}rec\text{-}uses(f) = \{f'\} \text{ then}$$
$$\quad\quad \text{let } focus = parent(parent(f'))$$
$$\quad\quad \text{case } !focus \text{ of}$$
$$\quad\quad (\text{app}(f', a) \Rightarrow$$
$$\quad\quad\quad \text{splice } n \text{ in place of } e$$
$$\quad\quad\quad \text{splice } m \text{ in place of } focus$$
$$\quad\quad\quad \text{let } (occs, redexes) = substAtom(x, a)$$
$$\quad\quad\quad reduceOccs(occs \cup cleanExp(a))$$
$$\quad\quad\quad reduceRedexes(redexes)$$

```
                    return true
                (_) ⇒ return false
            else return false
    (let x be ⌈val(v)⌉ in n) ⇒
        if uses(x) = ∅ then
                splice n in place of e
                reduceOccs(cleanExp(parent(v)))
                return true
        else if v is an atom a then
                splice n in place of e
                let (occs, redexes) = substAtom(x, a)
                reduceOccs(occs ∪ cleanExp(parent(a)))
                reduceRedexes(redexes)
                return true
        else case !v of
        (pair(a, b)) ⇒
                if initial then
                        let redexes = reduceProjections(e, x, a, b, uses(x))
                        if redexes = ∅ then return false
                        else
                                reduceRedexes(redexes)
                                reduce(false, e)
                                return true
                else return false
        (injᵢ(a)) ⇒
                if initial then
                        let (occs, redexes) = reduceCases(e, x, i, a, uses(x))
                        if redexes = ∅ then return false
                        else
                                reduceOccs(occs)
                                reduceRedexes(redexes)
                                reduce(false, e)
                                return true
                else return false
        (_) ⇒ return false
    (let y be e' in p) ⇒
        let redexes = reduceCC(e, y, e', p)
        for e'' ∈ redexes do reduce(false, e'')
        return true
    (_) ⇒ return false
```

The first case covers β-reductions on functions, with two sub-cases:

- $(\rightarrow .\beta_0)$ If the function is dead, its definition is removed, the continuation spliced in place of e, and any uses within the dead body deleted, possibly triggering new reductions.

- $(\to .\beta_1)$ If the function has one occurrence, which is non-recursive, it is inlined. The continuation of e is spliced in place of e, the function body is inlined with the argument substituted for the parameter, and the argument deleted. Substitution may trigger further reductions.

The second case covers β-reductions on computations as well as some instances of β-reduction on products and sums. It is divided into four sub-cases.

- $(T.\beta_0)$ If a value is dead, then its definition can be removed. The continuation is spliced in place of e. Then the uses inside the dead function body are deleted, possibly triggering new reductions.
- $(T.\beta_a)$ If a value is atomic, then it can be inlined. First the continuation of e is spliced in place of e. Then the atom is substituted for the bound variable. Finally the atom is deleted.
- $(\times.\beta)$ If a pair is bound to a variable x, and this is the initial visit of e, then any projections of x are reduced. For efficiency, new projections will subsequently be reduced as and when they are created.
- $(+.\beta)$ This follows exactly the same pattern as $\times.\beta$-reduction. The only difference is that the reduction itself is more complex, so can trigger new reductions in different ways.

The third case deals with commuting conversions.

The algorithm ensures that the current reduction is complete before any new reductions are triggered. Potential new redexes created by the current reduction are encoded and executed after the current reduction has completed.

$reduceUp(e)$ reduces above e as far as possible:

$$reduceUp(e) = \text{if } reduce(\text{false}, e) \text{ then } reduceUp(parent(e)) \text{ else skip}$$

$reduceRedexes$ reduces a set of expression redexes, whilst $reduceOccs$ reduces a set of occurrence redexes:

$$reduceRedexes(redexes) = \text{for each } e \in redexes \text{ do } reduceUp(e)$$
$$reduceOccs(xs) = \text{for each } r \in xs \text{ do}$$
$$\quad\text{if } isSmall(r) \text{ then } reduceUp(parent(def(r))) \text{ else skip}$$
$$isSmall(r) = r \notin \text{rec-uses}(r) \text{ and } |\text{non-rec-uses}(r)| \le 1$$

$cleanExp(e)$ removes all occurrences and subexpressions inside e and returns a set of occurrence redexes.

```
cleanExp(e) = case !e of
    (r) ⇒
        e := dead
        return deleteUse(r)
    (letfun f(x) be m in n) ⇒
        e, f, x := dead
        return cleanExp(m) ∪ cleanExp(n)
    (app(a, b)) ⇒
        e := dead
        return cleanExp(a) ∪ cleanExp(b)
    ...
```

Remark. Marking nodes as dead ensures that unnecessary work is not done on dead redexes. A crucial difference between the imperative algorithms and the improved quadratic one is that reduction in the former immediately detects new redexes, whereas the improved quadratic algorithm only detects new (non-local) redexes on a subsequent traversal.

deleteUse(r) removes r and returns a set of 0 or 1 occurrence redexes:

> *deleteUse*$(r) =$
>> if r is already dead then return $\emptyset$
>> let $s = nextOcc(r)$
>> $uses(s) := uses(s) - \{r\}$
>> return $\{s\}$

> *nextOcc*$(r) =$
>> let $x = def(r)$
>> if r is non-recursive then return $s \in (non\text{-}rec\text{-}uses(x) \cup \{x\}) - \{r\}$
>> else if r is recursive then return $s \in (rec\text{-}uses(x) \cup \{x\}) - \{r\}$

reduceProjections(e, x, a_1, a_2, xs) reduces projections indexed by xs. e is an expression node of the form let x be val(pair(a_1, a_2)) in m, and xs is a subset of the uses of x.

> *reduceProjections*$(e, x, a_1, a_2, xs) =$
>> let *redexes* $:= \emptyset$
>> for each $s \in xs$ do
>>> let *focus* $= parent(parent(s))$
>>> case !*focus* of
>>> (proj$_i(s)$) $\Rightarrow$
>>>> splice a copy of a_i in place of *focus*
>>>> *redexes* $:= redexes \cup \{parent(focus)\}$
>>> (_) $\Rightarrow$ skip
>> return *redexes*

All the projections in which a member of xs participates are reduced, and a set of expression redexes is constructed. Each projection can trigger the creation of a new $T.\beta_a$-redex. For instance, consider:

$$\text{let } x \text{ be val(pair}(a, b)) \text{ in let } y \text{ be val(proj}_1(x)) \text{ in } m$$
$$\longrightarrow_{\times.\beta} \text{ let } x \text{ be val(pair}(a, b)) \text{ in let } y \text{ be val}(a) \text{ in } m$$
$$\longrightarrow_{T.\beta_a} \text{ let } x \text{ be val(pair}(a, b)) \text{ in } m[y := a]$$

reduceCases(e, x, i, a, xs) reduces case-splits indexed by xs. e is an expression node of the form let x be val(inj$_i(a)$) in m, and xs is a subset of the uses of x.

> *reduceCases*$(e, x, i, a, xs) =$
>> let *occs* $:= \emptyset$
>> let *redexes* $:= \emptyset$

for each $s \in xs$ do
    let $focus = parent(parent(s))$
    case $!focus$ of
    (case s of $(x_1)n_1 \; ; (x_2)n_2) \Rightarrow$
        $occs := occs \cup cleanExp(n_{3-i})$
        $deleteUse(s)$
        splice n_i in place of $focus$
        let $(occs', redexes') = substAtom(x_i, a)$
        $occs := occs \cup occs'$
        $redexes := redexes \cup redexes' \cup \{parent(focus)\}$
        $x_1, x_2 := $ dead
    $(\_) \Rightarrow$ skip
    return $(occs, redexes)$

The structure of *reduceCases* is similar to that of *reduceProjections*. However, it is slightly more complex because a single $+.\beta$-reduction inlines multiple atoms, splices one branch of a case and discards the other. Discarding the branch which is not taken gives a set of occurrence redexes as well as the expression redexes.

5.2   Substitution

$substAtom(x, a)$ substitutes the atom a for all the uses of the defining occurrence x. It returns a pair of a set of occurrence redexes and a set of expression redexes.

$substAtom(x, a) = $ case $(!a)$ of
    $(r) \Rightarrow substUse(x, r)$
    $(\_) \Rightarrow$
        for each $r \in uses(x)$ do
            splice a copy of a in place of r
            $x := $ dead
        return $(\emptyset, \emptyset)$

This is straightforward for non-variable atoms, as it cannot generate new redexes. In contrast, substituting a variable can trigger $\times.\beta$- and $+.\beta$-reductions.

$substUse(x, r)$ substitutes r for all the uses of the defining occurrence x.

$substUse(x, r) = $
    let $xs = uses(x)$
    if $r \in rec\text{-}uses(r)$ then
        $rec\text{-}uses(r) := rec\text{-}uses(r) \cup xs$
    else if $r \in non\text{-}rec\text{-}uses(r)$
        $non\text{-}rec\text{-}uses(r) := non\text{-}rec\text{-}uses(r) \cup xs$
    $x := $ dead
    let $e = parent(def(r))$
    case $!e$ of
    (let y be val($\lceil$pair$(a_1, a_2)\rceil$) in m) $\Rightarrow$
        for each $s \in xs$ do $def(s) := def(r)$

$$\text{let } redexes = reduceProjections(e, y, a_1, a_2, xs)$$
$$\text{return } (\emptyset, redexes)$$
$$(\text{let } y \text{ be val}(\lceil \text{inj}_i(a_i) \rceil) \text{ in } m) \Rightarrow$$
$$\text{for each } s \in xs \text{ do } def(s) := def(r)$$
$$\text{let } (occs, redexes) = reduceCases(e, y, i, a_i, xs)$$
$$\text{return } (occs, redexes)$$
$$(\_) \Rightarrow \text{return } (\emptyset, \emptyset)$$

Substitution is implemented by merging two sets together. Concretely, this amounts to the constant-time operation of inserting one doubly-linked circular list inside another. In addition, if x is bound to a pair, then projections are reduced, or if x is bound to an injection, then case-splits are reduced.

6   Analysis

There are two obvious operations mapping terms from the functional to the imperative representations, which we call *mutify* and *demutify*, respectively. We have a semi-formal argument for the following:

Proposition 3. *Let e be a term and $e' = (demutify \circ contract \circ mutify)(e)$. Then e' is a normal form for e.*

The argument uses the invariants of Sect. 4, plus the invariant that the children of the current node are in normal form. When new redexes are created, this invariant is modified such that subterms may contain redexes, but only those stored in appropriate expression redex sets or occurrence redex sets. It is reasonably straightforward to verify that the operations which update the graph structure do in fact correspond to MIL reductions. When *contract* terminates, all the redex sets are empty and the term is in normal form.

6.1   Complexity Without Commuting Conversions

Although our approach of performing CCs on the way down the tree works well in practice, the worst case time complexity is still quadratic in the size of the term. We define a version of our algorithm $contract_\beta$ which does not perform commuting conversions. This is obtained simply by removing the call to $reduceCCs$ from *contract*, and the test for commuting conversions from *reduce*.

Proposition 4. $contract_\beta(e)$ *is linear in the size of e.*

The argument is very similar to that of Appel and Jim [1] for their imperative algorithm. Essentially most operations take constant time and shrink the size of the term. The only exception is substitution. In the case where a non-variable is substituted for a variable x, the operation is linear in the number of uses of x. But it is only possible to substitute a non-variable for a variable once, therefore the total time spent substituting atoms is linear. In the case where a variable y is substituted for a variable x, the operation is constant, providing y is not bound to a pair or an injection. If y is bound to a pair or an injection, then the operation is linear in the number of uses of x. Again, once bound to a pair or an injection, a variable cannot be rebound, so the time remains linear.

Crucially, this argument relies on the fact that back pointers from uses back to defining occurrences are only maintained for pairs and injections. In our SML.NET implementation we found that maintaining back pointers from *all* uses back to defining occurrences does not incur any significant cost in practice. Even when bootstrapping the compiler ($\sim$ 80,000 lines of code) there was no discernible difference in compile time. Maintaining back pointers also allows us to perform various other rewrites including η-reductions. In the presence of all back pointers, optimising the union operation to always add the smaller list to the larger one guarantees $O(n \ log \ n)$ behaviour. Using an efficient *union-find* algorithm would restore essentially linear complexity.

6.2 Complexity with Commuting Conversions

Naively reducing commuting conversions can give quadratic behaviour. For instance, consider the following (innermost first) reductions:

> let x_k be (let x_{k-1} be ... let x_1 be m_1 in m_2 in ... m_k) in n
> $\longrightarrow^*$ $(S(k-1)$ $T.CC$-reductions)
> let x_k be (let x_1 be m_1 in ... let x_{k-1} be m_{k-1} in m_k) in n
> $\longrightarrow^*$ $(k-1$ $T.CC$-reductions)
> let x_1 be m_1 in ... let x_k be m_k in n

The total number of reductions is given by the recurrence: $S(1) = 0, S(k) = S(k-1) + k - 1$. This has solution $S(k) = k(k-1)/2$. Assuming each of the m_is and n have constant size, then k is linear in the size of the term. Hence the number of reductions is quadratic in the size of the term. If the *contract* function directly performed these reductions, then it would also be quadratic.

Another problem is that $+.CC$-reductions can introduce 'useless functions':

> let z be (let y be (case a of $(x_1)n_1$; $(x_2)n_2$) in m) in p
> $\longrightarrow^*$ letfun $f(y)$ be m
> in let z be case a of (x_1)let y_1 be n_1 in app(f, y_1)
> $\qquad\qquad\qquad\quad$; (x_2)let y_2 be n_2 in app(f, y_2)
> $\qquad$ in p
> $\longrightarrow^*$ letfun $f(y)$ be m
> in letfun $g(z)$ be p
> in case a of (x_1)let y_1 be n_1 in let z_1 be app(f, y_1) in app(g, z_1)
> $\qquad\qquad$; (x_2)let y_2 be n_2 in let z_2 be app(f, y_2) in app(g, z_2)

The function g is useless in the sense that it is always applied to the result of applying f to an argument. One might hope that g be composed with f.

If we change the reduction order, such that the commuting conversions are performed outermost first, then it is:

$$\text{let } z \text{ be (let } y \text{ be (case } a \text{ of } (x_1)n_1 ; (x_2)n_2) \text{ in } m) \text{ in } p$$
$$\longrightarrow^* \text{ let } y \text{ be (case } a \text{ of } (x_1)n_1 ; (x_2)n_2) \text{ in let } z \text{ be } m \text{ in } n$$
$$\longrightarrow^* \text{ letfun } f(y) \text{ be let } z \text{ be } m \text{ in } p$$
$$\text{in case } a \text{ of } (x_1)\text{let } y_1 \text{ be } n_1 \text{ in app}(f, y_1)$$
$$; \ (x_2)\text{let } y_2 \text{ be } n_2 \text{ in app}(f, y_2)$$

Fortunately, given the limited ways in which commuting conversions can trigger other reductions, the full imperative algorithm can get away with performing commuting conversions outermost first, with an initial call to *reduceCCse* before recursively contracting e's children. The operation *reduceCCs(e)* repeatedly checks e to see if it is a CC-redex. If it is, then it performs the commuting conversion, and iterates. If not, then it returns.

The previous example of quadratic behaviour due to commuting conversions becomes linear with this reduction strategy. However, quadratic behaviour can still arise through inlining functions that trigger further commuting conversions:

$$\text{letfun} \quad f_k(x_k) \text{ be let } y_k \text{ be app}(g, x_k) \text{ in app}(g, y_k)$$
$$f_{k-1}(x_{k-1}) \text{ be let } y_{k-1} \text{ be app}(f_k, x_{k-1}) \text{ in app}(g, y_{k-1})$$
$$\vdots$$
$$f_1(x_1) \text{ be let } y_1 \text{ be app}(f_2, x_1) \text{ in app}(g, y_1)$$
$$\text{in} \quad \text{app}(f_1, a)$$

contract takes quadratic time to reduce this term. In order to get a linear number of reductions, one would have to inline all the functions first, before performing any commuting conversions.

7   Performance

We have extended our one-pass imperative algorithm *contract* to the whole of MIL and compared its performance with the current implementation of *simplify*. Replacing *simplify* with *contract* is not entirely straightforward, as all the other phases in the pipeline are written to work on a straightforward immutable tree datatype for terms, which is incompatible with the representation used in *contract*. We therefore make use of *mutify* and *demutify* to change representation before and after *contract*. Since both *mutify* and *demutify* completely rebuild the term, they are very expensive – calling *mutify* and *demutify* generally takes longer than *contract* itself. Ideally, of course, all the phases would use the same representation. However, using two representations allowed us to compare the running times of *simplify* and *contract* on real programs.

Table 1. Total compile time (in seconds)

Benchmark	Lines of code	SML/NJ		MLton	
		tsimplify	*tcontract*	*tsimplify*	*tcontract*
sort	70	2.11	3.47	0.46	0.52
xq	1,300	13.1	14.4	2.46	1.76
mllex	1,400	11.6	16.0	2.39	2.03
raytrace	2,500	18.1	24.0	4.30	3.03
mlyacc	6,200	57.3	43.8.	10.0	6.04
hamlet	20,000	219	156	43.7	26.2
bootstrap	80,000	1310	1190	289	221

Table 2. Shrinking reduction time (in seconds) under SML/NJ and MLton

Benchmark	Under SML/NJ					Under MLton				
	Total		Breakdown			Total		Breakdown		
	simp	*mcd*	*m*	*c*	*d*	*simp*	*mcd*	*m*	*c*	*d*
sort	1.00	2.00	0.87	0.70	0.43	0.22	0.11	0.02	0.07	0.02
xq	5.86	5.98	1.90	3.61	0.47	1.46	0.54	0.35	0.15	0.06
mllex	6.09	7.49	3.31	3.16	1.02	1.21	0.57	0.27	0.23	0.07
raytrace	9.32	11.8	5.16	5.44	1.17	2.13	0.65	0.37	0.19	0.09
mlyacc	33.2	20.0	9.42	8.60	1.94	5.63	1.26	0.68	0.37	0.21
hamlet	84.5	56.4	26.2	21.5	8.59	23.3	5.54	1.85	2.77	0.92
bootstrap	439	282	130	100	53.0	107	36.6	11.8	18.4	6.38

Table 1 compares the total compile times (*tsimplify* vs *tcontract*) of several benchmark programs for the existing compiler, using *simplify*, and for the modified one, using *demutify* ∘ *contract* ∘ *mutify*. Table 2 compares the time *simp* spent in *simplify* with the times *m*, *c*, *d* spent in each of *mutify*, *contract* and *demutify* and their sum *mcd*. Each benchmark was run under two different versions of SML.NET. One was compiled under SML/NJ [12] and the other under MLton [13]. Benchmarks were run on a 1.4Ghz AMD Athlon PC equipped with 512MB of RAM and Microsoft Windows XP SP1.

The first five benchmarks are demos distributed with SML.NET. The sort benchmark applies quicksort to a list of integers; xq is an interpreter for an XQuery-like language for querying XML documents; mllex and mlyacc are ports of SML/NJ's ml-lex and ml-yacc utilities; raytrace is a port to SML of the winning entry from the Third Annual ICFP Programming Contest. The remaining benchmarks are much larger: hamlet is Andreas Rossberg's SML interpreter, whilst bootstrap is SML.NET compiling itself.

Figure 4 gives a graphical comparison of both tables. On small benchmarks, the current compiler is faster (*tcontract*/*tsimplify*). But for medium and large benchmarks, we were surprised to discover that *contract* is faster than *simplify*, even though much of the time is spent in useless representation changes. Under SML/NJ, *tcontract*/*tsimplify* shows a decrease of nearly 30% in the total compile

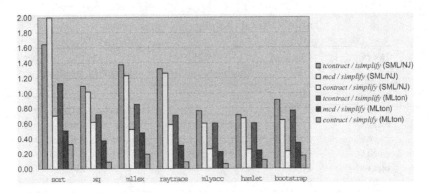

Fig. 4. Comparing *contract* with *simplify*

time in some cases; under MLton, there is a decrease of up to 40%. This is a significant improvement, given that in the existing compiler only around 50% of compile time is spent performing shrinking reductions. Comparing the actual shrinking reduction times *c* and *simp*, *contract* is up to four times faster than *simplify* under SML/NJ, and up to 15 times faster under MLton (on `mlyacc`). The level of improvement under MLton is striking. Our results suggest that MLton is considerably better than SML/NJ at compiling ML code which makes heavy use of references.

As an exercise, one of the other transformations *deunit*, which removes redundant unit values and types was translated to use the new representation. The *contract* function is called before and after *deunit*, so this enabled us to eliminate one call to *demutify* and one call to *mutify*. This translation was easy to do and did not change the performance of *deunit*. We believe that it should be reasonably straightforward, if somewhat tedious, to translate the rest of the transformations to work directly with the mutable representation.

8   Conclusions and Further Work

We have implemented and extended Appel and Jim's imperative algorithm for shrinking reductions and shown that it can yield significant reductions in compile times relative to the algorithm currently used in SML/NJ and SML.NET. The improvements are such that, for large programs, it is even worth completely changing representations before and after *contract*, but this is clearly suboptimal. The results of this experiment indicate that it would be worth the effort of rewriting other phases of the compiler to use the graph-based representation.

Making more extensive use of the pointer-based representation would allow many transformations to be written in a different style, for example replacing explicit environments with extra information on binding nodes, though this does not interact well with the hash-consing currently used for types. We also believe that 'code motion' transformations can be more easily and efficiently expressed.

It is unfortunate that CCs and inlining conspire to produce quadratic complexity. Sabry and Wadler's study of CPS translations offers an interesting insight [11]. In their variant of Moggi's computational lambda calculus λ_{c**}, terms are in CC-normal form by definition, and β-reduction of an application is combined with CC-normalisation of its enclosing let-expression: adopting this more refined notion of redex may allow us to achieve linear complexity.

More speculatively, we would like to investigate more principled mutable graph-based intermediate representations. There has been much theoretical work on graph-based representations of proofs and programs, yet these do not seem to have been exploited in compilers for higher-order languages (though of course, compilers for imperative languages have used a mutable flow-graph representations for decades). With a careful choice of representation, some of our transformations (such as $T.CC$) could simply be isomorphisms and we believe that a better treatment of shared continuations in the other commuting conversions would also be possible.

References

1. Andrew W. Appel and Trevor Jim. Shrinking lambda expressions in linear time. *Journal of Functional Programming*, 7(5):515–540, 1997.
2. N. Benton and A. Kennedy. Monads, effects and transformations. In *3rd International Workshop on Higher Order Operational Techniques in Semantics (HOOTS), Paris*, volume 26 of *ENTCS*. Elsevier, September 1999.
3. N. Benton, A. Kennedy, and C. Russo. SML.NET. http://www.cl.cam.ac.uk/Research/TSG/SMLNET/, June 2002.
4. N. Benton, A. Kennedy, and C. Russo. Adventures in interoperability: The SML.NET experience. In *Proc. 6th ACM-SIGPLAN International Conference on Principles and Practice of Declarative Programming (PPDP)*, August 2004.
5. Nick Benton, Andrew Kennedy, and George Russell. Compiling Standard ML to Java bytecodes. In *Proc. ACM SIGPLAN International Conference on Functional Programming (ICFP '98)*, volume 34(1), pages 129–140, 1999.
6. O. Danvy. A new one-pass transformation into monadic normal form. In *Proc. 12th International Conference on Compiler Construction*, number 2622 in Lecture Notes in Computer Science, pages 77–89. Springer, 2003.
7. Ecma International. ECMA Common Language Infrastructure standard, December 2002. http://www.ecma-international.org/publications/standards/Ecma-335.htm.
8. J. Hatcliff and O. Danvy. A generic account of continuation-passing styles. In *Proc. 21st Annual Symposium on Principles of Programming Languages*. ACM, 1994.
9. Sam Lindley. *Normalisation by evaluation in the compilation of typed functional programming languages*. PhD thesis, The University of Edinburgh, 2005.
10. S. L. Peyton Jones and A. L.M. Santos. A transformation-based optimiser for Haskell. *Science of Computer Programming*, 1998.
11. Amr Sabry and Philip Wadler. A reflection on call-by-value. *ACM Transactions on Programming Languages and Systems*, 19(6):916–941, 1997.
12. Standard ML of New Jersey (SML/NJ) compiler: http://smlnj.org/.
13. Stephen Weeks, Matthew Fluet, Henry Cejtin, and Suresh Jagannathan. MLton whole-program optimizing compiler: http://mlton.org/.

Dynamic Construction of Generic Functions

Ronny Wichers Schreur and Rinus Plasmeijer

Institute for Computing and Information Sciences
Radboud University Nijmegen
Toernooiveld 1, 6525 ED Nijmegen, The Netherlands
{ronny,rinus}@cs.ru.nl
http://www.cs.ru.nl/{~ronny,~rinus}

Abstract.. This paper presents a library for the run-time construction
and specialisation of generic or polytypic functions. This library utilises
the type information that is available in dynamics to implement generic
functions on their values. The library closely follows the static generic
framework, both in its use and in its implementation. It can dynamically
construct generic operations ranging from equality, *map* and parsers to
pretty printers and generic graphical editors. A special feature of the
library is that it can also be used to derive meaningful specialisations of
generic functions that operate on the type representation of the dynamic.

1   Introduction

This paper is about constructing generic functions for dynamically typed values
(or shortly, dynamics). Let us first explain what we mean by generic functions
and dynamics.

In Generic Haskell [13] as well as in Clean [15] it is possible to define *generic
functions* [4, 8]. A generic function is an ultimate reusable function that allows
reflection on the structure of data in a type-safe way.

Once defined, a generic function can be applied on any value of any given
concrete static type. Generic functions can be used to define work that is of a
general nature. The technique has successfully been applied to define functions
like equality, *map*, *fold*, to construct parsers and pretty printers, to create GUI
applications [3] and to generate test data [10].

A generic function is actually not a single function, but rather a special kind
of overloaded function. To define a generic function, instances for the generic
function are defined for a finite number of type constructors. Given these base
instances, the compiler can fully automatically derive an instance for the generic
function for any given concrete *static* type.

Both in Haskell as well as in Clean one can use *dynamics*. Dynamics allow the
programmer to associate a run-time value with its type. The are some differences
between dynamics in Haskell and in Clean. In Clean dynamics are incorporated
in the language while in Haskell dynamics are made available via a library facility. Dynamics in Clean can be of polymorphic type, and one can do run-time
type unification using type pattern variables [14]. Furthermore, dynamics (even

C. Grelck et al. (Eds.): IFL 2004, LNCS 3474, pp. 160–176, 2005.
© Springer-Verlag Berlin Heidelberg 2005

functions) can be serialised , stored to disk and read it in by some other running application. In this way one can easily create persistency, type-safe plug-ins, and mobile code [17]. The facility has been used to create a type safe functional operating system [16] that uses a typed file system in which all files are dynamics stored on disk.

Dynamics enable the type safe communication of data and code between independently programmed distributed applications. It would therefore be very nice if we would also be able to apply generic functions to a dynamic, in particular to a "foreign" dynamic. In theory it should be possible to construct such a generic function, since a dynamic contains information about its type.

The ability to construct such a generic function that can be applied on any value of any type stored in a dynamic would give us new possibilities. For instance, in our functional operating system we will be able to test the equality of two (unknown) dynamics. It also means that if we receive a dynamic from somewhere, we can automatically create a parser or pretty printer for it. From that moment on, the operating system shell is able to recognise expressions of the types involved.

Figure 1 gives an impression of what we want to achieve . The program at the top writes a tree value in a dynamic to disk. This dynamic value is read by the bottom application. Note that the Tree type is not available at compile time in the bottom application. By using the library it is still possible to create a graphical editor for the tree in the dynamic value.

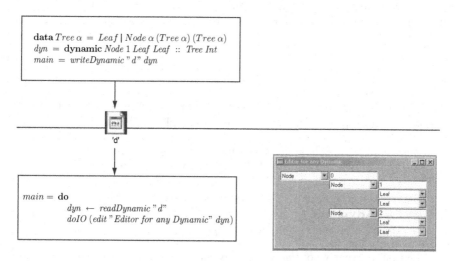

Fig. 1. A dynamically constructed generic editor

In practice this means that all the conversions and constructions that are currently done by the compiler at compile-time now somehow have to be accomplished at run-time. This is not so easy. A compiler can do full reflection on the representation of types and terms, but a running application (Clean uses compiled code) can only do some limited reflection on the representation of the types. Furthermore one has to be able to construct new functions at run-time. The research question is: is it nevertheless possible to create generic functions for dynamics? In this paper we explain how one can do it, and explain what language facilities are needed to realise it.

The main contributions of this paper are:

- We show that that our library enables the construction of generic functions at run-time in the same spirit as the well-known static generic translation scheme (section 6 and 4);
- We show that our generic functions cannot only be used on the value part but also on the type part of a dynamic (section 4).

The code and examples in this paper are presented in Haskell, because it is more widely known. In any case, the differences are insignificant. The library is implemented in Clean and available from the web-page that accompanies this paper (`http://www.cs.ru.nl/~ronny/DynGen/`).

The remainder of the paper is organised as follows. In section 2 we briefly recap the dynamic machinery. In section 3 we describe how a generic function is statically defined in the language. Then we explain in section 4 how, with help of our library, a generic function for dynamics can be constructed in a very similar way as in the static case. The translation scheme for generics as implemented in the compiler is illustrated in section 5. In section 6 we explain how we manage to realise this translation scheme at run-time. In section 7 we show some extensions, present example applications, and discuss the efficiency of the library. After discussing related work in section 8, we end in section 9 with conclusions and future work.

2   Dynamics

Dynamically typed values, or dynamics for short, combine a value with a representation of its type [1, 15]. Here are some examples of dynamics.

$$twoDynamics \ :: \ (Dynamic, Dynamic)$$
$$twoDynamics \ = \ (\textbf{dynamic } 3 :: Int, \ \textbf{dynamic } id :: \forall \alpha.\alpha \rightarrow \alpha)$$

$$dynApply \ :: \ Dynamic \rightarrow Dynamic \rightarrow Dynamic$$
$$dynApply \ (\textbf{dynamic } f :: a \rightarrow b) \ (\textbf{dynamic } x :: a) \ = \ dynamic \ f \ x :: b$$
$$dynApply \ \_\_ \ = \ error \ ``dynApply : type \ error"$$

The first alternative of $dynApply$ only matches if the first dynamic argument contains a function value and the second dynamic argument a value of a type that matches the argument type of the function. This example shows how matching on dynamic values involves dynamic unification of types. This guarantees that the application $f \ x$ is safe.

The type pattern variable in a dynamic can also arise from a type variable in the signature of the function. Such a type variable is postfixed with an upward arrow, as in the following two functions.

$$toDyn \; :: \; \forall \alpha. \, Typeable \; \alpha \Rightarrow \alpha \rightarrow Dynamic$$
$$toDyn \; x \; = \; dynamic \; x \; :: \; \alpha{\uparrow}$$

$$fromDyn \; :: \; \forall \alpha. \, Typeable \; \alpha \Rightarrow \; Dynamic \rightarrow \alpha$$
$$fromDyn \; (dynamic \; x \; :: \; \alpha{\uparrow}) \; = \; x$$
$$fromDyn \; \_ \; = \; error \; \text{``type mismatch''}$$

These so called *type dependent functions* [14] are overloaded in the type representation of that type variable, indicated by the *Typeable* class. For example in *fromDyn* the type of α is determined by the context in which the function is used.

The dynamic system in Clean has more features that are not used in this paper, but that do greatly enhance the applicability of dynamics. One can serialise any dynamic (even functions) and store its value to disk or send it over to another running application. Any other Clean application can read in or receive such a dynamic. Clean uses compiled code which means that a dynamic linker is required that is able to link in code to a running application [17].

2.1   Obtaining Additional Information About Dynamic Types

In Haskell access to the representations of types and data type definitions is available in the Data.Generics library that was developed to support the techniques in the "Scrap your boilerplate articles" [11, 12].

In Clean, dynamics, patterns match on dynamics, as well as dynamic unification are part of the language. Access to the representation of types and the type definitions is therefore less important to the average Clean user. To realise our library, we do need access to this type of information. The representation contains all the information needed to construct the generic representation for dynamic types at run-time. The actual representations of types and data types in both Haskell and Clean differ from the one presented in this paper. We have simplified it a bit to increase readability.

The following library functions are used to obtain additional information about types. The *typeOf* function returns the representation of a type.

$$typeOf \; :: \; \forall \alpha. \, Typeable \; \alpha \Rightarrow \alpha \rightarrow TypeRep$$
data *TypeRep*
$$= TyCon \; TyCon \mid TyApp \; TypeRep \; TypeRep$$
$$\mid \; TyForAll \; VarId \; TypeRep \mid TyVar \; VarId$$

The function *typeDefOf* returns a representation of the data type.

$$typeDefOf \; :: \; TyCon \rightarrow TyDef$$
data $TyDef \; = \; AlgType \; \{arity :: Int, \; conses :: [(Constr, [Type])]\} \mid NoType$

The *Constr* data type represents a data constructor from an algebraic type. It supports the following operations.

data *Constr* =   — abstract type
instance show Constr
build :: *Constr* → *Dynamic*
match :: *Constr* → *Dynamic*

The function *build* returns a dynamic that contains the constructor. The function *match* returns a dynamic with a function that matches on the constructor. For example for the *Cons* constructor in the *List* type these dynamics have the following values.

$build_{Cons}$ = **dynamic** *Cons*
$match_{Cons}$ = **dynamic** $\lambda\, l\, f\, x \to$ **case** l **of** *Cons* $h\, t \to f\, h\, t\,;\, \_ \to x$

3   Generic Programming

This section describes the basics of generic or *polytypic* programming à la Hinze [9]. Generic functions are defined on the sum-of-products structure of algebraic data types. The following code shows the generic constructors from which the generic structure is build and presents the generic structure for a user defined list type.

data 1   = 1   — unit
data $\alpha \times \beta$ = $\alpha \times \beta$ — product
data $\alpha + \beta$ = $InL\, \alpha \mid InR\, \beta$ — sum

data *List* α = $Nil \mid Cons\, \alpha\, (List\, \alpha)$ — user defined algebraic type
type $List°\, \alpha = 1 + (\alpha \times (List\, \alpha))$ —   and its generic structure

In the full blown generic framework the generic structure is much richer with information about data constructors and record fields (their name, arity, and so on). This information is necessary for generic parsers and pretty-printers, but we do not consider it further for clarity's sake.

The remainder of this section illustrates how a programmer defines and uses a generic function in the static generic framework. The running example is a generic equality function that is used to compare two integer lists.

3.1   Define the Type Signature of the Generic Function

The generic equality function is defined as follows.

type $Eq\, \alpha$ = $\alpha \to \alpha \to Bool$
generic $eq\, a$ :: $Eq\, a$

In this example there is only one generic variable before the double colon (a), but in general there can be several. The type after the double colon can also be polymorphic in other type variables. We do not consider higher-ranked types in this paper, so all polymorphic variables must be quantified at the top level.

3.2   Provide the Base Instances

The programmer provides each base instance by defining a function with the name of the generic function subscripted with the name of the type constructor.

$$
\begin{array}{ll}
eq_{Int}\ a\ b & = a == b \\
eq_1\ 1\ 1 & = True \\
eq_\times\ eq_1\ eq_2\ (a_1 \times a_2)\ (b_1 \times b_2) & = eq_1\ a_1\ b_1\ \&\&\ eq_2\ a_2\ b_2 \\
eq_+\ eq_l\ eq_r\ (InL\ a)\ (InL\ b) & = eq_l\ a\ b \\
eq_+\ eq_l\ eq_r\ (InR\ a)\ (InR\ a) & = eq_r\ a\ b \\
eq_+\ eq_l\ eq_r\ \_\ \_ & = False
\end{array}
$$

The number of arguments of a base instance depends on the arity of the type constructor. For example, $eq_\times$ receives equality functions for the first and second elements of the pairs.

3.3   Specialise the Generic Function for a Particular Type

A specialisation is denoted by putting the type between braces after the name of the generic function.

$$
main\ =\ print\ (eq\{List\ Int\}\ (Cons\ 1\ Nil)\ (Cons\ 2\ Nil))
$$

Here $eq\{List\ Int\}$ is the specialisation of the generic equality function for lists of integers. It is also possible to specialise for types of higher kind such as $List$ (kind $* \rightarrow *$). In this paper the type for which a generic function is specialised is assumed to be monomorphic.

4   Dynamic Generic Library

In the previous section 3 we showed how to statically define and use a generic equality function. Here we show how to do the same dynamically. For this purpose the library offers a number of functions to construct a generic function at run-time. Basically, we do the same steps as before. For each step a library function is offered (*defineGeneric*, *baseInstance*, *specialise*). All definitions of the dynamic generic function given so far are collected in an abstract type (*GenFun*).

```
data GenFun    — abstract data type
defineGeneric :: Int → Type → GenFun
baseInstance  :: TyCon → Dynamic → GenFun → GenFun
specialise    :: GenFun → Type → Dynamic
```

We will demonstrate the use of each library function for the equality example from section 2. Because several base instances have to be provided for any generic function, we make the notation a little lighter with an infix variant of the *baseInstance* function. It is defined as follows:

$$(:+:) \; \textit{infixl} \; 4$$
$$(:+:) \; :: \; \textit{GenFun} \; \rightarrow \; (\textit{TyCon}, \; \textit{Dynamic}) \; \rightarrow \; \textit{GenFun}$$
$$\textit{genFun} \; :+: \; (\textit{tyCon}, \; \textit{dyn}) \; = \; \textit{baseInstance} \; \textit{tyCon} \; \textit{dyn} \; \textit{genFun}$$

Below we use the notation $\lceil a \rceil$ as a short-cut for the representation of the type a. For example $\lceil \textit{List Int} \rceil$ denotes $\textit{typeOf} \; (\perp :: \textit{List Int})$. The same notation is also overloaded to denote the representation of a type constructor. For example $\lceil \textit{List} \rceil$ denotes the representation of the $\textit{List}$ type constructor. The context always indicates which of the two variants is meant.

4.1   Define the Type Signature of the Generic Function

The first step is to provide the signature of the generic function. For the generic equality it is:

$$\textit{defEq} \; :: \; \textit{GenFun}$$
$$\textit{defEq} \; = \; \textit{defineGeneric} \; 1 \; \lceil \forall a. \; \textit{Eq} \; a \rceil$$

The generic type variables and any other type variables are all bound by one quantifier in the second argument of *defineGereric*. By convention, the generic type variables are given first, and the integer argument indicates how many generic type variables the function takes. In the example the first variable (a) is the generic type variable.

4.2   Provide the Base Instances

After defining the type of the dynamic generic equality function, we extend it by providing the base instances.

$$\textit{baseEq} \; :: \; \textit{GenFun}$$
$$\textit{baseEq} = \textit{defEq} \quad :+: \; (\lceil \textit{Int} \rceil, \; \textbf{dynamic} \; \textit{eq}_{\textit{Int}})$$
$$:+: \; (\lceil \; 1 \; \rceil, \; \textbf{dynamic} \; \textit{eq}_1 \;)$$
$$:+: \; (\lceil \; \times \; \rceil, \; \textbf{dynamic} \; \textit{eq}_\times \;)$$
$$:+: \; (\lceil \; + \; \rceil, \; \textbf{dynamic} \; \textit{eq}_+ \;)$$

Assuming that we already have a static generic function for equality defined, the definition is rather straightforward. The instances of the static generic function *eq* can directly serve as the base instances for the dynamic generic equality.

This code shows that it can be tiresome to populate the generic function with the base instances for all base and primitive types (we should also have provided base instances for *Float*, *Char*, *Bool*). It may be useful to have some language support to make it easier to add all available static base instances.

4.3   Specialise the Generic Function for a Particular Type

Finally we can apply our dynamic generic function to check if two dynamics are equal.

$$genEq :: TypeRep \rightarrow Dynamic$$
$$genEq = specialise\ baseEq$$
$$main\ = print\ (genEq \lceil List\ \ Int \rceil$$
$$'dynApply'\ (\textbf{dynamic}\ Cons\ 1\ Nil)$$
$$'dynApply'\ (\textbf{dynamic}\ Cons\ 2\ Nil))$$

The example shows that using the dynamic generic library is very similar to using the static generic framework. In the example above we made good use of the static instances of the generic equality function to serve as the base instances of the dynamic generic equality. However, it is also possible to use the dynamic generic library without using the static generic framework.

5   Generic Translation

Before we explain how generic functions are constructed dynamically we first review the static translation scheme as originated from Hinze [8].

We present the translation scheme by studying the code that the compiler generates for our running example. The purpose of this exposition is to point out the information that is needed to perform the translation and to get an idea of the language features that are used in the generated code. In the next section we will then see how this corresponds to the dynamic setting.

5.1   Overview

The compiler uses the following information for the translation scheme (readily available from the compiler's syntax tree):

- the signature of the generic function;
- the base instances for this generic function;
- the type for which the generic function has to be specialised;
- the type definitions of all types that appear in this type.

The remainder of this section describes the different parts of the translation: the specialisation of the generic function for a type expression, the conversion between values and their generic representation, and the derivation of the generic function for an algebraic type.

5.2   Specialisation

The specialisation of a generic function for a specific type is an easy transformation. It is nothing more than replacing type constructors with the instance of the generic function for that type, and replacing type application by term application. For the specialisation of the generic equality function for list of integers the compiler performs the following transformation.

$$eq\{List\ Int\} \Longrightarrow eq_{List}\ eq_{Int}$$

The eq_{Int} function was provided by the programmer (Int is a primitive type), but the compiler must derive the eq_{List} function. The remainder of the section describes how this is accomplished.

5.3   Equality on the Generic Representation

The first step is to specialise the generic equality function for the generic representation type $List^\circ$, again by replacing each type constructor with the generic instance for that type.

$$eq_{List^\circ}\ \ :: \forall\alpha.\ Eq\ \alpha \rightarrow\ Eq\ (List^\circ\ \alpha)$$
$$eq_{List^\circ}\ a = eq_1\ `eq_+`\ (a\ `eq_\times`\ eq_{List}\ a)$$

5.4   Embedding Projection

We now have an equality function on the generic representation of lists, but we need an equality function on lists. We can adapt one to the other by using a so called *embedding projection*. Conveniently enough this embedding projection itself can be implemented as a generic function. It has the following definition.

data $\alpha \rightleftarrows \beta\ =\ EP\ \{from :: \alpha \rightarrow \beta,\ to :: \beta \rightarrow \alpha\}$
generic $ep\ a\ b = a \rightleftarrows b$

For the generic equality function only the conversion in one direction is needed because the generic type variable occurs on negative positions (to the left of an arrow), but to cover the general case we combine the conversions both ways.

The embedding projection for the equality function is the specialisation of the generic function ep on the structure of signature of the generic function, in our example the equality type $\alpha \rightarrow \alpha \rightarrow Bool$.

$$ep_{eq}\ \ :: \forall\alpha\beta.\ (\alpha \rightleftarrows \beta)\ \rightarrow\ (Eq\ \alpha \rightleftarrows Eq\ \beta)$$
$$ep_{eq}\ a = a\ `ep_\rightarrow`\ (a\ `ep_\rightarrow`\ ep_{id})$$

This specialisation deviates from the standard scheme in one place. The type constructor $Bool$ is replaced by ep_{id} (defined as $\{from = id,\ to = id\}$) instead of ep_{Bool}. In fact, the embedding projection for any type that does not involve a generic type variable is the identity projection. With this observation the number of embedding projections can be reduced.

The function $ep_\rightarrow$ composes the embedding projections for the argument type and the result type.

$$ep_\rightarrow\ arg\ res\ =\ EP\ (from\ arg\ o\ from\ result)\ (to\ result\ o\ to\ arg))$$

5.5   Conversion Functions

The implementation of the conversion functions from a list to its generic representation and the other way around is a simple exercise in case distinction, based on the algebraic structure of the type definition.

$$from_{List} :: \forall\alpha.List\ \alpha \rightarrow List^\circ\ \alpha \qquad to_{List}\ :: \forall\alpha.List^\circ\ \alpha \rightarrow List\ \alpha$$
$$from_{List}\ Nil = InL\ 1 \qquad\qquad to_{List}\ (InL\ 1) = Nil$$
$$from_{List}\ (Cons\ a\ b) = InR\ (a\times b) \qquad to_{List}\ (InR\ (a\times b)) = Cons\ a\ b$$

The two conversion functions are grouped by $convert_{List}$.

$$convert_{List} :: \forall \alpha.\ List\ \alpha \rightleftarrows List_o^\circ\ \alpha$$
$$convert_{List} = EP\ from_{List}\ to_{List}$$

5.6 Derived Function

The last step in the derivation is to combine the specialisation on the generic representation, the conversion function and the embedded projection for the generic function.

$$adapt_{List} :: \forall \alpha.\ Eq\ (List\ \alpha) \rightarrow Eq\ (List^\circ\ \alpha)$$
$$adapt_{List} = epfrom\ (ep_{eq}\ convert_{List})$$

$$eq_{List} \qquad :: \forall \alpha.\ Eq\ \alpha \rightarrow Eq\ (List\ \alpha)$$
$$eq_{List}\ a \quad = adapt_{List}\ (eq_{List^\circ}\ a)$$

Note that eq_{List} is a recursive function (indirectly through eq_{List°).

6   Dynamic Generic Translation

In this section we implement the dynamic generic library functions from section 4 by adapting the static generic transformations from section 5.

6.1   Basic Implementation

As can be seen from the type signatures in section 4, a *GenFun* value is passed between the library functions. It contains information about the generic function that was stored in the compiler's syntax tree in the static translation scheme. The abstract type is defined as a record with the following fields.

```
data GenFun  =  GenFun  {  arity      :: Int
                        ,  signature  :: TypeRep
                        ,  instances  :: FiniteMap TyCon Dynamic
                        ,  ep         :: Dynamic                  }
```

This record is created by the *defineGeneric* function that stores the arity and the type signature, creates an empty map of instances and constructs the embedding projection for the type signature. The *specialiseEP* function performs the specialisation for the embedding projection of the generic type signature as described in section 5.4.

```
defineGeneric    :: Int → Type → GenFun
defineGeneric a s = GenFun  {  arity      = a
                            ,  signature  = s
                            ,  instances  = emptyFM
                            ,  ep         = specialiseEP a s}
```

The *baseInstance* function adds an instance to the map of instances.

$$baseInstance \quad\quad :: TyCon \rightarrow Dynamic \rightarrow GenFun \rightarrow GenFun$$
$$baseInstance\ tc\ dyn\ gf = gf\ \{instances = addToFM\ (instances\ gf)\ tc\ dyn\}$$

Finally, *specialise* replaces all type constructors in the (monomorphic) type by the corresponding instance and all type applications by *dynApply* (see section 2). This corresponds to section 5.2.

$$specialise :: GenFun \rightarrow Type \rightarrow Dynamic$$
$$specialise\ gf\ (TyApp\ t\ a) = dynApply\ (specialise\ gf\ t)\ (specialise\ gf\ a)$$
$$specialise\ gf\ (TyCon\ tc)\ =\ \textbf{case}\ lookupFM\ (instances\ gf)\ tc\ \textbf{of}$$
$$Nothing\ \rightarrow\ derive\ gf\ tc$$
$$Just\ inst\ \rightarrow\ inst$$

This is a slight simplification of the actual library function that operates on a *State* monad, adding newly derived instances to the finite map of instances in the *GenFun* record.

Now all that is left to do is implement the *derive* function. We will do so in the next section.

6.2   Functions

The dynamic function that *derive* has to construct corresponds to eq_{List} in section 5.6. Here we see the first problem: The static translation introduces new function definitions. In the dynamic setting the dynamics can contain function values and we can apply dynamics to other dynamics, but we cannot create new function definitions.

To solve this problem we enrich the term language with lambda expressions and variables.

$$\textbf{data}\ Dynamic_\lambda = Term\ Dynamic\ |\ App\ Dynamic_\lambda\ Dynamic_\lambda$$
$$|\ Lambda\ Int\ Dynamic_\lambda\ |\ Var\ Int$$

In this language we can construct the derived function (the λ subscripts indicate that we are working in $Dynamic_\lambda$).

$$derive_\lambda \quad\quad :: GenFun \rightarrow TyCon \rightarrow Dynamic_\lambda$$
$$derive_\lambda\ gf\ tc = foldr\ Lambda\ (adapt\ \text{`}App\text{`}\ derived)\ varIds$$
$$\quad\textbf{where}$$
$$\quad\quad typeDef = typeDefOf\ tc$$
$$\quad\quad varIds\ =[1..arity\ typeDef]$$
$$\quad\quad adapt\ \ = Term\ (adaptor_\lambda\ gf\ typeDef)$$
$$\quad\quad derived = foldl\ App\ derive_\lambda\ gf\ typeDef)\ (map\ Var\ varIds)$$

The function $derive_\lambda^\circ$ constructs the derived function for the generic representation of the type definition. As we have seen in section 5.2 this is simply a matter of specialising the generic structure of the type definition. The function $adaptor_\lambda$ is more difficult and we postpone its implementation to the next subsection.

The enriched dynamics can be translated to regular dynamics by the well-known bracket abstraction algorithm that removes all lambdas and variables with the use of the S, K, and I combinators. These combinators can be defined in our term language, because dynamics can contain polymorphic functions.

$$derive \quad :: GenFun \rightarrow TyCon \rightarrow Dynamic$$
$$derive\ gf\ tc = bracketAbstract\ (derive_\lambda\ gf\ tc)$$

6.3   Pattern Matching

The function $adaptor_\lambda$ constructs the conversion function between values and their structural representation. It corresponds to $convert_{List}$ in section 5.5. Here the next problem appears.

The conversion function performs pattern matches. In the dynamic library the constructors on which we have to match are not know until run-time. In the previous function we showed how to dynamically introduce lambda expressions, but our term language does not contain pattern matching or case distinction.

Instead we use the *match* functions (see 2.1) that can be applied to the constructor info. This match function takes a value (a list in this example) and a function that should replace the constructor. If the value matches, this function is applied to the arguments of the constructor, otherwise it returns nothing. By chaining the match functions for all the constructors in a data type we can build the required conversion function.

6.4   Recursive Functions

There is one more hurdle to take. Recursive types lead to recursive functions in the translation. This means that to derive an instance for a recursive type we need the instance for this type. To escape from this loop we construct recursive functions with the use of a fix-point combinator. We could also have introduced the fix-points at the type level, this amounts to the same thing. The dynamic fix-point operator has the following definition.

$$fix\ f \quad = \textbf{let}\ x\ =\ f\ x\ \textbf{in}\ x$$
$$dynFix :: Dynamic$$
$$dynFix = \textbf{dynamic}\ fix :: \forall\alpha.(\alpha \rightarrow \alpha) \rightarrow \alpha$$

Unfortunately, this fix-point combinator can only express limited forms of recursion. The type of fix shows that the recursive calls should all have the same type as the function itself. On the type level this means that this method does not work for non-uniform types, such as

data $Nested\ \alpha\ =\ One \mid Two\ (Nested\ (\alpha,\ \alpha))$

In the static scenario instances for non-uniform types can only be expressed because Haskell supports polymorphic recursion.

Perhaps these non-uniform types can be handled with more advanced fix-point combinators, but the details have not been worked out.

7   Applications and Extensions

We present some examples of the use of the library, describe some extensions and discuss the efficiency of our solution.

7.1   Defining the Instance for Dynamic

In section 4 we saw how to derive an equality function to compare two dynamics. In the example below this example is extended to define a base instance of the static generic equality function for the type *Dynamic*.

$$eq_{Dynamic}\ x@(\textbf{dynamic}\ \_\ ::\ a)\ y@(\textbf{dynamic}\ \_\ ::\ a)\ =\ eqDyn\ \lceil a\rceil\ x\ y$$
  where
    $convert_{Dyn}\ ::\ \forall\alpha.\ Typeable\ \alpha\ \Rightarrow\ \alpha\ \rightleftarrows\ Dynamic$
    $convert_{Dyn}\ =EP\ toDyn\ fromDyn$

    $eqDyn\ type\ =liftDynEq\ (genEq\ type)$

    $liftDynEq\ ::\ Dynamic\ \rightarrow\ Eq\ Dynamic$
    $liftDynEq\ =\lambda(dynamic\ eq\ ::\ Eq\ a)\ \rightarrow\ epfrom\ (ep\{Eq\}\ convert_{Dyn})\ eq$
$eq_{Dynamic}\ \_\ \_\ =\ False$

The first alternative of $eq_{Dynamic}$ only applies if the two dynamics have a matching type. In that case the representation of this type is used to specialise the dynamic generic equality (with the function *genEq* from section 4.3). The *liftDynEq* function transforms the equality function in the dynamic (type *Eq a*) to an equality function on two values of type *Dynamic*. Such a lift function can be defined for any generic function in a similar way.

7.2   Deriving a Generic Function for the Types

So far we have only looked at how the generic function can operate on the values in the dynamics. But we also have to consider the type in the dynamic. A generic pretty printer for dynamics should not only print the value in the dynamic, but also its type.

  generic *pprint t* :: $t->$ *String*
  pprint (**dynamic** *Cons* 1 *Nil* :: *List Int*)
$\Rightarrow$ "dynamic Cons 1 Nil :: List Int"

A naive specialisation of the pretty printer for the representation of the type gives the rather unsatisfactory result "TyApp (TyCon List) (TyCon Int)".
    The library provides a function that helps in this situation.

  specialiseForType :: [*TypCon*] $\rightarrow$ *GenFun* $\rightarrow$ *Dynamic*

In the case of the pretty printer the dynamic constructed *specialiseForType* contains a pretty printer of type *TypeRep* $\rightarrow$ *String*, but it behaves as if it were defined on the type universe that is formed by the list of type constructors.

For example for the types *Int*, *Bool* and *List* this universe can be presented by the following algebraic type.

data *Type* = *Int* | *Bool* | *List Type*

Note that *Int*, *Bool* and *List* are data constructors in this type.

The library function *specialiseForType* can be used for many other generic functions. A parser for dynamics can first apply the parser generated with *specialiseForType* to parse the type string. This parser delivers a representation of the type which is then used to construct the parser for the value string. In test data generation first a type can be generated and then a value of this type. The graphical editor for dynamic values from the introduction can also be extended so that the user can also edit the type as well as the values for that type.

7.3   Error Handling

So far we have ignored the errors that can occur during the dynamic construction of generic functions. Compile-time errors from the static framework have become run-time errors in our library and this means that all the library functions we have used so far are inherently partial.

The *defineGeneric* function can fail if there is no embedding projection defined for one of the type constructors in the signature of the dynamic function. The *baseInstance* function can fail if the type of the function in the dynamic does not correspond to the type signature of the dynamic function. The *specialise* function can fail if the instance for a type cannot be derived, for example because it is an abstract type.

The library provide versions of all the functions that return proper error codes in case something goes wrong. Because of the explicit manner in which the generic functions are constructed in the library, the application programmer can use the error codes to recover from the situation.

7.4   Efficiency

The efficiency of the dynamically constructed generic functions is in the same order as the efficiency of unoptimised static generic functions. The construction of functions with combinators may seem costly, but under graph rewriting semantics each introduced combinator is only evaluated once.

A compiler does have more optimisation opportunities. Fusion for example has proved to be powerful enough to completely remove the overhead of the construction of the generic representation of values for most generic functions [5, 6]. This optimisation is not possible in our dynamic setting. The library cannot analyse the base instances that are provided by the programmer, because these dynamics contain compiled code.

8   Related Work

Earlier work by one of the authors [2] can be seen as a prequel to the present paper. In that paper the representation of types is also used implement generic function on dynamics, but it assumed compiler support to generate many of the functions that are constructed at run-time in the current approach. The system was limited to generics function with one generic variable.

Cheney and Hinze [7] combined dynamics and generics from the outset. Their implementation is lightweight in the number of language features that are used. The dynamics already contain values with the generic structure and the programmer has to write the conversions functions between values and their generic representation. The dynamics in the current paper contain the actual values with sharing fully preserved, which makes them more efficient.

The "Boilerplate" articles [11, 12] use the same run-time information about types and type definitions to build generic traversal schemes. Because this information is present in dynamics the traversal schemes can also be applied to the values in dynamics. The library presented in the current paper makes the approach from Generic Haskell or Clean available for dynamic values, but the library does require a more powerful dynamic typing system (dynamics with polymorphic types and run-time unification). Many functions can be implemented with either system and experience will have to show which approach is more convenient in what situation.

9   Conclusions and Future Work

We have developed a library in Clean that enables a programmer to create an instance for a generic function for values of type Dynamic. A dynamic can contain any value of any type which can both be inspected at run-time using a pattern match. Dynamics can be stored on disk or send to another application over the internet.

Using our new library, one is now able at run-time to apply generic functions on dynamics of any value and (almost) any type. Such a dynamic might even have been created by other applications. One cannot only apply "consuming" generic functions like equality and pretty printing, but also typical "producing" generic functions like parsers. Furthermore, one cannot only define generic functions on values but one can define generic functions on their types as well. It is possible, for example, to create a generic editor to edit a type stored in a dynamic. It can be used to compose a new type using the available ones. Now one can create another generic editor to construct a value of this newly constructed type.

The library is very easy to use for someone familiar with the static generic approach. The definition of a dynamic generic function can be given in a very mechanical way. It is even imaginable that the dynamic definition can be created automatically by a compiler from the static description.

The library is implemented in Clean. The implementation actually provides a run-time variant of the static generic transformation scheme as implemented in the Clean compiler. To realise this, one among others has to be able to construct new functions at run-time. We have accomplished this by using bracket abstraction. For dealing with recursive types one has to be able to construct recursive functions for which we have used a fix-point combinator. Currently we can only deal with uniform recursive types.

In principle it should be possible to adopt our library for Haskell if the dynamic typing system would be more powerfull. Our solution needs dynamics that contain polymorphic types and run-time unification.

In the future we would like to investigate if it is possible to remove the current restriction that dynamic generic functions cannot be applied to non-uniform recursive types. Furthermore we want to create some larger applications to test the library. Feedback from our users is highly appreciated.

Acknowledgement

Many thanks to Artem Alimarine for valuable discussions and the anonymous referees for numerous suggestions for improvement.

References

1. M. Abadi, L. Cardelli, B. Pierce, G. Plotkin, and D. Rèmy. Dynamic typing in polymorphic languages. In *Proceedings of the ACM SIGPLAN Workshop on ML and its Applications*, San Francisco, June 1992.
2. P. Achten, A. Alimarine, and R. Plasmeijer. When generic functions use dynamic values. In R. Peña, editor, *The 14th International workshop on the Implementation of Functional Languages, IFL'02, Selected Papers*, volume 2670 of *LNCS*, pages 17–33. Madrid, Spain, Springer, Sept. 2002.
3. Achten, Peter, van Eekelen, Marko and Plasmeijer, Rinus. Generic Graphical User Interfaces. In Greg Michaelson and Phil Trinder, editors, *Selected Papers of the 15th Int. Workshop on the Implementation of Functional Languages, IFL03*, volume 3145 of *LNCS*. Edinburgh, UK, Springer, 2003.
4. A. Alimarine and R. Plasmeijer. A Generic Programming Extension for Clean. In T. Arts and M. Mohnen, editors, *The 13th International workshop on the Implementation of Functional Languages, IFL'01, Selected Papers*, volume 2312 of *LNCS*, pages 168–186. Älvsjö, Sweden, Springer, Sept. 2002.
5. A. Alimarine and S. Smetsers. Optimizing generic functions. In D. Kozen, editor, *The 7th International Conference, Mathematics of Program Construction*, number 3125 in LNCS, pages 16 – 31. Stirling, Scotland, UK, Springer, July 2004.
6. A. Alimarine and S. Smetsers. Improved fusion for optimizing generics. In M. Hermenegildo and D. Cabeza, editors, *Proceedings of Seventh International Symposium on Practical Aspects of Declarative Languages*, number 3350 in LNCS, pages 203 – 218. Long Beach, CA, USA, Springer, Jan. 2005.
7. J. Cheney and R. Hinze. A lightweight implementation of generics and dynamics, 2002.
8. R. Hinze. A new approach to generic functional programming. In *The 27th Annual ACM SIGPLAN-SIGACT Symposium on Principles of Programming Languages*, pages 119–132. Boston, Massachusetts, January 2000.

9. R. Hinze and S. Peyton Jones. Derivable Type Classes. In G. Hutton, editor, *2000 ACM SIGPLAN Haskell Workshop*, volume 41(1) of *ENTCS*. Montreal, Canada, Elsevier Science, 2001.

10. P. Koopman, A. Alimarine, J. Tretmans, and R. Plasmeijer. Gast: Generic automated software testing. In R. Peña and T. Arts, editors, *The 14th International Workshop on the Implementation of Functional Languages, IFL'02, Selected Papers*, volume 2670 of *LNCS*, pages 84–100. Springer, 2003.

11. R. Lämmel and S. Peyton Jones. Scrap your boilerplate: a practical design pattern for generic programming. *ACM SIGPLAN Notices*, 38(3):26–37, Mar. 2003. Proc. of the ACM SIGPLAN Workshop on Types in Language Design and Implementation (TLDI 2003).

12. R. Lämmel and S. Peyton Jones. Scrap more boilerplate: reflection, zips, and generalised casts. In *Proceedings; International Conference on Functional Programming (ICFP 2004)*. ACM Press, Sept. 2004. 12 pages; To appear.

13. S. Peyton Jones and Hughes J. et al. *Report on the programming language Haskell 98*. University of Yale, 1999. http://www.haskell.org/definition/.

14. M. Pil. Dynamic types and type dependent functions. In K. Hammond, T. Davie, and C. Clack, editors, *Implementation of Functional Languages (IFL '98)*, LNCS, pages 169–185. Springer Verlag, 1999.

15. R. Plasmeijer and M. van Eekelen. *Concurrent CLEAN Language Report (version 2.0)*, December 2001. http://www.cs.kun.nl/~clean/contents/contents.html.

16. A. van Weelden and R. Plasmeijer. Towards a strongly typed functional operating system. In R. Peña and T. Arts, editors, *The 14th International Workshop on the Implementation of Functional Languages, IFL'02, Selected Papers*, volume 2670 of *LNCS*, pages 215–231. Springer, Sept. 2003.

17. M. Vervoort and R. Plasmeijer. Lazy dynamic input/output in the lazy functional language Clean. In R. Peña and T. Arts, editors, *The 14th International Workshop on the Implementation of Functional Languages, IFL'02, Selected Papers*, volume 2670 of *LNCS*, pages 101–117. Springer, Sept. 2003.

Reasoning About Deterministic Concurrent Functional I/O

Malcolm Dowse[1,*], Andrew Butterfield[1], and Marko van Eekelen[2]

[1] Trinity College Dublin, Ireland
{Malcolm.Dowse, Andrew.Butterfield}@cs.tcd.ie
[2] University of Nijmegen, The Netherlands
M.vanEekelen@science.ru.nl

Abstract. This paper develops a language for reasoning about concurrent functional I/O. We assume that the API is specified as state-transformers on a single world state. We then prove that under certain conditions evaluation in this language is deterministic, and give some examples. All properties were machine-verified using the Sparkle proof-assistant and using Core-Clean as a meta-language.

1 Introduction

In pure functional languages, I/O is usually achieved using some method of explicitly sequencing actions on the external world (monads [13]; unique types [1]). However, solutions to I/O tasks are sometimes more easily expressed and understood when written in a style that allows for the specification of concurrent I/O.

> "All I/O operations [are] strictly sequenced along a single "trunk". Sometimes, though, such strict sequencing is unwanted." [13]

In Clean [14], a limited form of concurrent I/O is permitted. The unique type-system allows the global world state to be "split" into distinct parts resulting in, for example, a file and the rest of the file system. This leaves the relative ordering of actions on each distinct part of the global-state unspecified, but since the regions are distinct, evaluation still remains deterministic.

Concurrent Haskell [12], on the other hand, introduces powerful concurrency primitives into the language. Processes may perform I/O, fork and communicate with one another. Although this has many practical uses, it has the unavoidable effect of introducing non-determinism.

In this paper we introduce a small language with monad-like constructs which is designed for reasoning about the effect of concurrency in state-based functional I/O. We then show how given some pre-conditions on the state and some extra run-time checks we call *contexts* one can loosen the explicit sequencing of

---

* Supported by Enterprise Ireland Basic Research Grant SC-2002-283.

C. Grelck et al. (Eds.): IFL 2004, LNCS 3474, pp. 177–194, 2005.
© Springer-Verlag Berlin Heidelberg 2005

actions without introducing non-determinism. The resultant language is rather dynamic in nature, requiring more run-time checks. However, it does provide greater flexibility compared with the strict sequencing of I/O actions currently required by Haskell if we wish to retain deterministic behaviour.

1.1   This Paper

Section 2 introduces our state-based model of I/O, APIs and contexts. Section 3 then implements a non-deterministic language with monad-like I/O and a `fork` concurrency primitive, and Section 4 proves that under certain specific conditions the language is confluent with respect to evaluation. Finally, Sections 5 and 6 give detailed examples of contexts being used to allow safe concurrency on separate parts of the one file system.

We use Core-Clean as a meta-language for implementing the API, modelling global-state and sequencing I/O actions. Our only axioms are pieces of Clean/Core-Clean code. Proofs were all machine-verified using the Sparkle proof-assistant [4], a semi-automated LCF-style proof-assistant designed specifically for reasoning about Core-Clean. Core-Clean supports a large subset of the functionality of the Clean programming language, including parametric polymorphism and strictness annotation – but not I/O, hence the need for meta-proofs.

This work generally builds on existing research by the authors [2, 6, 5] into examining how the different ways of expressing (functional) I/O affect our ability to do formal reasoning. We use Clean to model the language, but our results are in no way bound by Clean's actual implementation.

1.2   Related Work

An enormous amount of literature has been published on the subjects of concurrency, state and I/O in functional languages. Most of it has only a limited relevance to our work, which is concerned, ultimately, with the semantics of I/O with a view to proving useful properties about actual programs.

For us, state is strictly global with a fixed interface. This distinguishes our work from literature on memory allocation, deallocation and sharing. When explicit concurrency is mentioned with reference to functional languages, it usually includes inter-process communication and other typically non-deterministic constructs (for example, the CCS-style approach adopted in [12]). Most mathematical results concerning functional I/O tend to be high-level and axiomatic (monads and monad-transformers [11]; using CCS to structure the ordering of actions [7]). In general, the specifics of actual APIs are ignored.

Deterministic concurrent I/O in functional languages has, however, been studied before. This has mainly been in implementation-driven attempts to provide a smoother I/O interface: the Clean file system API [14]; some implementation techniques for deterministic concurrency [3]; state-splitting using a special form of lazy functional state-thread [9]. Building models of the specifics of the I/O system is not new either [10, 8]. As with our approach, these systems are also state-based.

Nonetheless, this paper, as far as we know, is the first to tackle the semantic issues of concurrency in state-based I/O, incorporating a full-blown formal model of the global state as part of the language's semantics. Our results also have been machine verified.

1.3   A Note on Sparkle and Clean

Occasionally we modify the actual Clean syntax in this paper to make up for small shortcomings in Sparkle. In the actual Clean code: functions are usually used in an uncurried fashion; records are replaced with tuples; lambda abstractions are replaced by named functions; `Chars` are replaced with `Ints`.

Sometimes strict tuple and strict list types are used:

```
:: STup a b = STup  !a !b
:: SList :a = SCons !a !(SList a) | SNull
```

For the purposes of clarity, we change these types to `!(a,b)` and `![a]` respectively, retaining the names of the standard operations (`fst`, `length` etc.)

The benefit of using Sparkle is that lazy functional semantics are already encoded within the theorem prover. We only need to wrap the pure language in a small exterior which allows I/O to be expressed. Any small pitfalls concerning name-capture, strict/lazy semantics or the Hindley-Milner type system will (hopefully) be detected automatically.

One disadvantage of using Sparkle is that it is not ideal for modelling a world-state. For example, there is, as of yet, no facility for modelling sets easily in Sparkle. Also, since we are always reasoning about actual programs which may not terminate, all types must necessarily contain a bottom element.

We use Clean syntax, but it is mostly very similar to that of Haskell. The most obvious difference is that a type `a -> b -> c` in Haskell is written as `a b -> c` in Clean.

2   State-Based I/O and Contexts

In this paper we incorporate a `fork`-like primitive into I/O in a functional language. To introduce concurrency without causing non-determinism we must be able to isolate certain classes of legitimate I/O actions which don't interfere with one another. Only actions with this property can be performed concurrently.

The solution is based around *contexts*. A context identifies a set of permitted actions. Each program fragment is executed within a particular context and, along with the global state, it affects what the program does and is allowed to do. If the current context forbids certain actions then any attempt to execute these actions will result in a catchable run-time error.

2.1   Modelling I/O

To talk about non-interference we resort to an entirely state-based model of I/O. The meaning of each action is defined as a state-transformer on some global state.

Similarly, we regard the meaning of a whole program as being the resultant effect it has on global state.[1]

An instance of the Clean record type `IOSystem` defines both the semantics of each I/O action and how concurrency can be performed.

```
:: IOSystem v a p w c :== { af :: a w -> (w,v)
                          , ap :: c a -> Bool
                          , pf :: p c -> (c,c)}
```

The above structure – three functions parameterised by five types, and one additional pre-condition which we discuss below – is enough to formally model an I/O system with deterministic concurrency. The following subsections explain each component in turn.

2.2   af – The Semantics of Actions

The function `af :: a w -> (w,v)` models the effect of each action on the world state. The type `w` is that of the world, or global state. `a` is the API, with each element identifying an I/O action that can be performed. Type `v` denotes return values. This is typically a sum type capable of storing `Ints`, `Bools`, `Chars` or any other value that an action needs to return.

For any action `a`, `af a :: w -> (w,v)` defines the state-transformer for that action.

2.3   ap - Contexts and Non-interference

Contexts are denoted by the type `c` and the meaning of each context is defined by `ap :: c a -> Bool`. `ap c a` is a `Bool` which indicates whether action a is permitted by context c. A context c can be thought of as the set of actions a such that `ap c a = True`.

The original purpose of contexts was to isolate certain groups of actions which don't interfere. We can say that two actions a_l and a_r won't interfere with one another if, for all world states, the order in which they are performed is irrelevant. This is expressed as $a_l \;|||\; a_r$:

$$a_l \;|||\; a_r \triangleq \forall w.\forall w_2.\forall v_l.\forall v_r$$
$$(\exists w_1.\text{af } a_l\; w = (w_1,v_l) \wedge \text{af } a_r\; w_1 = (w_2,v_r))$$
$$\Leftrightarrow$$
$$(\exists w_1.\text{af } a_r\; w = (w_1,v_r) \wedge \text{af } a_l\; w_1 = (w_2,v_l))$$

---

[1] This means that any two non-terminating programs become indistinguishable – a rather worrying problem. The CCS approach to modelling I/O [12] doesn't suffer from this, however, and since we see no immediate reason why one can't have the best of both worlds, this will be a topic of future work.

Now we can define two important relations on contexts:

$$c_1 \;|||\; c_2 \triangleq \forall a_1.\forall a_2.\text{ap } c_1\, a_1 \wedge \text{ap } c_2\, a_2 \implies a_1 \;|||\; a_2$$

$$c \sqsubseteq c_1 \triangleq \forall a.\text{ap } c\, a \implies \text{ap } c_1\, a$$

$c_1 \;|||\; c_2$ states that for all actions a_1 permitted under context c_1 and for all actions a_2 permitted under context c_2, the ordering of actions a_1 and a_2 is irrelevant. $c \sqsubseteq c_1$ states that if an action is permitted to run in context c then it will also be permitted in context c_1.

$|||$ is symmetric and $\sqsubseteq$ is a pre-order – both by definition.

2.4 pf - Enforcing Non-interference

Assume that we have modelled our API and created a set of contexts which model all the different permissions a program might well be allowed to have. We would now like to guarantee that if a program running in context c performs a `fork` which results in two programs with contexts c_l and c_r, then

1. neither process will interfere with one another: $c_l \;|||\; c_r$.
2. neither process will be capable of performing an action forbidden by the enclosing parent context: $c_l \sqsubseteq c \wedge c_r \sqsubseteq c$.

We solve this problem by defining a function `pf :: p c -> (c,c)`, which we assume obeys that very pre-condition:

$$\mathrm{PRE}_{\text{af,ap,pf}} \triangleq \forall c.\forall c_l.\forall c_r.\forall p.\ \text{pf } p\, c = (c_l,c_r) \implies c_l \;|||\; c_r \wedge c_l \sqsubseteq c \wedge c_r \sqsubseteq c$$

A value of type `p` is an extra parameter which gives the programmer some flexibility with regard to how he wishes the current context to be split. If a program is running in context c, the programmer `fork`s supplying the value p, and $\text{pf } p\, c = (c_l,c_r)$, then the new left- and right-hand processes will execute in contexts c_l and c_r respectively. When both of these terminate, the execution of the parent process will continue again in context c.

To prevent visual clutter, for the rest of the paper we assume the existence of some implicit `IOSystem` called $s_{\text{af,ap,pf}}$. We assume this defines the functions `af`, `ap` and `pf`, and binds the types `v`, `a`, `w`, `c` and `p`. Unless stated otherwise, all results generalise over all of these values.

3   A Language with Concurrent I/O

In this section we define a language which implements concurrency as described in the previous section in a functional style.

3.1   Syntax

The language is defined directly in Clean. Programs are elements of the higher-order algebraic data-type `Prog v a p`.

```
:: Prog v a p = Bind (Prog v a p) (v -> Prog v a p)
              | Ret v
              | Act a (Prog v a p)
              | Par p (Prog v a p) (Prog v a p) (v v -> v)
```

Ret and Bind are similar in spirit to Haskell's monadic return and >>= respectively. Ret v returns v without changing the global state. Bind m f performs m, and if m terminates with some resultant value v, it then performs the program f v. The program Act a m performs action a if it is permitted in the current context. If it isn't permitted it runs program m instead, where m would typically act as a sort of exception handler, providing an alternative return value indicating that the action wasn't allowed. Par p ml mr vf runs ml and mr in parallel, splitting the context as determined by p. If both ml and mr terminate with values vl and vr respectively, the whole program yields a return value vf vl vr.

Since we are using a normal algebraic type, the type signatures of the four constructors are quite a lot weaker than we would like – especially those of Bind and Par. The upshot is that all return values must be an element of the same fixed type v.

These problems could be solved using an extra type variable to indicate the program's resultant return type (as opposed to the return type of actions) and some existential typing. We don't do this. One reason is that Sparkle has no facilities for reasoning about existential types. More importantly, the problem doesn't really limit the flexibility of our results. Since the type-variable v isn't constrained in any way, intuitively it can be made polymorphic. The only reason that we use an algebraic type at all is to make explicit the fact that there are four and only four ways of constructing a Prog.

3.2   Single-Step Reduction Rules

We define the operational semantics for the language at a high level of abstraction using non-deterministic single-step reduction.

We use the following syntactic sugar, choosing infix notation for Bind, Par and the function vf :: v v -> v.

$$m_l \overset{*\;p}{\|} m_r \overset{\triangle}{=} \text{Par } p\; m_l\; m_r\; (*)$$

$$m \ggg f \overset{\triangle}{=} \text{Bind } m\; f$$

$$w \Vdash m \longrightarrow_c w_1 \Vdash m_1 \overset{\triangle}{=} \text{"program } m \text{ with world-state } w \text{ may single-step}$$
$$\text{reduce under context } c \text{ to program } m_1 \text{ with}$$
$$\text{world-state } w_1\text{."}$$

The seven reduction rules can be found in Figure 1.

The first two refer to the interaction between Ret and Bind: evaluation always proceeds (recursively) from left to right. The third and fourth describe the behaviour of Act a m as described above. The final three rules refer to concurrency. The first of these states that when both sides are finished then the parallel execution of both has finished. It is the final two rules which introduce non-determinism into the single-step semantics: if the left-hand-side or the right-hand-side can be reduced then any arbitrary one may chosen.

$$w \Vdash \textbf{Ret } v \ggeq f \quad \longrightarrow_c \quad w \Vdash f\, v \tag{1}$$

$$\frac{w \Vdash m \quad \longrightarrow_c \quad w' \Vdash m'}{w \Vdash m \ggeq f \quad \longrightarrow_c \quad w' \Vdash m' \ggeq f} \tag{2}$$

$$\frac{\textbf{af } a\, w = (w',v') \quad \textbf{ap } c\, a = \textbf{True}}{w \Vdash \textbf{Act } a\, m \quad \longrightarrow_c \quad w' \Vdash \textbf{Ret } v'} \tag{3}$$

$$\frac{\textbf{ap } c\, a = \textbf{False}}{w \Vdash \textbf{Act } a\, m \quad \longrightarrow_c \quad w \Vdash m} \tag{4}$$

$$\frac{}{w \Vdash (\textbf{Ret } v_l) \overset{*\,p}{\|} (\textbf{Ret } v_r) \quad \longrightarrow_c \quad w \Vdash \textbf{Ret } v_l * v_r} \quad \textbf{pf } p\, c = (c_l,c_r) \tag{5}$$

$$\frac{w \Vdash m_l \quad \longrightarrow_{c_l} \quad w' \Vdash m_l'}{w \Vdash m_l \overset{*\,p}{\|} m_r \quad \longrightarrow_c \quad w' \Vdash m_l' \overset{*\,p}{\|} m_r} \quad \textbf{pf } p\, c = (c_l,c_r) \tag{6}$$

$$\frac{w \Vdash m_r \quad \longrightarrow_{c_r} \quad w' \Vdash m_r'}{w \Vdash m_l \overset{*\,p}{\|} m_r \quad \longrightarrow_c \quad w' \Vdash m_l \overset{*\,p}{\|} m_r'} \quad \textbf{pf } p\, c = (c_l,c_r) \tag{7}$$

Fig. 1. Single-Step Reduction Rules

3.3   Implementation

We implement single-step reduction as a Clean function which modifies the program/state pair given the context it has to be reduced in. However, the above language aims to leave the order in which concurrent actions are performed unspecified. Since we are reasoning about an implementation in a deterministic language like Core-Clean it is necessary to emulate this randomness or lack of knowledge. One approach might be for the reduction function to return a list containing the possible resultant programs after single-step reduction. Instead, the solution we chose was to supply an extra argument to the single-step reduction function.

```
:: Random   :== ![Bool]
next :: (IOSystem v a p w c) c Random (Prog v a p, w) -> (Prog v a p, w)
```

next implements single-step reduction. The extra argument mentioned is of type Random and acts as a sort of random number generator. One individual

Random (that is, strict list of Bool[2]) is consumed for each single-step reduction – one boolean value for each syntactic level of parallelism. The boolean values are only referred to when a non-deterministic choice needs to be made between reducing the left- or right-hand-side of a parallel computation. If it's False, go left; if it's True, go right. If the list isn't long enough the evaluator just defaults to the value False.

We can now define the implementation of single-step reduction by existentially quantifying over the possible Random values.

$$w \Vdash m \longrightarrow_c w_1 \Vdash m_1 \triangleq \exists r.r \neq \bot \wedge \mathsf{next}\ \mathsf{s_{af,ap,pf}}\ c\ r\ (m,w) = (m_1,w_1)$$

3.4   Evaluation

Evaluation is the process of continually single-step reducing a program until it becomes a single value of the form Ret v. Although we can write a function which does just that, in order to prove properties formally we must be precise about the number of reduction steps required.

```
:: Random2 :== ![Random]
rdce :: Int (IOSystem v a p w c) c Random2 (Prog v a p,w)->(Prog v a p,w)
```

rdce iterates the single-step reduction function next a specific non-negative number of times. It requires a value of type Random2 (a strict list of Random) as a parameter because each application of next on its own needs a fresh Random. With every iteration another Random is consumed from the list, defaulting to [] if the list is exhausted.

Like with reduction, we again define some more syntactic sugar.

$$w \Vdash m \overset{c}{\Downarrow} \langle v, w_1 \rangle \triangleq \exists q.q \neq \bot \wedge \exists i.\mathsf{rdce}\ i\ \mathsf{s_{af,ap,pf}}\ c\ q\ (m,w) = (\mathsf{Ret}\ v, w_1)$$

$$w \Vdash m \overset{c}{\Downarrow} \langle v, w_1 \rangle \triangleq \forall q.q \neq \bot \implies \exists i.\mathsf{rdce}\ i\ \mathsf{s_{af,ap,pf}}\ c\ q\ (m,w) = (\mathsf{Ret}\ v, w_1)$$

The first, $w \Vdash m \overset{c}{\Downarrow} \langle v, w_1 \rangle$, states that $w \Vdash m$ may possibly evaluate to $w_1 \Vdash \mathsf{Ret}\ v$ in context c, depending on which non-deterministic choices are made. $w \Vdash m \overset{c}{\Downarrow} \langle v, w_1 \rangle$, on the other hand, is stronger. It states that $w \Vdash m$ *always* evaluates to $w_1 \Vdash \mathsf{Ret}\ v$ in context c (which, of course, if true, implies that it possibly can). It is the second, stronger property which we want and the purpose of the confluence proof is to show that if $\mathbb{PRE}_{\mathsf{af,ap,pf}}$ holds then the two are in fact the same: if a program can evaluate to some resultant state then it won't ever do anything else.

---

[2] An infinite, lazy stream of Bool might seem more appropriate but this isn't the case. Laziness also introduces partiality and we then need a messy pre-condition on every stream ensuring that each individual Bool is defined. With a strict list r we get this condition automatically by asserting simply that $r \neq \bot$.

Quite often we need to be explicit about the number of reduction steps performed. In these situations we annotate the evaluation with that number, as follows:

$$w \Vdash m \stackrel{c}{\Downarrow_i} \langle v, w_1 \rangle \triangleq \exists q. q \neq \bot \wedge \mathbf{rdce}\ i\ \mathbf{s}_{\mathtt{af,ap,pf}}\ c\ q\ (m, w) = (\mathtt{Ret}\ v, w_1)$$

$$w \Vdash m \stackrel{c}{\Downarrow_i} \langle v, w_1 \rangle \triangleq \forall q. q \neq \bot \Longrightarrow \mathbf{rdce}\ i\ \mathbf{s}_{\mathtt{af,ap,pf}}\ c\ q\ (m, w) = (\mathtt{Ret}\ v, w_1)$$

3.5   Failure

Since the language's semantics and individual programs contain arbitrary functions, it is clear that reduction can fail or not terminate. We define failure simply to be the case that no number of reduction steps would ever yield a single value. It can happen in a number of different ways:

- An action fails - that is, for some action a, $\mathtt{ap}\ a\ w = \bot$.
- When running program $m \ggg f$, f doesn't terminate when applied to m's return value.
- A program is syntactically ill-defined. For example: $\bot \stackrel{*\ p}{\|} \bot$.
- The functions $\mathtt{ap}$ and $\mathtt{pf}$ happen to return $\bot$.
- The program loops infinitely, continually performing I/O actions.

4   Proving Confluence

In this section we show that if $\mathbb{PRE}_{\mathtt{af,ap,pf}}$ holds then the non-deterministic single-step semantics are confluent with respect to program evaluation. In other words, the arbitrary choices made when reducing any given program have no effect on the resultant global-state and return value.

The full confluence proof is large and requires many smaller results. Only the more important ones are shown below.

Lemma 1. *If* $\mathbb{PRE}_{af,ap,pf}$ *holds and single-step reducing a program is successful, either it didn't change the world-state at all or it performed a single action which was permitted by that program's context.*

Proof. Structural induction over $\mathtt{Prog}^3$. The only way the world-state can be changed is by performing an action. Because of the properties guaranteed by $\mathbb{PRE}_{\mathtt{af,ap,pf}}$, no forbidden action can be performed at a deeper lever which might have been forbidden at the top level.

Lemma 2.

$$\mathbb{PRE}_{af,ap,pf}\ \wedge\ (\exists p. \exists c. \mathbf{pf}\ p\ c = (c_l, c_r)) \Longrightarrow$$
$$(\exists w_1.\ w \Vdash m_l \longrightarrow_{c_l}\ w_1 \Vdash m_{l1}\ \wedge\ w_1 \Vdash m_r \longrightarrow_{c_r}\ w_2 \Vdash m_{r1})$$
$$\Leftrightarrow$$
$$(\exists w_1.\ w \Vdash m_r \longrightarrow_{c_r}\ w_1 \Vdash m_{r1}\ \wedge\ w_1 \Vdash m_l \longrightarrow_{c_l}\ w_2 \Vdash m_{l1})$$

---

[3] This isn't usually possible. On this one occasion we have no need to reason about f in a program of the form $m \ggg f$.

If two contexts don't interfere then the order in which one single-step reduces those two program in the different contexts is irrelevant.

Proof. A direct application of Lemma 1 and the non-interference properties guaranteed by $\mathrm{PRE}_{af,ap,pf}$. If both both m_l and m_r performed an action then their order was irrelevant.

Lemma 3.

$$\mathrm{PRE}_{af,ap,pf} \ \wedge \ (\exists p.\exists c.\textbf{pf}\ p\ c = (c_l, c_r)) \Longrightarrow$$

$$(\exists w_1.\ w \Vdash m_l \ \Downarrow_{i_l}^{c_l}\ \langle v_l, w_1\rangle \ \wedge \ w_1 \Vdash m_r \ \Downarrow_{i_r}^{c_r}\ \langle v_r, w_2\rangle)$$

$$\Leftrightarrow$$

$$(\exists w_1.\ w \Vdash m_r \ \Downarrow_{i_r}^{c_r}\ \langle v_r, w_1\rangle \ \wedge \ w_1 \Vdash m_l \ \Downarrow_{i_l}^{c_l}\ \langle v_l, w_2\rangle)$$

The evaluation order of two programs in two non-interfering contexts is irrelevant.

Proof. Induction over both i_l and i_r. Each single-step reduction in m_l is, in turn, exchanged with the other reductions in m_r so that it happens after m_r instead of before it, applying Lemma 2.

Lemma 4.

$$\frac{w \Vdash m \ggg f \ \Downarrow_i^c\ \langle v_2, w_2\rangle}{\exists i_1.\exists v_1.\exists w_1.i_1 \geq 0 \ \wedge \ w \Vdash m \ \Downarrow_{i_1}^c\ \langle v_1, w_1\rangle \ \wedge \ w_1 \Vdash f\ v_1 \ \Downarrow_{i-i_1-1}^c\ \langle v_2, w_2\rangle}$$

If $m \ggg f$ evaluates with some specific reduction order then there exists a specific reduction order for m which yields a value v_1 and another reduction order for $f\ v_1$ which, together, has the same resultant effect.

Proof. Induction on i. The initial **Random2** list, which determines the reduction order, is effectively sliced into two parts. The first part is the ordering for m, the second that for $f\ v_1$.

Lemma 5.

$$\frac{w \Vdash m \ \Downarrow_{i_1}^c\ \langle v_1, w_1\rangle \qquad w_1 \Vdash f\ v_1 \ \Downarrow_{i_2}^c\ \langle v_2, w_2\rangle}{w \Vdash m \ggg f \ \Downarrow_{i_1+1+i_2}^c\ \langle v_2, w_2\rangle}$$

If evaluation of m is confluent, always returning value v_1, and $f\ v_1$ is also confluent, then so is the evaluation of $m \ggg f$.

Proof. Induction on i_1.

Lemma 6.

$$w \Vdash m_l \overset{*\,p}{\|} m_r \overset{c}{\Downarrow}_i \langle v, w_2 \rangle \wedge \mathrm{PRE}_{af,ap,pf} \wedge \mathit{pf}\, p\, c = (c_l, c_r)$$
$$\Longrightarrow$$
$$\exists i_1. \exists v_l. \exists v_r. \exists w_1. \left(\begin{array}{c} i_1 \geq 0 \wedge v = v_l * v_r \wedge \\ w \Vdash m_l \overset{c_l}{\Downarrow}_{i_1} \langle v_l, w_1 \rangle \wedge \\ w_1 \Vdash m_r \overset{c_r}{\Downarrow}_{i - i_1 - 1} \langle v_r, w_2 \rangle \end{array} \right)$$

If $m_l \overset{*\,p}{\|} m_r$ evaluates with some arbitrary reduction order then there exists a reduction order for m_l and a reduction order for m_r such that executing both separately, one after the other, has exactly the same effect.

Proof. Induction on i. We split the `Random2` list used for both m_l and m_r, filtering the `Random` values into two separate lists depending on which of the two sub-programs received each value originally.

Lemma 7. *if* $\mathit{pf}\, p\, c = (c_l, c_r)$ *and* $\mathrm{PRE}_{af,ap,pf}$,

$$\frac{w \Vdash m_l \overset{c_l}{\Downarrow}_{i_l} \langle v_l, w_1 \rangle \quad w_1 \Vdash m_r \overset{c_r}{\Downarrow}_{i - i_l - 1} \langle v_r, w_2 \rangle \quad i \geq 0}{w \Vdash m_l \overset{*\,p}{\|} m_r \overset{c}{\Downarrow}_i \langle v_l * v_r, w_2 \rangle}$$

If evaluation of m_l and m_r are both confluent on their own when run sequentially in two non-interfering contexts c_l and c_r, then $m_l \overset{*\,p}{\|} m_r$ is also confluent when run in an enclosing context c.

Proof. Induction over i. Depending on the random values, each reduction step in the parallel computation may pick either to reduce m_l or m_r. If it's m_l it is relatively easy. If m_r has to be single-step reduced we must show that reducing it once at the start is no different to doing it after m_l has been fully evaluated.

One awkward technicality is the proof that failure propagates sensibly: if neither m_l nor m_r fail, then it must be shown that failure cannot occur at a higher level either, regardless of reduction order.

Theorem 1. Confluence
$$\text{if } \mathrm{PRE}_{af,ap,pf}, \text{ then } w \Vdash m \overset{c}{\Downarrow}_i \langle v, w_1 \rangle \Longrightarrow w \Vdash m \overset{c}{\Downarrow}_i \langle v, w_1 \rangle$$

Proof. Strong induction over i. The base case, $i = 0$, is trivial since m is just a value. In the inductive case we perform case analysis on the three different recursive constructors (`Bind`, `Act` and `Par`). For each constructor, we

1. Decompose $w \Vdash m \overset{c}{\Downarrow}_i \langle v, w_1 \rangle$ into the separate, sequential evaluation of m's constituent sub-programs.

2. Apply the inductive hypothesis, thus guaranteeing that the different sub-programs are confluent when run in isolation. (The number of reduction steps in each sub-program must be strictly less than i – and in this case it always is.)
3. Show that the confluence of reduction is preserved when the sub-programs are executed as individual parts of the one program again.

Proving this for Act is not difficult. For Bind, steps 1 and 3 above are performed by Lemmas 4 and 5, and for Par, by Lemmas 6 and 7.

Corollary 1. *If* $\mathbb{PRE}_{af,ap,pf}$, *then if a program can fail, it always will.*

Proof. By contradiction. If it didn't always fail, then it would for some reduction order succeed in evaluating, and therefore, by confluence, always evaluate.

5   An Example: A File System

5.1   Design Criteria

We want the file system to contain a potentially infinite number of files, each file containing any finite amount of data. Files can be opened for shared reading with multiple read-pointers, as well as (non-shared) reading and writing. Files can also be created and deleted.

The design and implementation of the file system is also influenced by the fact that we want the behaviour of certain actions to be independent of one another. Most notably:

– Actions on different files.
– Actions on different read-handles of the same file.

The model is not meant to be industrial strength. Nonetheless, we would like to think that it is a plausible simplification, capturing many reasonable everyday properties one would expect of a real file system.

5.2   File System State

The FS type models our file system:

```
:: FS     :== MapN (Maybe FData)
:: OpenSt = Closed | Open ![Maybe Ptr] | ReadWrite !Ptr
:: Hnd    = ReadH !Nam !FileDes | WriteH !Nam
:: Maybe a = Just !a | Nothing

:: FData   :== !(Data,OpenSt)        :: Data :== ![Char]
:: MapN d  :== Nam -> d              :: Nam  :== Int
:: FileDes :== Int                   :: Ptr  :== Int
```

A file system is a mapping from names to Maybe FData - a file either doesn't exist or has a FData associated with it. File data itself consists of a (strict) list of characters and an `OpenSt` which indicates whether the file is closed, open for (shared) reading or open for both reading and writing.

If it's open for reading then the file maintains a list of active pointers. This list grows with each new shared-read. Each time a handle is closed it is replaced by `Nothing`, and if all handles have been closed then the entire file is then closed. If the file is open for writing then it just stores the one pointer. Once files are opened, they are accessed via handles of type `Hnd`. This structure contains enough information to find out where the required file-pointer is stored within the global-state.

5.3 File API and Return Values

There are fourteen primitive file system actions in our API, which we encode as an algebraic type. As in [5], we trim the meaning of each action down to its bare, logical minimum. That is: lots of actions, each doing a very specific task.

```
:: FSAction = FOpen Nam Bool  | HClose Hnd  | FClose Nam  | HRead Hnd
            | HWrite Hnd Char | HNext Hnd   | HEOF Hnd    | HRewind Hnd
            | HValid Hnd      | FIsOpen Nam | FIsRead Nam | FCreate Nam
            | FDelete Nam     | FExists Nam
```

Seven of the fourteen actions act on handles (which themselves refer to specific files); the others just act on filenames.

Each action can return information using the dynamic return type `RV`.

```
:: RV = RInt !Int | RChar !Char | RBool !Bool | RHnd !Hnd | RNull
```

We also define two useful look-up functions with the following types and the obvious definitions.

```
actNam :: FSAction -> Nam            hndNam :: Hnd      -> Nam
```

5.4 Defining a State-Transformer

The common patterns of behaviour to do with non-interference mentioned above are much easier to guarantee and reason about if they are enforced directly.

We can be certain that two actions on different pieces of global state don't interfere if:

- They only modify their own piece of global state.
- Both their resultant return value and the way that they modify the state is solely determined by the action's own parameters and the original value of that piece of local state.

For this reason, all API-calls are modelled as state-transformers on individual *files*. Additionally, API-calls on file-handles are (mostly) modelled as state-transformers on individual *file-pointers* (for one specific file).

Actions on Individual Files. The meaning of each action is given by a function of type (Maybe FData) -> (Maybe FData, RV). This is converted into a state-transformer on FS with the function liftMapN (the details are omitted).

```
liftMapN :: !Nam (d -> (d,r)) (MapN d) -> (MapN d, r)
```

Lemma 8. *if $n_1 \neq n_2$, then, for any two state-transformers f_1 and f_2, the execution of* liftMapN n_1 f_1 *and* liftMapN n_2 f_2 *is order independent.*

Proof. Relatively easy in the absence of failure. The definition of liftMapN must strictly evaluate the local state before and after the (local) state-transformer is applied to guarantee that failure propagates symmetrically.

Actions on Individual Pointers. Certain actions only modify the value of one pointer in a file, the identity of that pointer being determined by a handle. These actions may examine the contents of that file, but cannot examine the values of any other file-pointers. This interface is enforced using liftPtrsMapN.

```
liftPtrsMapN :: (![Char] (Maybe Ptr) -> (Maybe Ptr, r)) Hnd ->
  (Maybe FData -> (Maybe FData, r))
```

Lemma 9. *If h_1 and h_2 are both read-handles referring to the same file but referring to different pointers, then the execution of* liftPtrsMapN f_1 h_1 *and* liftPtrsMapN f_2 h_2 *is order independent.*

Proof. Not too difficult, but does require a library of standard strict list theorems.

5.5 Implementing the API

Finally, we build the full API state-transformer afFS using the liftMapN function. An individual API-call may also employ liftPtrsMapN.

To save space we just show the implementation of FOpen and HRead.[4]

```
afFS :: FSAction FS -> (FS,RV)
afFS a w = liftMapN (actNam a) (actFn a) w

actFn :: (Maybe FData) -> (Maybe FData, RV)
actFn (FOpen n b)  = fOpen_ n b
actFn (HRead h)    = liftPtrsMapN hRead_ h
actFn (HWrite h c) = // .....

fOpen_ :: !Nam Bool (Maybe FData) -> (Maybe FData, RV)
fOpen_ n False (Just (cs,Closed))  =
            (Just (cs, Open [Just 0]), RHnd (ReadH n 0))
fOpen_ n False (Just (cs,Read ps)) =
```

---

[4] The HRead action is a little different to a normal POSIX-style read. It only reads the character - to increment the file pointer afterwards one must then use HNext.

```
               (Just (cs, Open ps++[Just 0]), RHnd (ReadH n (length ps)))
fOpen_ n True  (Just (cs,Closed))  =
               (Just (cs, ReadWrite 0), RHnd (WriteH n))

hRead_ :: ![Char] (Maybe Ptr) -> (Maybe Ptr, RV)
hRead_ cs (SJust p) = (SJust p, RChar (cs!!p))
```

5.6   Resultant Properties

The above file system partially defines an `IOSystem` with type variables `v`, `a` and `w` bound to `RV`, `FSAction` and `FS` respectively. The function `afFS` gives the semantics of each action.

The file system implementation obeys two important properties.

Lemma 10. *If* $actNam\, a_1 \neq actNam\, a_2$, *then* $a_1 \;|||\; a_2$

Proof. A direct consequence of Lemma 8.

Lemma 11. *If* a_1 *and* a_2 *are actions which act on the same file but different read-pointers, then* $a_1 \;|||\; a_2$

Proof. The actions `HRead`, `HEOF`, `HNext`, `HRewind` are straightforward (using Lemma 9) since they are defined directly using `liftPtrsMapN`. `HValid` and `HClose` are a little special and require more work.

6   File System Contexts

6.1   Partitioning Contexts on Files

A simple but useful example is to identify contexts with sets of files that a program is allowed to access. The context is a map from `Nam` to `Bool` – a look-up table used to determine if files of a particular name can be accessed.

```
:: CEasy :== MapN Bool
:: PEasy :== [Nam]

apEasy :: CEasy FSAction -> Bool
apEasy c a = c (actNam a)

pfEasy :: PEasy CEasy -> (CEasy,CEasy)
pfEasy p c  = (\n -> c n && not (isMember n p),
               \n -> c n && isMember n p)
```

Lemma 12. $\mathbb{PRE}_{afFS,\, apEasy,\, pfEasy}$

Proof. The properties $c_l \sqsubseteq c$ and $c_r \sqsubseteq c$ are trivial ((`c n && not (isMember n p)`) and (`c n && isMember n p`) both imply (`c n`)). The property $c_l \;|||\; c_r$ is proved by first showing that any respective left- and right-hand action a_l and a_r

permitted by these contexts can't act on the same file. (If it did, that filename simultaneously would and would not be an element of the list p.) Once we know this, use Lemma 10.

The lemma proved above guarantees confluence. The program `Par ns ml mr vf` runs programs `ml` and `mr` in parallel. It attempts to give `mr` access to as many of the files referred to in `ns` as possible. `ml` is allowed to access any remaining files.

6.2   Example of File-Based Partitioning

Figure 2 gives a small example of file-based partitioning.

The program `totalLength ns` calculates concurrently the sum-total of the lengths of each of the files named in list `ns`. If one filename appears twice in `ns`, only one process will be able to access it. If a file is "locked-out" by the current context, `fileLength` will simply return 0.

```
totalLength :: [Nam] -> Prog RV FSAction PEasy
totalLength ns = foldr (\n1 m1 ->
  Par [n1] m1 (fileLength n1)
              (\(RInt i1) (RInt i2) -> RInt (i1+i2))
  (Ret (RInt 0)) ns

fileLength :: Nam -> Prog RV FSAction PEasy
fileLength n =
  Bind (Act (FOpen n) (Ret RNull))
    (\v -> case v of
      RNull -> Ret (RInt 0)    // (if file access is denied)
      RHnd h -> Bind (fileLenLoop n 0)
                (\l -> Bind (Act (HClose h) undef) (\_ -> Ret l)))

// keep incrementing the handle, counting the length.
fileLenLoop :: Hnd Int -> Prog RV FSAction PEasy
```

Fig. 2. Computing File Lengths

6.3   Shared Reads

The context data doesn't have to just include what files the programmer is allowed to access. It can also be modified to include information about what specific actions the programmer is allowed to perform on those files.

By modifying the contexts to incorporate information about which specific handles one is allowed to read from, a limited kind of shared reads are permitted. It is limited because an `FOpen` on one file cannot run concurrently with any action on that file – all read-handles must be opened before any concurrency takes place at all. The problem is that while contexts can enforce a property such as "don't allow a `HRead` read from handle h", it can't be expected to enforce a property like "don't permit a `FOpen` to run if it possibly could return a handle h".

So the current file system model is slightly inadequate. However, by modifying it a little so as to separate the creation of a handle from the opening of a file, this problem should be avoidable. This will be the subject of future work.

7   Conclusions and Future Work

We have developed a language for expressing and reasoning about state-based I/O with concurrency. By adding contexts to the language it can be shown that with certain pre-conditions concurrent evaluation is deterministic.

Future work shall involve more sophisticated and realistic I/O models, including models of non-state-based I/O such as stream I/O. Stream I/O is perhaps the most pressing issue since at the moment two concurrent sub-programs are unable communicate with one another. Also important is the ability to properly distinguish non-terminating programs. Two other possible future directions are the development of Hoare-like proof rules for reasoning about languages with context and an investigation into whether types could be used to statically check some of the run-time properties required by contexts.

Acknowledgments

The authors would like to thank the anonymous referees, and Glenn Strong and Shane O'Conchuir. Their helpful suggestions improved the quality of this paper.

References

1. E. Barendsen and S. Smetsers. Uniqueness typing for functional languages with graph rewriting semantics. *Mathematical Structures in Computer Science*, 6(6):579–612, 1996.
2. A. Butterfield and G. Strong. Proving correctness of programs with I/O – a paradigm comparison. In T. Arts and M. Mohnen, editors, *Proceedings of the 13th International Workshop, IFL2001*, volume LNCS2312, pages 72–87, 2001.
3. D. Carter. Deterministic concurrency. Master's thesis, Department of Computer Science, University of Bristol, September 1994.
4. M. de Mol, M. van Eekelen, and R. Plasmeijer. Sparkle: A functional theorem prover. In T. Arts and M. Mohnen, editors, *Proceedings of the 13th International Workshop, IFL2001*, number LNCS2312, page 55. Springer-Verlag, 2001.
5. M. Dowse, A. Butterfield, M. van Eekelen, M. de Mol, and R. Plasmeijer. Towards machine verified proofs for I/O. Technical Report NIII-R0415, University of Nijmegen, April 2004.
6. M. Dowse, G. Strong, and A. Butterfield. Proving make correct – I/O proofs in Haskell and Clean. In R. Peña and T. Arts, editors, *Proceedings of the IFL 2002*, volume LNCS2670, pages 68–83, 2002.
7. A. D. Gordon. An operational semantics for I/O in a lazy functional language. In *Proceedings of the Conference on Functional Programming Languages and Computer Architecture*, pages 136–145, New York, NY, USA, June 1993. ACM Press.

8. C. Hall and K. Hammond. A dynamic semantics for haskell (draft), May 20 1993.
9. I. Holyer and E. Spiliopoulou. Concurrent monadic interfacing. In *IFL '98, 10th International Workshop, Selected Papers, London, UK, September 1998*, pages 73–89. Lecture Notes in Computer Science, Volume 1595, Springer Verlag, June 1999.
10. P. Hudak and R. S. Sundaresh. On the expressiveness of purely functional I/O systems. Technical report, Yale University, 1989.
11. M. P. Jones and L. Duponcheel. Composing monads. Technical report, Yale University, December 1993.
12. S. Peyton Jones, A. Gordon, and S. Finne. Concurrent Haskell. In ACM, editor, *POPL '96: Florida, 21–24 January 1996*, pages 295–308, New York, NY, USA, 1996. ACM Press.
13. S. Peyton Jones and P. Wadler. Imperative functional programming. In ACM, editor, *POPL '93: Charleston, January 10–13, 1993*, pages 71–84, New York, NY, USA, 1993. ACM Press.
14. R. Plasmeijer and M. van Eekelen. Concurrent clean version 2.0 language report. http://www.cs.kun.nl/~clean/, December 2001.

A   Sparkle Section Files

The Sparkle section files, which contains the proofs of all lemmas, theorems and numbered equations in this paper, can be obtained from:

http://www.cs.tcd.ie/research_groups/fmg/archive/ifl2004proofs.html

General Homomorphic Overloading

Alex Shafarenko and Sven-Bodo Scholz

Dept of Computer Science, University of Hertfordshire, United Kingdom
{A.Shafarenko, S.Scholz}@herts.ac.uk

Abstract. A general homomorphic overloading in a first-order type system is discussed and its attendant subtype inference problem is formulated. We propose a computationally efficient type inference algorithm by converting the attendant constraint-satisfaction problem into the algebraic path problem for a constraint graph weighted with elements of a specially constructed non-commutative star semiring. The elements of the semiring are monotonic functions from integers to integers (including $\pm\infty$) with pointwise maximum and function composition as semiring operations. The computational efficiency of our method is due to Kleene's algebraic path method's cubic complexity.

1 Introduction

The concept of homomorphic overloading (h-overloading for short) is not completely new, although to the best of our knowledge it has not been laid into the foundations of any type system before. The original idea probably goes at least as far back as Reynolds's paper [6], where he remarked that "the key to ensuring that implicit conversions[1] and generic operators mesh nicely is to require a commutative relationship between implicit conversions and homomorphisms". To illustrate this, consider the following example. Let a generic operator f be defined on two types: $f_1 : a_1 \rightarrow b_1$ and $f_2 : a_2 \rightarrow b_2$, and let also $a_1 \sqsubseteq a_2$ and $b_1 \sqsubseteq b_2$. Under such conditions, the operator application $f\,x$ is naturally ambiguous. Indeed if $x : a_1$ it has the type a_2 as well so then which of the results $f_1\,x$ or $f_2\,x$ is expected? The usual principle is to choose the least type, i.e. that of f_1, so the result is $(f_1\,x) : b_1$. However this is coercible to b_2 which gives rise to the question: what is the relationship between the *value* of $f_1\,x$ raised to the type b_2 and the value of $f_2\,x$?

Reynolds suggests that the results for so overloaded operators must be the same. For instance, if we consider, following [6], $+_1 : (int, int) \rightarrow int$ and $+_2 : (real, real) \rightarrow real$ we find that $x +_1 y$ coerces to type $real$ to give precisely the value of $x +_2 y$ (assuming that the available range of integers can be represented as floats without rounding, which is usually the correct assumption). It is easy to see that in this example the coercion from integer to real serves as a homomorphism from $(int, +)$ to $(real, +)$, hence our term "homomorphic overloading". Paper

---

[1] i.e., coercions.

C. Grelck et al. (Eds.): IFL 2004, LNCS 3474, pp. 195–210, 2005.
© Springer-Verlag Berlin Heidelberg 2005

[6] does not treat this homomorphism as a vehicle of type inference, but rather as a category-theoretical basis for formal semantics of a language that includes generic operators and coercions. By contrast, our concern is exactly the former.

In [4] we showed that a primitive form of h-overloading, where the type signature was constrained to fixed supertypes and subtypes of participating type variables, allowed fast type inference in the presence of unknown external types. The resulting types were inferred as explicit functions of the external types using the longest path algorithm on a constraint graph. We further showed the utility of h-overloading by giving an example of a language for stream processing that benefited from it. However, our solution was not generic, as it limited the variety of overloaded operators to a very restricted set of "offset-homomorphic" operators with a special type signature. Thus arbitrary h-overloading was not supported, in particular, there was no provision for arbitrary user-defined generic operators.

In this paper we shall lift restrictions on the h-overloaded signatures, which will make user-defined families of h-overloaded operators possible, while retaining the original complete inferability of types shown in [4]. We will introduce a combined overloading scheme which uses h-overloaded types within archetypes, which are groups of types belonging to disjoint subtyping hierarchies. This makes it possible to combine general type checking with automatic inference of homomorphic types.

The rest of the paper is organised as follows. In the next section we will review some of the basic concepts of the homomorphic type theory. Section 3 will introduce a new abstraction for defining type constraints: a star semiring of integer functions. We shall re-formulate the type inference problem as an *algebraic path* one and will find the solution to the former in terms of the latter. Section 4 focuses on the solution algorithms and implementation issues. Section 5 discusses recursion issues that arise when combining several modules into programs. Related work is presented in Section 6, and finally there are some conclusions.

2   H-Overloading

Before introducing homomorphic overloading formally, we must note that h-overloading does not need to be the only overloading mechanism in a language that benefits from it. Indeed, one important reason to use overloaded operators is to avoid the proliferation of notation by reusing symbols based on their informal, mnemonic aspect. Where h-overloading is possible, it can be left implicit since, as we shall show, its disambiguation is always automatic and computationally efficient. By contrast, non-homomorphic overloading requires explicit declarations of type (or class of types, as in Haskell) since genuine ambiguity may arise when the program context does not constrain the choice of an overloading tightly enough. Using another of Reynolds's examples, if '+' were to denote both string concatenation and arithmetic addition, an assignment such as $a := b + c$, without further type constraints, would leave the type ambiguous, requiring an explicit declaration of type. H-overloading of the numerical instances of '+' would enable generic declarations like a, b, c : *numeric* rather than requiring, for example, a more specific (and restrictive) a, b, c : *int* but it would not eliminate type declarations completely, since the possibility for a, b and c to be of string type cannot be ruled out automatically.

Thus we consider types as being qualified by an 'archetype' specification, which is explicitly declared and is not subject to inference (although it is, of course, subject to type checking in a standard way). Here by archetype we mean a set of all subtypes of a well-defined type. For instance, numbers form an archetype with the usual subtyping into integers, reals and complex numbers; pairs of numbers form an archetype which contains a lattice of subtypes, etc.

One archetype may qualify several so-called *type attributes* at the same time. For instance, numerical arrays can be assumed to have the following attribute structure:

$$narray(etype, rank),$$

where *narray* is an archetype of numerical arrays, which is declared, *etype* is the type of the array element taken from the subtyping hierarchy $int \sqsubset real \sqsubset complex$ and *rank* is the number of array dimensions taken from the hierarchy $0 < 1 < \ldots < r_{max}$, where the coercion from lower to higher rank is achieved by infinite replication of the corresponding array in the extra dimensions. This archetype was assumed in [4] in defining a stream processing language, where all operators were overloaded homomorphically in *etype* and *rank*. Another example could be the string archetype: *text(len)*, where *len* is the maximum size of the string, with obvious subtyping. Our subtyping scheme is, at the moment, first-order as we do not allow functional subtyping, the reason being that contravariance of function-argument types destroys the semiring construction described in Section 3, making type inference inefficient. This circumstance prevents our typing scheme from being used in a general functional language. We do nevertheless take full account of contravariance of non-functional types, making our approach applicable to first-order, single assignment languages, such as SAC[12] and ASTL[11]. Here contravariance manifests itself in the *downward* coercion of a left hand side of an assignment and is the reason that the least type of a variable is required to be sufficiently high.

In the rest of the paper, we shall assume the archetype qualifiers of all (sub)expressions in a program to have been deduced from the archetype declarations and the program text, so that they can be omitted from type signatures without creating an ambiguity. We also assume that two types can be in a subtype relation only if they come from the same archetype; in this sense all archetypes are disjoint. An n-ary operator is assumed to act on the Cartesian product of types, on which subtyping is defined in the standard way, i.e. component-wise.

Our focus will be on the inference of the least permissible types in a program where all operator overloadings are required to satisfy the following

Homomorphism Restriction. *For any (overloaded) operator F, an instance $F_2 : a_2 \to b_2$ is said to be homomorphic to an instance $F_1 : a_1 \to b_1$ iff $a_1 \sqsubseteq a_2$,*

$b_1 \sqsubseteq b_2$ and $(\forall x : a_1)b_{21}F_1x = F_2a_{21}x$, where a_{21} is the type coercion $a_1 \to a_2$ and b_{21} is the coercion $b_1 \to b_2$. For any overloaded operator F and any pair of its instances $F_{1,2}$ having identically qualified signatures, one instance must be homomorphic to the other.

Proposition 2.1. *The set of identically qualified instances of an overloaded operator that satisfies the homomorphism restriction is linearly ordered.*

This follows from the fact that homomorphism is an antisymmetric relation, which is also transitive since the coercions are compositional, i.e. $(\forall t_1 t_2 t_3 : t_1 \sqsubseteq t_2 \sqsubseteq t_3)c_{31} = c_{32} \circ c_{21}$, where c_{ij} is the coercion $t_j \to t_i$). Note that the linear order of instances induces a linear order on the operand and result subtypes. This does not mean that the subtyping structure of an archetype must be a chain; it only has to *contain* a chain for every overloaded operator family defined on it. Thus, different operator families can potentially use different chains within the archetype without violating the homomorphism restriction. For any h-overloaded n-ary operator family F with k instances, we will write its type signature as follows: $F : \omega_1 \times \omega_2 \times \ldots \omega_n \to \omega_0$, where all ω_i are chains of length k in their respective archetypes. The potential confusion with the type signature of a single operator where ω_i are sets of *values* will be avoided by using small Greek letters only for chains of types. A type signature in this form does not by itself define the relationship between the output type of the operator family and its input types, it only defines the ranges of those types within their corresponding archetypes.

The homomorphic restriction has two important consequences. Firstly, it completely disambiguates operator application: $F\,x$ can always be interpreted as the application of the *lowest* instance of F compatible with the type of x. If the programmer meant a higher instance and applied a further operator to the result assuming that type, this is not a problem, since the result of applying the lower instance is coercible to the output type of the higher one, *yielding exactly the same value.*

Secondly, since Proposition 2.1 places the input and output types on chains in subtyping orders, in any well-typed expression the output type chain ω_1 of an operator F_1 belonging to the expression must *mesh* with the input chain ω_2 of the next operator F_2 up the expression tree. This means that, firstly, the output archetype of F_1 should be the same as the input archetype of F_2, which is not our concern since the archetype checking is assumed to have been done. Secondly, at least one element of ω_1 must be a subtype of some element of ω_2 so that the result of F_1 can be coerced to an input type of F_2. Let $x_{\max}$ be the greatest element of ω_1 coercible to ω_2:

$$x_{\max} = \max_{\omega_1}\{x \mid (\exists y \in \omega_2)x \sqsubseteq y\}.$$

Then the operator F_1 can be restricted (without loss of generality) to just those overloadings for which the output type is at most $x_{\max}$. On the other hand F_2 can be restricted, also without loss of generality, to just those overloadings for which the input type is at most $x_{\max}$ (for arity 1). Similar conditions must be satisfied in all operands of F_2 if its arity is greater than 1. Finally, a coercion map $c : \omega_1' \to \omega_2$ can be constructed:

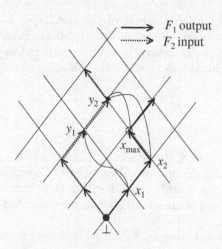

Fig. 1. Meshing type chains

$$c\,x = \min_{\omega_2}\{y \mid x \sqsubseteq y\}\,,$$

where

$$\omega_1' = \{x \mid x \in \omega_1 \wedge x \sqsubseteq x_{\max}\}\,,$$

and inserted between F_1 and F_2. It is obvious from the existence of $x_{\max}$ that for any $x \in \omega_1'$ the set on the right-hand side is nonempty, and so the function is well-defined. It is also easy to see that $c\,x$ is a non-decreasing function. Figure 1 gives an example of two meshed chains, where their common archetype is a lattice. The coercion map is depicted by curvy arrows: $c\perp = \perp$, $c\,x_1 = y_1$ and $c\,x_2 = c\,x_{\max} = y_2$

Another source of coercion is occurrences of program variables. When a variable occurs in a contravariant context, e.g. on the left-hand side of an assignment, the context defines a type chain (corresponding to the top-level operator on the right-hand side) and the type of the variable must be upwards of an output type belonging to that chain. The latter will be subject to type inference and is a priori unknown. Since there can potentially be several contravariant contexts in the program involving the same variable, the variable type must be the least upper bound of the corresponding output types.[2] The variable may also occur in a covariant context, at which point the type derived from the contravariant contexts will be coerced up to the least member of the input type chain assumed by that covariant context.

The difference between meshing a variable with an operator and meshing two operators is subtle. The procedure exemplified in fig 1 effectively maps a chain onto another chain preserving the order, whereas in the case of variable-to-operator meshing, the least upper bound of the elements of the output chains

---

[2] Note here, that these may arise in single assigment context, iff multiple assigments to disjoint parts of structured data such as arrays are supported.

is represented as a partially ordered subset of the archetype. A coercion map has to map this partially ordered subset onto the input chain of its associated operator. There is a useful factorisation, however, which reduces this kind of meshing to the previous kind. Let us consider the following example program

```
x := F (x,y);
...
x := G y
```

where $F : \alpha_1 \times \alpha_2 \to \beta$, $G : \alpha_3 \to \gamma$, the type of x, t_x is given by $t_x \sqsupseteq (b \sqcup g)$, where $b \in \beta$, $g \in \gamma$ are the (unknown) output subtypes of the operators. Note that depending on the shape of the β and γ chains within their common archetype, the least upper bound of b and g can sweep an arbitrary bounded subset, which does not have to be a chain.

For illustration, let us insert coercion functions into the program explicitly:

```
x := CxF F (CFx x, CFy y)
...
x := CxG G (CGy y)
```

Obviously, the output type of CFx is

$$\min_{\alpha_1}\{w \mid w \sqsupseteq (b \sqcup g)\} = \max(\min_{\alpha_1}\{w \mid w \sqsupseteq b\}, \min_{\alpha_1}\{w \mid w \sqsupseteq g\}),$$

which can be simplified to $\max_{\alpha_1}(c_b b, c_g g)$ where c_b and c_g are coercion maps of the kind discussed earlier. Observe that the agreement in type only involves operator output types, b and g with the type of the variable x being directly dependent upon them. Thus the types of program variables can be eliminated from the typing scheme; the output type variables of the corresponding top-level operators hold sufficient information.

In the general case the dependency of an input type of an operator on the output types of other operators via a variable has the form $\max_{i=1}^{n}(f_i\, x_i)$ for some n, where f_i is a map from a specific output chain to the common input chain. This construction is very important as it makes it possible to replace f_i by functions mapping a chain *offset* (which is a nonnegative integer representing the distance of a particular type along the chain from its bottom end) onto a chain offset. One can then reason about types solely in terms of those offset numbers. This follows from the factorisation exemplified above, i.e. from the fact that for any chain ω in a partial order P and any bounded set $S \subseteq P$

$$\min_{\omega}\{x \mid x \sqsupseteq (\bigsqcup S)\} = \max_{\omega}\{By \mid y \in S\}$$

where $B : P \to \omega$ is given by

$$Bx = \min_{\omega}\{y \mid y \sqsupseteq x\}$$

provided that such Bx exist.

Crucially, under h-overloading, a similar type representation exists for the operators themselves with respect to their multiple operands. It is given by the following

Proposition 2.2. *For any homomorphically-overloaded n-ary operator F : $(a_1, a_2, \ldots, a_n) \to b$, the output type offset $\hat{b}$ can be expressed as a function of the input type offsets $\hat{a}_i$ as follows:*

$$\hat{b}(\hat{a}_1, \hat{a}_2, \ldots, \hat{a}_n) = \max(f_1\hat{a}_1, f_2\hat{a}_2, \ldots, f_n\hat{a}_n),$$

where $f_i : \mathbb{I}_i \to \mathbb{I}_0$ are some non-decreasing functions, $1 \leq i \leq n$, $\mathbb{I}_i = [0, k_i]$ is the offset range of the ith operand, k_i is the type offset of the highest overloading in the ith operand relative to the lowest overloading operand type, and $\mathbb{I}_0 = [0, k_0]$ is the output type offset range, with k_0 the difference between the maximum and the minimum output types along the subtype chain.

The proof of Proposition 2.2 follows from the observation that each operand separately demands a certain lowest overloading, and that it is also compatible with all overloadings higher than that one. Consequently, the least output type corresponds to the highest demand, which explains the maximum in the formula. The non-decreasing nature of the functions f_i comes from the fact that raising the type of ith operand along its chain can only make it too high for the current overloading and hence demand a higher one, with a higher output type.

For convenience, we extend the function domains so that $\mathbb{I}_i = \mathbb{I}_0 = \mathbb{Z} \cup \{-\infty, +\infty\} = \mathbb{Z}^\infty$ for all i and assume that $(\forall x < 0, i) f_i x = -\infty$ and $(\forall x > k_i, i) f_i x = +\infty$. The latter assumption models a type error by yielding an infinitely high supertype when the input type range is exceeded, and the former one is motivated by the semiring construction in Section 3. We shall call functions such as f_i and the above-mentioned coercion map c type *maps* when they are expressed in offset form $\mathbb{Z}^\infty \to \mathbb{Z}^\infty$. The range of $x \geq 0$ in which $f x < \infty$ is the *carrier* of the type map f. Since our type maps are based on finite subtype chains, we shall assume that all carriers are finite. The set of all such functions will be denoted as $\mathbb{F}$ below.

To summarise, the type analysis of a program written in a language with h-homomorphic operators breaks down into the following stages:

1. analysis of the explicit archetype declarations contained in the program.
2. analysis of the operator definitions, including the structure of h-homomorphism within each archetype.
3. archetype checking throughout the program
4. determination of coercion maps induced by meshing, with a subsequent conversion into offset form; elimination of variables by connecting co- and contravariant occurrences by type maps.
5. recording of all type signatures and converting them into offset form; recording of the type maps.
6. subtype inference

Type checking in a language with explicit declarations is well known and does not present a problem. Hence the first three tasks on the list are straightforward.

Item 4 has been explained in previous sections as well as item 5. It is the last stage, item 6, that presents a major challenge, which we focus on in the next section.

3   Subtype Inference

The language. To illustrate the subtype inference algorithm, we shall introduce a simple single-assignment language, which models some features of both SAC[12] and ASTL [4] (as well as possibly other single-assignment languages where subtyping can be introduced) that are relevant to the type inference method proposed. The syntax of the language is given in figure 2, where a single module is defined. A complete program is a set of modules.

⟨module⟩ → **function** ⟨name⟩ (⟨par-tuple⟩) ⟨body⟩

⟨par-tuple⟩ → ⟨var⟩ [, ⟨var⟩]*

⟨body⟩ → ⟨assig⟩ [; ⟨assig⟩]*

⟨assig⟩ → ⟨var⟩ [⟨selector⟩] := ⟨exp⟩

⟨exp⟩ → ⟨var⟩ | ⟨op⟩ ⟨exp-tuple⟩ | ⟨function⟩ ⟨exp-tuple⟩

⟨exp-tuple⟩ → (⟨exp⟩ [, ⟨exp⟩]*)

⟨function⟩ → ⟨id⟩

Fig. 2. The model language

A module defines a function whose body is a set of assignments. An assignment assigns the value of the right-hand side to the object signified by the left-hand side. The optional selector defines which part of the object has been assigned a value, for example which index of an array. All such parts are required to have the same subtype, i.e. the data structure is assumed to be homogeneous. There is a semantic constraint that the the selectors applied to the same variable define the partitioning of that variable associated object, i.e. the selected parts are disjoint and the coverage is complete, hence a single-assignment semantics is assured. SAC achieves this by syntactic means (with a static guarantee), whilst ASTL has a dynamic check for the singleness of assignment, but these details are irrelevant to subtype inference. All that is important for the treatment below is that

1. the same variable can be used repeatedly on the left-hand side of assignment representing different parts of a homogeneous data structure;
2. all these occurrences are type-contravariant, i.e. $\tau_{var} \geq \tau_{RHS}$
3. all occurrences of a variable on the right-hand side are covariant, i.e. $\tau_{var} \leq \tau_{op}$ where τ_{op} is the maximum subtype that the operator applied to the variable in the right-hand side allows it to have.

Each operator $<op>$ is predefined with a homomorphic subtype signature defined by Proposition 2.2. Function calls name the function to be called explicitly, and all functions are assumed to be first-order. Function subtype signatures are *not* required to be provided by the programmer but are inferred in the process of subtype inference.

A primary constraint set Subtype inference begins with associating fresh type variables with all subexpressions in the program. In our case, these variables represent type offsets from $\mathbb{Z}^\infty$ rather than type values for the reasons explained earlier. For every operator occurrence, the operator type maps are invoked to produce a type constraint in the form:

$$v_0 = \max_{i=1}^{n}(f_i v_i),$$

where v_i, $i = 0 \ldots n$ are any of the type variables just introduced. The constraints can be broken down into a set of simpler constraints in what we shall call *canonical form*:

$$\forall_{i=1}^{n} \tau_0 \geq f_i \tau_i,$$

on the assumption that the minimum type assignment is sought. All canonical constraints in a program constitute the *primary constraint set*. This set can be assumed to contain exactly one constraint for every pair of types a and b. Indeed, if there are two constraints between these types, $a \geq f_1 b$ and $a \geq f_2 b$, then they can be replaced by an equivalent constraint $a \geq f_{1 \oplus 2} b$, where for all $x \in \mathbb{Z}^\infty$, $f_{1 \oplus 2} x = \max(f_1 x, f_2 x) = (f_1 \oplus f_2) x$. (We denote the operator of the pointwise maximum of two functions by $\oplus$.) On the other hand, if there are no constraints between a and b, then the constraint $a \geq \mathbf{0} b$ can be added, where $\mathbf{0} : \mathbb{Z}^\infty \to \mathbb{Z}^\infty$ such that for all $x \in \mathbb{Z}^\infty$, $\mathbf{0} x = -\infty$. Thus one can speak of an $n \times n$ constraint matrix C_{ij} defining the primary constraint set for n type variables. Each element of C_{ij} is the function $\mathbb{Z}^\infty \to \mathbb{Z}^\infty$ that occurs in the constraint between types x_i and x_j in canonical form.

Note that some of the type variables are associated with program variables which are external to the program unit being compiled and which are, consequently, not subject to inference. The purpose of type inference is to express the least type of each program variable as a function of those external types.

Constraint set expansion The simplest type inference procedure would be to initially assign 0 to all type variables associated with internal variables, and then iterate the constraint set until a fixed point is reached or a type variable acquires the value of infinity. In matrix form, we seek a solution to the constraint satisfaction problem $x = C x$ as a fixed point of the iterative process:

$$x^{[0]} = \mathbf{0}; \ x^{[k+1]} = C x^{[k]}.$$

Here $C x$ denotes $\bigoplus_{i=1}^{n} C_{ij} x_j$.

The procedure is sound, since at each iteration it delivers a lower bound of all types implied by the primary constraint set. Also, due to the non-decreasing nature of all matrix elements of C, at each iteration which does not deliver a fixed point, it produces an increased lower bound for at least some type variables. Since the carriers of all matrix elements are finite, a fixed point exists and is reachable. Obviously, the constraint set is satisfiable iff none of the lower bounds delivered at the fixed point is infinite.

This solution has two potential problems. First of all, the number of iterations is only bounded from above by the total length of all type chains, since at each iteration (which does not result in a fixed point) only one type variable has to increase. Secondly, since the numerical values of the external type parameters are unknown, iterations have to be performed with the matrix C by raising it to a power (using function composition as multiplication and $\oplus$ as addition). This by itself is a costly operation, to perform even once.

We propose a more efficient algorithm, based on the algebraic path problem, which we consider next.

Algebraic structure of $\mathbb{F}$ Recall that the elements of the constraint matrix are drawn from the set $\mathbb{F}$ of nondecreasing functions $\mathbb{Z}^\infty \to \mathbb{Z}^\infty$ that yield $-\infty$ on all $x < 0$ and $+\infty$ on sufficiently large $x \geq 0$. Consider a six-tuple $\Phi = (\mathbb{F}, \oplus, \odot, *, \mathbf{0}, \mathbf{1})$ where $\oplus$ is as defined above, $\odot : \mathbb{F} \times \mathbb{F} \to \mathbb{F}$ is a function composition, $* : \mathbb{F} \to \mathbb{F}$ is Kleene's star operation:

$$f^* = \mathbf{1} \oplus f \oplus (f \odot f) \oplus (f \odot f \odot f) \oplus \dots,$$

$\mathbf{0} \in \mathbb{F}$ is as defined above and $\mathbf{1} \in \mathbb{F}$ is the identity function[3]: $\mathbf{1}x = x$ for $x \geq 0$, $\mathbf{1}x = -\infty$ otherwise.

Proposition 3.1. $\oplus$, $\odot$ *and* $*$ *are closed in* $\mathbb{F}$.

Indeed, the $\oplus$ operation is closed in $\mathbb{F}$ since the point-wise maximum of two nondecreasing functions is a nondecreasing function, whose carrier is included in the union of the carriers of the arguments and so is finite. Likewise, the composition of two nondecreasing functions is a nondecreasing function. The behaviour of this function at negative arguments and $\pm\infty$ is proven immediately by substitution; the carrier of the result is the same as that of the first operand, so $\odot$ is closed in $\mathbb{F}$.

Finally, the star operator is defined in terms of the fixed point of a series, each member of which is computed from elements of $\mathbb{F}$ using the operators $\oplus$ and $\odot$. Since they are both closed in $\mathbb{F}$, the star operator itself is closed in $\mathbb{F}$ if the fixed point exists. The fixed point does exist, since the series of partial sums is point-wise nondecreasing and since $\mathbb{Z}^\infty$ includes $+\infty$. In fact, we will show below that the fixed point can be computed in a finite number of steps by an efficient algorithm, which means that the series for the star operator is always

---

[3] Strictly speaking the identity function is not in $\mathbb{F}$ since it does not have a finite carrier; nor is $\mathbf{0}$. However, we include them in $\mathbb{F}$ as special elements. The use of both $\mathbf{1}$ abd $\mathbf{0}$ with $\oplus$, $\odot$ and $*$ does not lead to further infinite-carrier elements.

finite for any element of $\mathbb{F}$. This obviates the proof that the star construct is well behaved; such a proof would usually be required for an infinite star series. ‡

Proposition 3.2. $(\mathbb{F}, \oplus, \mathbf{0})$ and $(\mathbb{F}, \odot, \mathbf{1})$ are monoids, the former is commutative. Indeed, function composition is associative and so is point-wise maximum. The elements $\mathbf{0}$ and $\mathbf{1}$ are obviously the identities of the respective operations. ‡

Proposition 3.3. Operation $\odot$ distributes over $\oplus$ both on the left and on the right:

$$a \odot (b \oplus c) = (a \odot b) \oplus (a \odot c) \text{ and } (b \oplus c) \odot a = (b \odot a) \oplus (c \odot a).$$

The proof is by point-wise application, using the nondecreasing nature of functions a, b and c. ‡

Proposition 3.4. $\mathbf{0}$ is a null with respect to $\odot$: $\mathbf{0} \odot x = x \odot \mathbf{0} = \mathbf{0}$ The proof follows immediately from the construction of the element $\mathbf{0}$. ‡

Propositions 3.1-4 form the proof of the following

Lemma 3.5. Φ is a star semiring.

Inference procedure Now consider the constraint satisfaction problem again. Let us associate every type variable with a vertex of a weighted, directed graph G. Each edge (v_i, v_j, f) of the graph represents the constraint

$$v_i \geq f\, v_j\,.$$

Since the (internal) program variables occur in both covariant and contravariant contexts, the graph is not necessarily acyclic, and may contain infinite as well as finite walks. Each walk corresponds to a chain of primary constraints connecting its ends, and hence to a *secondary* constraint corresponding to the (finite or infinite) $\odot$-product of the weights of the participating edges. The tightest constraint between any types v_i and v_j due to the primary constraint set is the $\oplus$-sum of the weights of all walks W_{ij} in graph G from vertex i to vertex j:

$$P_{ij} = \bigoplus_{w \in W_{ij}} \left(\bigodot_{e \in w} f_e \right),$$

where the selection of edges e from the walk w in the $\odot$-product is in the walk order. This is a formulation of the classical *algebraic path problem* [8] for the semiring Φ and graph G.

The solution to the algebraic path problem is the matrix P_{ij} of semiring values. We will define an efficient algorithm for its computation below. For now let us assume P_{ij} has been computed, and proceed to the type assignment.

Proposition 3.6. Divide the set of type variables $\{v_k \mid 1 \leq k \leq n\}$, into external ones $k \leq n_e$, which correspond to the program variables from the parameter tuple of the function, see figure 2 (and which consequently are not subject to type assignment) and the rest $n_e < k \leq n$. The least type assignment is given by the following formula:

$$v_k = \min_{v_k^*}\{x \mid x \geq \max_{i=1}^{n_e}(P_{ki}\, v_i)\} = P_{kk} \odot \max_{i=1}^{n_e}(P_{ki}\, v_i)\,,$$

where v_k^* is the set of solutions of the equation $x = P_{kk}x$. The outline of the proof is as follows. First of all, observe that any type assignment for the variable v_k has to satisfy the secondary type constraint $v_k \geq P_{kk}v_k$. Since $P_{kk} \geq 1$ point-wise (since at any rate $v_k \geq v_k$), only the fixed points of P_{kk} are suitable as potential type assignments for v_k. Secondly, v_k must be large enough to satisfy all primary and secondary constraints induced by the external types, which explains the above formula. The third part of the equation is due to the fact that P_{kk} is the point-wise maximum of all cyclic chains on vertex k, hence $P_{kk} \odot P_{kk} = P_{kk}$ and so, for all $x \in \mathbb{Z}^\infty$, $P_{kk}(P_{kk}\,x) = P_{kk}x$. This means that $P_{kk}x$ is a fixed point of P_{kk}. The fact that this fixed point is the least one greater than or equal to x is due to $P_{kk} \geq 1$ point-wise and to its nondecreasing nature.

One might think that v_k must be large enough to satisfy the constraint induced by any other internal variable v_j: $v_k \geq (P_{kj}v_j)$. We claim that this happens automatically. Indeed, assume the contrary, i.e. that for some j, $v_k < (P_{kj}v_j)$. By the above assignment $v_j \geq P_{jj} \odot P_{ji}v_i$ (recall that P_{jj} is a nondecreasing function, so it distributes over the maximum), and so $v_k < P_{kj} \odot P_{jj} \odot P_{ji}v_i$ for any external v_i. The right-hand side reduces to $P_{ki}v_i$ by definition of P and semiring distributivity. Hence $v_k < P_{ki}v_i$, which contradicts our type assignment and proves its validity. ‡

4   Implementation

The type inference method proposed in the previous section requires the ability to compute the algebraic path matrix P_{ij} efficiently. This is achieved by Kleene's algorithm in $O(n^3)$ semiring operations using the following iterative process. Set the initial value $P_{ij}^{[0]}$ according to the primary constraint graph. For any edges (i,j) not found in the graph set $P_{ij}^{[0]} = \mathbf{0}$. For $k = 1 \ldots n$ do:

$$(\forall i,j)P_{ij}^{[k]} = P_{ij}^{[k-1]} \oplus (P_{ik}^{[k-1]} \odot (P_{kk}^{[k-1]})^* \odot P_{kj}^{[k-1]})$$

The solution is $P_{ij} = P_{ij}^{[n]}$.

At each iteration, the algorithm requires $2n^2$ semiring multiplications and n^2 semiring additions as well as one star operation. We consider the implementation of those next.

We propose the representation of semiring elements as sorted lists of pairs (a,v) where $a \geq 0$ is the value of the function argument and v is its result. The list is sorted in the ascending order of a. The value of the function for the arguments greater than the last one listed are assumed to be $+\infty$. The empty list corresponds to the maximum element of Φ, $\phi_{\max}$: $(\forall x \in \Phi)x \oplus \phi_{\max} = \phi_{max}$. The elements $\mathbf{0}$ and $\mathbf{1}$ are represented as special values recognised by all three operators.

It is easy to see that the $\odot$ operation in this representation is little more than the classical database *join* of the operands equating the v field of the first operand and the a field of the second; it yields a sorted list as a result. Both source lists are only traversed once, thanks to the nondecreasing nature of the semiring elements and the fact that any emerging lists are already sorted. The $\oplus$ operator is implemented as a join in the field a of both lists followed by the pointwise maximum of the corresponding v fields. Of course the a field does not even need to be stored, as it contains merely the sequential number of the list element.

The star operator is slightly trickier to implement. Observe that since $\oplus$ is idempotent (i.e., $(\forall x \in \Phi) x \oplus x = x$), $(f \oplus 1)^* = f^*$, which can be proven by substitution. Hence without any loss of generality we can assume that $f x \geq x$ for all nonnegative x. The first step is to identify closed intervals of x, $[b_i, e_i]$ such that:

$$f(b_i - 1) \leq b_i - 1,$$
$$f k > k \text{ for } b_i \leq k < e_i \text{ and}$$
$$f e_i = e_i.$$

If no such interval exists, it is easy to see that $f x = x$ for all $x \geq 0$, in which case $f^* = f = 1$. Indeed, since for any $f \in \Phi$, $f(-1) = -\infty$ and $f(+\infty) = +\infty$, there is at least one suitable pair of e_i and b_i. Hence the middle condition is not satisfied, which means that for all k $f k \leq k$, hence $f \oplus 1 = 1$.

In the general case, the carrier of f is partitioned into one or more closed intervals of the above sort with possibly intervals where $f x \leq x$ occurring in between those. We then apply the following

Proposition 4.1. *Within each interval* $[b_i, e_i]$, $f^* x = e_i$.

Indeed acting f on any point within the interval will produce a greater result not exceeding e_i (which is the value of a nondecreasing function at the right end of the interval where it is nondecreasing, hence the maximum). Therefore, repeated application of f will eventually reach e_i which is a fixed point.

The star algorithm should consequently proceed in two passes. In the first pass, the closed intervals are identified by scanning the list and comparing the current and previous elements. At the same time any elements for which $v < a$ are adjusted to $v = a$. In the second pass, the answer is computed by filling up the intervals with their final value of a. This is best accomplished by placing the list elements on top of a stack during the first pass, and reading them off the top of the stack in the second, so that the ends of intervals could propagate backwards.

One last observation: in the previous section we stated that f^* maps any x to the nearest fixed point equal or exceeding x. Clearly our algorithm has this property.

From the description of the semiring algorithms, it is clear that their computational cost is $O(L)$ where L is the length of the longest chain in the subtyping system. An obvious optimisation would be to exploit the fact that there are usually much fewer instances to an operator than there are different subtypes in a type. Consequently, the type maps are likely to be step functions with many different a corresponding to the same v. The above algorithms can easily be modified for such functions: only the first record with the same v need be kept, the join algorithm must compare for $\geq$ instead of equality, etc. As a result the computational cost of semiring operations could be reduced to $O(V)$ where V is the maximum number of overloadings defined for any operator in the program.

5   Linkage

The inference procedure described in Section 3 delivers the subtypes of all variables (including the function result) in terms of the types of the function parameter tuple. It can only do that if the subtype transformation of all function applications in the function body is known. If recursive functions are not present, this is easily achievable as the invocation graph for the program is acyclic, and so functions must exist that call no further functions. Inference starts with those. When their subtype signatures (the mapping of the parameter tuple types onto the function result type) becomes known, they can be used to perform subtype inference in functions that depend on those, etc., until inference for the whole program is complete.

Recursive functions can be included into the subtype inference framework by applying the following fixed-point calculation.

1. Assume that each function $F_j : (p_1, \ldots, p_{m_j}) \to t_j$ returns the lowest subtype of the corresponding supertype: $t_j = \max_k f_{jk} p_k$ with all $f_{jk} = f_{jk}^{[0]} = \mathbf{0}$
2. Perform subtype inference in each of the bodies using the above assumption for any function applications occurring in it. The result is a new approximation $f_{jk}^{[1]}$.
3. Iterate step 2 until $(\forall jk) f_{jk}^{[m+1]} = f_{jk}^{[m]}$

The existence of the fixed point follows from the fact that the "sum of product" formula for P_{ij} from Proposition 3.6 is monotonic with respect to all f_i. Indeed, define partial order on Φ thus: $f_1 \sqsubseteq f_2$ iff $f_1 \oplus f_2 = f_2$. Then using semiring distributivity show that for any edge k, its weighting f_k, and any semiring element f, if $f_k \sqsubseteq f$ then $(\forall ij) P_{ij}(f_k) \sqsubseteq P_{ij}(f)$. Informally, this means that if a type function f is replaced by a pointwise same-or-higher function, this can only make any other type function in the constraint set pointwise same-or-higher. This, of course, automatically guarantees a fixed point if the codomain of all type functions here is finite, which is the case.

Note that the fixed-point procedure does not necessarily require a repeated solution of the entire algebraic path problem. Each iteration only changes weightings on a few edges corresponding to function applications. The other edges that correspond to the operator applications retain their weightings, and in any practical program these would be the majority. Consequently, one can introduce a vertex enumeration that leaves all function-application vertices at the end. Only those vertices will require Kleene's algorithm iterations to be re-done, thus giving a cost estimate of $O(mn^2) \ll n^3$, where $m \ll n$ is the number of type variables associated with function applications in the expression tree. In a practical system this estimate can be reduced further by taking into account the locality of type dependencies in the abstract syntax tree.

6   Discussion and Related Work

The issue of type inference with atomic subtyping has a long history. We cite papers [1, 2, 6, 9, 7] as ones where foundation work was done. Of these, paper [7] is probably the most relevant as it tackles the issue of decidability of general type inference in the presence of subtyping, but it does not bound its cost. The main thrust of our work is towards homomorphism of types and effective constraint-satisfaction algorithms that make type inference possible. This issue was not approached systematically until a simplified theory was given by us in [4]. Our concept of type homomorphism is consonant to Lievant's idea of "discrete polymorphism" proposed in [3], where it was suggested that overloadings should be treated as models of a single theory. We believe that h-overloading is less restrictive as it allows higher instances to "expand" the functionality of the lower ones without destroying the consistency between them.

Technically, the most relevant to our work could be the paper by Rehof and Mogensen [10], where a method is described for what they termed a "definite constraint satisfaction problem". Here all constraints are presented in a form similar to ours: $v_0 \geq f(v_1, \ldots, v_k)$, where f is a nondecreasing function. Then an algorithm is presented, with a complexity linear in the number of constraints, (i.e. quadratic in the number of variables n) which finds the least solution. The main difference is that in [10] the system of constraints is assumed to be *closed*, i.e. all variables are subject to type minimisation within the constraints. In the present paper, we approach a more general problem of constraint satisfaction with unknown external parameters, which are types of the external variables that are *not* subject to minimisation. In our case, the solution is a function of those types. The algorithm from [10] does not apply to such situations. We have proposed a slightly more costly solution, with the cost $O(n^3)$, but which allows external types to be parameters in the type assignment.

7   Conclusions

A type inference solution for a general first-order, atomic subtyping with homomorphic overloading has been proposed. We have shown that after archetype checking, an h-overloaded operator produces type constraints characterisable by nondecreasing functions on the expanded integer set. A star semiring Φ was proposed to capture algebraic properties of such functions. Using Φ, we have built a type inference procedure based on Kleene's algorithm. The procedure infers the least types of all internal variables in the program as explicit functions of the external types.

Future work will proceed towards introducing homomorphic subtyping to SAC and implementing the subtype inference algorithm. More thought is required to improve the efficiency of linking, perhaps by using some heuristics for the first approximation. It would also be interesting to tackle higher-order functional subtyping for which the present technique is not immediately applicable.

References

1. L.Cardelli and P.Wegner. On understanding types, data abstraction, and polymorphism. *Computing Surveys*, 17(4):471-522, 1985.
2. J.Mitchell. Type inference with simple subtypes. *Journal of Functional Programming*, 1:245–285, 1991.
3. D. Lievant Discrete Polymorphism. *Proc. 1990 ACM Conference on LISP and Functional Programming*, pp. 288–297, 1990.
4. A. Shafarenko. Coercion as homomorphism: type inference in a system with subtyping and overloading. PPDP'2002, Pittsburg, PA. October 6-8, 2002
5. A.Shafarenko. RETRAN: a Recurrent Paradigm for Data-Parallel Computing. *Computer Systems Science and Engineering*, vol 11, No 4, July 1996, pp 201-209
6. J.C. Reynolds. Using category theory to design implicit conversions and generic operators. In: *SemanticsDirected Compiler Generation*, LNCS vol 94, pages 211-258. SpringerVerlag, 1980.
7. S.Kaes. Type inference in the presence of overloading, subtyping and recursive types. *Proceedings of the 1992 ACM conference on LISP and functional programming. San Francisco, California, United States* 1992. pp. 193–204
8. G. Rote, "Path Problems in Graphs", in G. Tinhofer, E. Noltemeier, M. Syslo (eds.), Computational Graph Theory, Springer-Verlag, Computing Suppl. 7, Wien, 1990, pp. 155–198.
9. Y. Fuh and P. Mishra. Type inference with subtypes. *Theoretical Computer Science* 73:155-175, 1990.
10. J. Rehof and T. Mogensen. Tractable constraints in finite semilattices. In R. Cousot and D. Schmidt, editors, Proc. of 3rd Int. Static Analysis Symposium (SAS'96), pages 285–300. Springer LNCS vol. 1145, 1996.
11. A. Shafarenko. Stream Processing on the Grid: an Array Stream Transforming Language. *SNPD 2003*, pp. 268-276
12. Sven-Bodo Scholz: Single Assignment C: efficient support for high-level array operations in a functional setting. *J. Funct. Program.* 13(6) pp. 1005-1059 (2003)

Simple, Effective Code-Size Reduction
for Functional Programs

Ekaterina Stefanov and Anthony M. Sloane

Department of Computing, Macquarie University
{kate, asloane}@ics.mq.edu.au

Abstract. Code-size reduction is an important area of investigation
for computer system developers due to the increasing use of technologies such as communication networks and embedded systems for which
program size is an important factor. A new software-based method of
program compression for languages with interpreter-based runtime systems is described. The method employs a modified version of a standard
dictionary-based text compression algorithm to produce a shorter encoding for a given program and a runtime system tailored for it. In comparison with previous software-based code-size reduction methods the new
method is simpler to implement and imposes lower overhead at compile
time. Its performance on a representative suite of Haskell programs is
analysed. Executable space savings of 16–26% are achieved as a result
of code compression, exclusion of unused instructions from the runtime,
and inclusion of the standard library in the optimisation. To the best
of the authors' knowledge, this is the first work on running compressed
code for a purely declarative and functional language.

1   Introduction

The size of computer programs is important in many modern computing environments. For example, communication networks are often used to transport
programs for execution on remote platforms such as Web browsers or mobile
phones. Cost and latency considerations demand that developers trade off program functionality (and hence size) with communication bandwidth. Similarly,
embedded computer systems are increasingly part of our day-to-day lives. The
cost of embedded systems is closely related to the amount of code and data that
must be included.

These sorts of concerns have lead to a growing interest in *code-size reduction
methods* that can be applied automatically to any program. Thus a developer
can gain the benefits of reduced program size without having to artificially limit
the functionality of their program as much.

Code-size reduction methods based on hardware modifications have arguably
the most potential for success. However, they are also the most costly to implement, at least until such hardware becomes available in most machines. Hence,
we focus on software-based approaches in this paper.

C. Grelck et al. (Eds.): IFL 2004, LNCS 3474, pp. 211–225, 2005.
© Springer-Verlag Berlin Heidelberg 2005

Our method targets the embedded systems and small device application areas, where traditionally the language of choice has been C due to its ability to produce small fast executables. Alternatives to C for these platforms are desirable due to reasons such as enhanced safety, developmental efficiency, and higher-level language features.

We are primarily interested in code-size reduction approaches for languages whose execution models are based on bytecoded abstract machines. Prominent examples include Java and the Java Virtual Machine [1], Prolog and the Warren Abstract Machine [2], and Haskell and the G-machine [3, 4]. These sorts of languages are not traditionally used for size-critical applications. We are investigating ways in which the compiled bytecode size of programs can be reduced and how the associated runtime systems can be tailored to specific programs to further reduce program size.

In this paper we describe a new, simple and effective method of code-size reduction called *LZW-based Code Compression (LZW-CC)* that uses a slightly modified version of the well-known Lempel-Ziv-Welch (LZW) text compression algorithm [5, 6, 7]. LZW was chosen as the basis of our approach because of its simplicity and its use of a fixed-size codeword which matches the encodings of most bytecode languages.

Input to LZW-CC is the bytecode for both a program and the standard library routines used by that program. The output is equivalent but shorter bytecode for the program and library routines using a customised instruction set. The added instruction codes stand for sequences of instructions from the original code as identified by the modified LZW algorithm.

As well as compressing the bytecode, we also modify the interpreter component of the run-time system so that is capable of executing programs that use the extended instruction set but doesn't have support for instructions that are not used in the program or library routines under consideration.

Our experience so far with LZW-CC shows that it compares favourably with existing software-based approaches to code-size reduction. It is relatively straightforward to implement, yields reasonable compression ratios for typical programs, and should not impose a high runtime overhead. Compilation times for individual modules are slightly slower than usual. When the entire standard library is included in the compression phase, overall compilation times are naturally longer than a regular compilation that can use precompiled library modules. However, LZW-CC imposes less compile-time overhead than other similar methods. It is also simple to implement.

The rest of the paper is structured as follows. The next section places LZW-CC in context with previous work by introducing the main terminology of the area. Section 3 describes LZW-CC in detail by way of an artificial example. In Section 4 we describe a limited experimental evaluation of LZW-CC based on a prototype implementation in the nhc98 compiler [8] [9] applied to a suite of typical Haskell programs. We also undertake a brief analysis of the theoretical optimal performance of compression on this data. Section 5 compares the performance of the method with other notable software code-size reduction methods. Finally, in Section 6 we sum up and point toward future work.

2   Background

Code-size reduction methods are usually categorised as *code compaction* or *code compression* [10]. Code compression requires partial or full decompression before execution, while compacted code is directly executable in the same sense as the original code. Code compaction achieves program size reduction by replacing part of the code with equivalent shorter code.

For example, Cooper and McIntosh developed a compaction method for an optimising compiler [11]. They used techniques such as procedural abstraction to identify repeated sequences of code in the compiler's intermediate representation and replace them with single instances. A related compaction method called *Squeeze* was developed by Muth, Debray et. al. [12]. It uses similar techniques to Cooper and McIntosh but operates on linked code rather than the compiler intermediate representation. Thus it has access to the full program and has more opportunity for identifying repeated code sequences.

Other software-based techniques for code-size reduction fall under the code compression banner. In contrast with code compaction methods, these approaches end up with a code representation that is not directly executable. Rather, some form of decompression must be performed before the code can be executed.

The Slim Binaries approach of Franz and Kistler transmits a program in an efficiently encoded abstract syntax tree accompanied by a code generator [13]. When the program is executed the code generator is first applied to the tree to produce native code, then the native code is executed. The startup time of the program is significantly increased since code generation is happening at runtime.

When runtime performance is important, it has been suggested that only infrequently executed code should be compressed, thus achieving significant code reduction while minimising the runtime penalty [DE03].

For our purposes, the most relevant of the code compression methods are those based on an underlying interpreter or just-in-time (JIT) compilation infrastructure. For example, Ernst et. al. have developed an approach specifically aimed at code that is transmitted to be executed on another machine [14]. Their compiler identifies patterns in its intermediate representation and compresses them. The transmitted reduced code comes with a dictionary that can be used to construct the native code. This reconstruction process can involve significant overhead.

An unpublished variant of this method by Fraser and Proebsting starts with the tree-based intermediate representation produced by a C compiler [15]. Patterns of operations in the intermediate code tree are identified so as to reduce its size in an optimal way for a given maximum pattern size. The tree is then replaced by a smaller equivalent version where instances of the new operations replace the pattern occurrences. A customised interpreter is generated that is capable of executing all of the old operations that remain plus any new ones that have been created. The new program and its interpreter can then be transported to an execution environment.

Another relevant project by Clausen et. al. considered compression of Java bytecode for embedded systems [16]. They "factorize" recurring instruction sequences to form new instructions. Patterns are identified by growing groups of equivalent instruction sequences. A Java Virtual Machine extended with macro support for these new instructions can then execute the compressed program.

3   LZW-CC: LZW-Based Program Compression

Before we detail LZW-CC, a few words are in order to explain some of our design choices. We prefer a code compression approach to code compaction, because the latter usually involves significant effort at the compiler end. We would like language implementors to be able to use our method without having to invest significantly in compiler infrastructure to support complex pattern detection or optimisation.

Of previous work, LZW-CC is most similar to the approaches of Fraser and Proebsting [15] and Clausen et. al [16]. Compared to Fraser and Proebsting we also identify patterns in the code but we work with the linear byte-code rather than with a tree-based intermediate representation. Also, to reduce the implementation effort and compile-time overhead we do not follow Fraser and Proebsting and try to produce an optimal covering for a given pattern size. However, we do include library routines in the compression which they do not. Clausen et. al. work with bytecode like us but use a more complex method for identifying patterns thereby imposing more overhead on the compiler writer.

Our target area is languages whose runtime systems involve some form of interpretation of abstract machine instructions. Fraser and Proebsting were working with C. However, C is not usually interpreted so a price must be paid for the addition of an interpreter that must be transmitted or stored along with the program and the increase in runtime compared with compilation to machine code. In contrast, the programs we are interested in are usually bundled with an interpretive runtime anyway so there is no fundamental change.

Compared to compaction-based methods, compressed code implies some runtime overhead to decompress the program. LZW-CC certainly has some overhead but we try to limit it by using a simple dictionary-based compression method. As in the closely related methods our compression produces new interpreter instructions corresponding to patterns in the original code. None of the methods need complicated infrastructure to decompress instructions. In our case a direct lookup using static pattern definitions suffices.

3.1   Overview

The input to LZW-CC is a program comprising:

1. Compiled user code. We assume the code consists of a) a code segment containing bytecode instructions and b) zero or more other segments containing constant data such as strings or initialised structures.
2. A collection of standard library modules that are used by the program from (1). Each library module is assumed to be of the same form as the program

(i.e., bytecode and data segments). (Thus we do not need the source code of the library.)

3. A runtime system that is capable of executing the program and routines from (1) and (2). We assume there is a component of the runtime designed to interpret bytecode instructions and use the program's data segments (if any). Other parts of the runtime may provide support but they play no role in the compression approach so we do not consider their form here.

LZW-CC attempts to reduce the size of the user code, library and runtime system combination by compressing the bytecode segments (program and library) and producing a customised interpreter that knows how to execute exactly those instructions present in the bytecode. We do not currently apply any compression to the data segments.

LZW-CC carries out the following steps:

1. Identify bytecode patterns. A modified version of LZW is applied to the bytecode segments. The result is a set of patterns that might be used in the compressed program and static occurrence counts for each pattern.
2. Select patterns to use and replace their occurrences in the bytecode segments. Patterns are selected on the basis of a static measure of space savings that would result from their use. The result is a new set of program and library bytecode segments that utilise a combination of old instruction types and new instruction types based on the applied patterns.
3. Modify the interpreter. The bytecode interpreter is changed to include code that handles the new instruction types and remove code that handles instruction types that are not present in any bytecode segment.

Once LZW-CC is finished, the modified user code, library routines and runtime system are combined to form an executable using the usual mechanisms.

The following sections detail the operation of LZW-CC with the use of an example language and program described next.

3.2   A Simple Abstract Machine and Program

To illustrate the operation of LZW-CC we will use a simple stack-based abstract machine based on the one described by Aho et al. [17]. The machine consists of an operand stack and separate instruction and data memories.

The instruction set of the stack machine has 14 instruction types. These are grouped into instructions for stack manipulation (*push, rvalue, lvalue, pop, assign* and *copy*), arithmetic operations (*mul, sub, add* and *div*) and control flow instructions (*goto, gotrue, gofalse* and *halt*).

Figure 1 shows a small C-like code snippet (left) and the equivalent stack machine code (middle). (The compressed code on the right will be discussed in Section 3.4.) The intention of this example is to illustrate LZW-CC in a situation where a number of non-trivial patterns can be found. Section 4 evaluates the method on real programs.

```
answer = 0;                    0: lvalue 1          0: C4
                               2: push 0
                               4: assign            1: assign
if (n1 == m) answer = 1;       5: rvalue 2          2: C2
                               7: rvalue 3          3: rvalue 3
                               9: sub               5: C7
                              10: gotrue 21
                              12: lvalue 1          6: C1
                              14: rvalue 1
                              16: assign
                              17: push 1
                              19: gotrue 67         7: C3

if (n2 == m) answer = 1;      21: rvalue 2          8: C2
                              23: rvalue 4          9: rvalue 4
                              25: sub              11: C6
                              26: gotrue 37
                              28: lvalue 1         12: C1
                              30: rvalue 1
                              32: assign
                              33: push 1
                              35: gotrue 67        13: C3

if (n3 == m) answer = 1;      37: rvalue 2         14: C2
                              39: rvalue 5         15: rvalue 5
                              41: sub              17: C5
                              42: gotrue 53
                              44: lvalue 1         18: C1
                              46: rvalue 1
                              48: assign
                              49: push 1
                              51: gotrue 67        19: C3

if (n4 == m) answer = 1;      53: rvalue 2         20: C2
                              55: rvalue 6         21: C8
                              57: sub
                              58: gotrue 67        22: C3
                              60: lvalue 1         23: C1
                              62: rvalue 1
                              64: assign
                              65: push 1

                              67: halt            24: halt
```

Fig. 1. A small C-like code snippet (left), corresponding stack machine code (middle) and compressed code (right)

3.3   Pattern Identification

First we describe the standard LZW text compression algorithm, then the modified LZW-CC version.

Create initial dictionary containing encodings of input text alphabet characters as themselves.
pattern = ""
While not end of input
    char = next character from input text
    newpattern = *pattern* ++ *char*
    If *newpattern* is in the dictionary then
        pattern = *newpattern*
    else
        code = new output encoding, add *newpattern*
        to the dictionary with encoding *code*, output the code for
        pattern to the output stream, and *pattern* = *char*.
    End If
End While

Fig. 2. Standard LZW text compression algorithm

LZW Algorithm. Figure 2 shows pseudo-code for the standard LZW text compression algorithm [5, 6, 7]. A dictionary is used to map patterns to their output encodings. By default, each possible input character is a pattern that maps to itself. We assume that non-character output encodings are also available to encode patterns. The algorithm reads the text one character at a time and creates patterns if a sequence of characters is not already in the dictionary.

LZW-CC Algorithm. The LZW-CC version of LZW incorporates changes motivated by the following considerations:

1. In LZW, when a pattern is first recognised (Step 5(b) of Figure 2)), its encoding is entered into the dictionary, but it is not used until its second and subsequent occurrences (if any). This strategy means that patterns occurring only once will not be used. Also, it enables the dictionary to be reconstructed on-the-fly during decompression, rather than having to be stored with the compressed text.
   LZW-CC uses patterns from their first occurrence but only if they occur more than once. We have a static definition of each pattern so that we don't have to pay the significant cost of recomputing the dictionary at runtime. Decompression of a pattern turns into a transfer of control to its static definition (see Section 3.5).
2. LZW regards the input stream as one contiguous sequence of characters. For our purposes, however, this is not possible because basic block entry points must still be directly addressable after compression so they cannot be allowed to occur inside patterns other than at the beginning. Thus LZW-CC does not allow patterns to cross basic block boundaries.

3. In LZW, the unit of compression is the character whereas in LZW-CC it is the instruction (meaning both the byte containing the operation code and any bytes containing operands). Thus in LZW-CC the initial dictionary is loaded with the instructions from the original program, rather than all of the bytecodes as separate entries.
4. In LZW-CC not all instructions are regarded as compressible. For example, some instructions contain combinations of data and code, or embody complex control flow and are therefore hard to compress sensibly. These *incompressible* instructions are ignored by LZW-CC.

Pattern-based compression algorithms can be divided into two basic functions: *modelling* to determine the patterns, and *coding* to apply the patterns to the data. LZW performs both of these functions during a single pass through the input text. In contrast, LZW-CC performs the two functions in separate phases so that it can apply patterns at all of their occurrences.

Create initial dictionary containing encodings of input program instructions encoded as themselves, with counts of zero.
Foreach basic block
    pattern = ""
    While not end of basic block
        byte = next byte from basic block
        If *byte* is an operation code for an incompressible instruction then
            increment the count for *pattern* if *pattern* is not empty,
            pattern = "", continue.
        End If
        newpattern = *pattern* ++ *byte* ++ following operand bytes (updating *byte*).
        If *newpattern* is in the dictionary then
            pattern = *newpattern*
        else
            code = new instruction operation code, add
            newpattern to the dictionary with encoding *code*,
            increment the count for *pattern*, and if *byte* is an
            operand then *pattern* = "" else *pattern* = *byte*.
        End If
    End While
End Foreach

Fig. 3. LZW-CC modelling algorithm

Figure 3 shows the LZW-CC modelling algorithm. We assume that the input is well-formed so that operands cannot appear without an earlier operation code. The encodings of patterns other than the original instructions are new instruction operation codes with zero operands.

For the example program this algorithm identifies 46 patterns. The patterns shown in Table 1 are considered to be included in the final encoding since their application would result in saving space.

Table 1. Patterns identified in the program from Figure 1

	Pattern	Count	Space Saved	Chosen?
1	lvalue 1 rvalue 1 assign push 1	4	24	yes: C1
2	lvalue 1 rvalue 1 assign	4	16	
3	lvalue 1 rvalue 1	4	12	
4	assign push 1 gotrue 67	3	12	
5	push 1 gotrue 67	3	9	
6	rvalue 1 assign	4	8	
7	assign push 1	4	8	
8	lvalue 1	5	5	
9	rvalue 2	4	4	yes: C2
10	rvalue 1	4	4	
11	push 1	4	4	
12	gotrue 67	4	4	yes: C3
13	rvalue 2 rvalue 6	1	3	
14	rvalue 2 rvalue 5	1	3	
15	rvalue 2 rvalue 4	1	3	
16	rvalue 2 rvalue 3	1	3	
17	lvalue 1 push 0	1	3	yes: C4
18	gotrue 67 lvalue 1	1	3	
19	gotrue 53 lvalue 1	1	3	
20	gotrue 37 lvalue 1	1	3	
21	gotrue 21 lvalue 1	1	3	
22	sub gotrue 67	1	2	
23	sub gotrue 53	1	2	yes: C5
24	sub gotrue 37	1	2	yes: C6
25	sub gotrue 21	1	2	yes: C7
26	rvalue 6 sub	1	2	yes: C8
27	rvalue 5 sub	1	2	
28	rvalue 4 sub	1	2	
29	rvalue 3 sub	1	2	
30	push 0 assign	1	2	
31	assign rvalue 2	1	2	

3.4   Pattern Selection and Replacement

After the modelling phase is complete, the encoding phase creates new instructions based on the patterns found. We don't necessarily use all of the patterns found by the modeller to create new instructions, however.

We only select patterns that can statically be determined to result in a reduction of bytecode size. Recall that we will have a single static copy of each pattern to perform decompression. Thus there is a tradeoff between the space taken by the old instructions and the space taken by the static copy and the bytecodes that invoke the new instructions. Formally, we require the following condition to be satisfied before we select a pattern:

$$n_j * l_j > n_j + l_j + 1$$

where n_j is the static number of occurrences of pattern j in the input and l_j is the length of pattern j. The extra 1 on the left-hand side is there to account for a termination byte on the static copy. The last three columns of Table 1 show the tradeoffs for the patterns identified in the example program and notes which patterns are chosen.

Once a set of patterns has been selected the encoding phase simply makes a pass over the bytecode segments replacing pattern occurrences with their encodings. Not all of the selected patterns will actually get used. It is common for chosen patterns to prevent other patterns from being used. For example, for the given code, if we choose pattern 1 then we cannot use patterns 2 to 7. Some of these are subsequences of pattern 1, other overlap with it. Once a long pattern is used, the occurrence count of its subpaterns has to be updated (reduced). For example, after we have applied pattern number 1, pattern 8 will have a count of 1.

The right-hand column of Figure 1 shows the compressed code that results from applying the selected patterns to the example program. The new program is 24 bytes long compared to the original 67 bytes. Operation codes beginning with "C" denote new instructions. The numeric suffix indicates a pattern from Table 1. Note that addresses in branch instructions need to be recalculated to reflect the deletion of instructions. Patterns that contain branch instructions need to be updated as well. For example, pattern 7 must be updated to refer to address 8 which is the new location of the instruction formerly at location 21.

3.5   Interpreter Modification

Naturally the details of interpreter modification depend on how the interpreter is implemented. Interpreter implementation and optimisation strategies are beyond the scope of this paper. However, to keep our discussion concrete we assume the common design of a fetch-decode-execute cycle implemented by a loop that dispatches to sections of code responsible for implementing each of the possible instructions. The bytecode instruction stream is accessed by a software instruction pointer.

Our interpreter modifications aim to: 1) enable the execution of the new instructions corresponding to pattern instances, and 2) reclaim the space used by interpreter code that is not needed for the particular program under consideration.

The scheme described here for adding support for the new compressed instructions is simplistic but has the advantage that it is easy to implement and should have little runtime overhead. As we have seen, each new instruction type corresponds to a pattern. For each pattern that has been used in the compressed program, we define a static array that contains the bytecode that comprises the pattern, terminated by a sentinel byte.

Code is added to the interpreter loop to dispatch to the static array when an instruction corresponding to the pattern is seen in the main instruction stream. Dispatching simply involves saving the instruction pointer, making the instruction pointer refer to the relevant static array, executing as normal, and reversing the redirection when a sentinel byte is seen. This dispatch code is only a few instructions on most machines and can be duplicated for each new instruction type. Even so, the dispatch code is usually bigger than a pointer, so slightly less space is used if a single copy is used for all new instruction types, indirecting through an array of pointers to the static arrays.

While we are compressing the program it is easy to keep track of the instructions that are used. Thus it is possible to remove support for these instructions from the interpreter. Often this just reduces to removing the corresponding sections of code from the main interpreter loop. For example, in our example program the *pop, copy, add, div, mul, goto* and *gofalse* instructions are not used so support for them can be removed.

4   Experimental Evaluation

In this section we present some preliminary experimental results and analysis from applying the LZW-CC method to real programs. We have a prototype implementation for the nhc98 Haskell compiler [8]. nhc98 uses a bytecode instruction set for a variant of the G-machine [3, 4]. The runtime system contains a bytecode interpreter implemented in the straight-forward fashion outlined earlier. The prototype implements all of the aspects discussed in the previous section including inclusion of library code and removal of unnecessary instructions from the interpreter.

Table 2 contains data from running our implementation on Haskell programs from the *nofib* benchmark suite [18]. The programs listed were chosen to reflect a range of possible Haskell applications. For example, *mkprog* and *maillist* are

Table 2. Experimental results from compressing a variety of Haskell programs in an nhc98-based prototype implementation

Program	Space Savings (%)			Program Entropy	
	Exe	Interp	Program	Bits	Savings bound (%)
putc	26%	50.4%	19.6%	5.27	34.1%
life	25.1%	49.5%	14.9%	5.37	32.9%
ansi	25%	48.5%	17.5%	5.36	33%
fish	25%	50.1%	17.9%	5.45	31.9%
puzzle	24.6%	49.5%	13.2%	5.35	33%
multiplier	23.9%	52.8%	14.6%	5.43	32%
rewrite	21.9%	50.1%	13.9%	5.43	32.1%
eliza	20.5%	46.8%	12.8%	5.36	33%
maillist	20.4%	49.5%	6.7%	5.43	32.5%
mkhprog	20%	47.5%	6.9%	5.49	31.5%
lambda	19.4%	52.3%	3.5%	5.49	31.5%
power	18.6%	42.9%	5.6%	5.43	32.1%
paraffins	17.4%	43.2%	3.6%	5.48	31.5%
x2n1	17.4%	43.2%	4.3%	5.45	31.9%
atom	16.2%	35%	3.9%	5.50	31.3%

typical real applications, *eliza* makes extensive use of strings, and *multiplier* performs a large number of calculations and output operations.

Overall our results show space savings for complete executables in the range of 16–26% (Exe column). When the interpreter is considered by itself (Interp column) the savings are bigger. Around 50% of the interpreter space usage is saved as a result of the optimisations to remove unnecessary instruction support and despite the increase in space usage due to the new instructions. (The programs induce around 50–60 new instructions compared to 159 instructions in the standard nhc98 implementation.)

The size of the interpreter is between 16 and 22% of the original executable and just by excluding unused original instruction code, we save between 8 and 11%. This saving represents about half of the overall saving that we observe for these programs.

On the other hand, the program code does not compress as well, on the order of 5–15% (Program column). This data includes both the bytecode of the program plus any data segments. At this stage we believe that the difference between these results and those typically obtained by LZW is accounted for by the fact that the data segments are not being compressed and by the effects of basic blocks on the algorithm. Basic blocks in functional programs tend to be pretty small (in our experiments the average size of a basic block is 20 bytes) so the impact is higher than it might be in languages that induce larger blocks.

It also has to be noted that C compiler optimizations performed on the newly generated code do not affect the compression because Haskell code in nhc98 is kept in an array in the data segment of the C program. Thus it is not visible to the C compiler optimiser.

4.1   Optimal Encoding

Choosing an optimal set of patterns is an NP-complete problem [19]. However, we can try to obtain a theoretical upper bound for the amount of space savings for which we can strive.

Shannon showed that the upper limit of compression for a given source is given by its entropy [20]. The entropy of a source is a measurement of its statistical properties and is measured in bits per character. Entropy depends on the probability of encountering each character in the input text. Shannon has defined six models for the source, depending on the correlations between occurrences of symbols.

Most usefully for our purposes, in Shannon's first-order model input symbols are statistically independent but not equally likely:

$$H = \sum_{i=1}^{m} p_i \log_2 p_i$$

where m is the size of the input alphabet, p_i is the probability of the i-th symbol of the input alphabet.

This model has been used previously in the literature to calculate the entropy of program code [21]. The entropy of the code in our experiments was calculated using the first-order model and is shown in the last two columns of Table 2. We show the calculated best possible bit count per character encoding (Bits column) for the source and the corresponding theoretical upper limit of achievable space savings (Savings bound column).

The entropy results are very similar across our test programs. By this measure, at least 5.3 bits are required per byte of code. This translates into a possible space saving in the program code of around 31–33%.

A number of factors appear to influence the difference between this theoretical optimum and the program savings results we obtained. First, our use of LZW sacrifices optimality for benefits such as a fixed-length codeword and its simplicity. Also, these figures apply to the entire program code but we are not compressing data segments. Finally, the entropy calculation is performed on the program code as a single sequence of characters but our algorithm must respect basic block boundaries.

5   Performance Comparison to Related Methods

In this section the experimental results achieved are compared to those of the two projects closest to this work: Fraser and Proebsting's interpreted C-code [15] and the Java bytecode compression of Clausen et. al. [16]. The three methods are compared with regards to their space savings and pattern selection overhead.

It has to be noted that any comparison of the performance of the three methods cannot be definitive as not all information necessary for comparison has been published and because the three projects have considered different languages and platforms. Nevertheless, a comparison might be useful to implementors interested in choosing the best language and approach for a particular platform.

5.1   Space Savings

Fraser and Proebsting report space savings for conventional text segments of two sample programs (lcc and burg) between 30% and 50% depending on the size of patterns used. The overhead of the interpreter's code is taken into account, but library code and other parts of the executable like literal code and branch tables have not been considered. Thus the overall space savings is lower than the reported savings.

Clausen et. al. report space savings of 15.3% on average (between 9.4% and 28%). These figures are reported for the memory footprint of the programs and as the authors note there is no guarantee that the memory footprint of a JavaCard program is a good indicator for the size of the program at runtime.

Our method achieves space savings between 16.2 and 26% for the executables of the chosen set of Haskell programs. This result compares favourably with the Java project. Even if all parts of the executable are taken into account, the C project is likely to better than our method. However, since this method spends much more time searching (see below) for an optimal pattern coverage we would expect it to do better.

5.2   Pattern Selection Overhead

Fraser and Proebsting use tree pattern matching to identify patterns. Very good results are reported for tree patterns containing more than four operations: the text segment's size is halved. For patterns with more than seven nodes, however, the authors report that the pattern selection (for *lcc*) takes hours.

Clausen et. al. use heuristics for selecting the set of patterns to be used for the final encoding. They start with an *occurrence group* of patterns applied greedily to achieve most savings first and keep on adding patterns until they run out of instruction operation codes or occurrence groups that save space. Pattern selection is reported to take ten to fifteen minutes.

Both of these methods use a compute-intensive pattern selection algorithm in comparison to the LZW-CC approach where a new program encoding can be computed in less than a minute and the whole re-compilation process (including library code) takes between six and seven minutes on a typical workstation.

6   Conclusion and Future Work

This paper presented LZW-CC, a new method of compressing interpreted language bytecode and creating a customised runtime system for a given program. Experimental results for a Haskell implementation were presented that show that LZW-CC can achieve overall space savings for executables of around 20–25%. LZW-CC is a simple algorithm so it can be implemented easily and has little overhead at compile time.

Several issues have to be investigated in the future. Firstly, the runtime penalty for running compressed code has to be evaluated in practice. We believe that our simple dispatch strategy means that the overhead is low but this claim still has to be verified. Second, we plan to investigate strategies for compressing data segments which constitute a large proportion of many executables. Any approach to this problem must take into account the way the data is accessed by the bytecode (for example, lazily in Haskell).

LZW-CC is based on LZW. We plan to investigate the use of other modelling algorithms to determine their effectiveness. Also, we plan to pursue more analysis of the optimal possible encoding. In this paper we have used Shannon's first-order model for entropy but it is arguable that second or higher order models are more appropriate because of dependences between instructions.

Finally, the method described here is not dependent on Haskell so we plan to apply it to other languages with interpreter-based implementations such as Prolog and Java. We expect that similar results can be achieved for these languages but are yet to investigate the effect of different virtual machine designs on the effectiveness of the compression.

References

1. Lindholm, T., Yellin, F.: The Java Virtual Machine Specification (2nd Edition). Addison-Wesley (1999)
2. Aït-Kaci, H.: Warren's Abstract Machine: A Tutorial Reconstruction. MIT Press (1991)
3. Peyton Jones, S.: Implementing lazy functional languages on stock hardware: the Spineless Tagless G-machine. Journal of Functional Programming **2** (1992) 127–202
4. Peyton Jones, S., Lester, D.: Implementing Functional Languages: A Tutorial. Prentice Hall (1992)
5. Ziv, J., Lempel, A.: A universal algorithm for sequential data compression. IEEE Transactions of Information Theory **23** (1977) 337–343
6. Ziv, J., Lempel, A.: Compression of individual sequences via variable-rate coding. IEEE Transactions of Information Theory **24** (1978) 530–536
7. Welch, T.: A technique for high performance data compression. IEEE Computer **17** (1984) 8–19
8. Rojemo, N.: Garbage collection, and memory efficiency, in lazy functional languages. PhD Thesis, Chalmers University of Technology, Sweden (1995)
9. Krastev, K.: Prototype implementation of LZW-CC for nhc98 [Online]. Available: www.comp.mq.edu.au/~kate/lzw-cc.tar (2004)
10. Beszedes, A., Ferenc, R., Gyimothy, T., Dolenc, A., Karsisto, K.: Survey of code-size reduction methods. ACM Computing Surveys **35** (2003) 223–267
11. Cooper, K., McIntosh, N.: Enhanced code compression for embedded risk processors. In: Proceedings of ACM SIGPLAN'99 Conference on Programming Language Design and Implementation. (1999) 139–149
12. Debray, S., Evans, W., Muth, R., de Sutter, B.: Compiler techniques for code compaction. ACM Transactions on Programming Languages and Systems **22** (2000) 378–415
13. Franz, M., Kistler, T.: Slim binaries. Communications of the ACM **40** (1997) 87–94
14. Ernst, J., Evans, W., Fraser, C., Lucco, S., Proebsting, T.: Code compression. In: Proceedings of ACM SIGPLAN'97 Conference on Programming Language Design and Implementation. (1997) 358–365
15. Fraser, C.W., Proebsting, T.A.: Custom instruction sets for code compression. Available at http://research.microsoft.com/~toddpro/papers/pldi2.ps (1995)
16. Clausen, L.R., Schultz, U.P., Consel, C., Muller, G.: Java bytecode compression for low-end embedded systems. ACM Transactions on Programming Languages and Systems **22** (2000) 471–489
17. Aho, A.V., Sethi, R., Ullman, J.: Compilers - Principles, Techniques, and Tools. Addison-Wesley (1986)
18. Partain, W.: The nofib benchmark suite of Haskell programs. In: Proceedings of the 1992 Glasgow Workshop on Functional Programming, Springer Verlag (1992) 195–202
19. Garey, M.R., Johnson, D.S.: Computers and Intractability: A Guide to the Theory of NP-Completeness. W. H. Freeman and Co. (1979)
20. Shannon, C.E.: A mathematical theory of communication. Bell System Technology Journal **27** (1948) 379–423 and 623–656
21. Latendresse, M., Feeley, M.: Fast and compact decoding of Huffman-encoded virtual instructions. In: ACM IVME'03, San Diego, California. (2003)

Author Index